D0790655

EXPLORER'S GUIDE

ADIRONDACKS

EIGHTH EDITION

ANNIE STOLTIE, LISA BRAMEN,
AND NIKI KOUROFSKY

THE COUNTRYMAN PRESS
A division of W. W. Norton & Company
Independent Publishers Since 1923

Copyright © 2018, 2003, 2000, 1996, and 1992 by by The Countryman Press
Copyright © 2008 by Annie Stoltie and Elizabeth Folwell
Copyright © 2012 by Annie Stoltie

All rights reserved
Printed in the United States of America

For information about permission to reproduce selections from this book, write to Permissions,
The Countryman Press, 500 Fifth Avenue, New York, NY 10110

For information about special discounts for bulk purchases, please contact
W. W. Norton Special Sales at specialsales@wwnorton.com or 800-233-4830

Manufacturing by Versa Press
Book design by Chris Welch
Production manager: Lauren Abbate

The Countryman Press
www.countrymanpress.com

A division of W. W. Norton & Company, Inc.
500 Fifth Avenue, New York, NY 10110
www.wwnorton.com

978-1-68268-108-4 (pbk.)

10 9 8 7 6 5 4 3 2 1

ACKNOWLEDGMENTS

It's because of Elizabeth "Betsy" Folwell that this guidebook exists. In 1992, Betsy wrote the first edition of what was called *The Adirondack Book,* a clearinghouse for all things Adirondack, in meticulous, exhaustive detail, with the usual dining and lodging material but also folksy stuff, like firehouse suppers and where to score Stoddard stereoviews. Although we've updated and added and changed and reorganized, this book's foundation is all Betsy—we've even double-checked much of what you'll read in these chapters with her, our Adirondack guru.

We're also thankful for help from other Adirondack friends, all intrepid reporters who shared their thoughts and meals and experiences as we compiled this book. They include Galen Crane, of Lake Placid; Tom Henry, of Charlotte, Vermont; and Mary Thill, of Saranac Lake. A special thank you goes to Saratogian Amy Godine, too, whose knowledge of Adirondack history and Spa City happenings—tossed with super, snappy writing—make the Adirondack history section and the Gateway Cities chapter so much fun.

Ted Comstock, of Saranac Lake, deserves thanks: he was kind enough to sort through his extensive collection of Adirondackana to find just the right historical postcards for this book.

This book shares the best of the Adirondacks through the talents of some of the finest photographers in the Northeast. We are indebted to Adirondack photographers Nancie Battaglia, Mark Bowie, John DiGiacomo, Eric Dresser, Johnathan Esper, Drew Haas, Carl Heilman II, Mark Kurtz, Kevin MacKenzie, Jeff Nadler, Shaun Ondak, Ben Stechschulte, and Melody Thomas. If you like what you see in these pages, check out these photographers' websites.

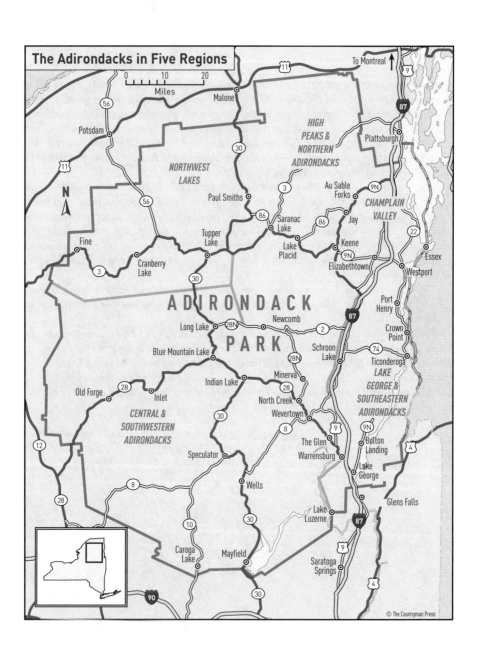

The Adirondacks in Five Regions

CONTENTS

MAPS

INTRODUCTION

New York's Adirondack Park is a big park—bigger than Yellowstone and Yosemite put together and larger than any of the national parks in the lower 48 states. This park is better than national parks in many ways, too. You don't pay an entry fee when you cross the so-called Blue Line, the park's boundary; you don't need a permit to hike, climb a mountain, canoe, or explore the backcountry. People make this park their home and have lived here for many generations, giving this region a distinctive culture and offering an array of services to visitors.

The park has a year-round population of about 130,000 residents and covers 6 million acres, about the size of the state of Vermont. Land owned by New York State—the Adirondack Forest Preserve—is about 2.5 million acres, and large landowners own another million acres and contribute significantly to the forested landscape and the local economy.

Through the years we've enjoyed visiting many different communities, exploring wild places, and learning about the region. Although the territory appears timeless, human endeavors change frequently. That's the impetus behind the eighth edition of this book—to supply information about new places and updates on classic spots.

We hope that these pages encourage you to explore this great place.

COURTESY OF ORDA/DAVE SCHMIDT

HOW THIS BOOK WORKS

To cover the Adirondack region, each geographic section of the park—and the towns, listed alphabetically within those sections—has been broken down to better serve those who are planning a trip to, say, Old Forge. However, in the Adirondack Park, it's not unusual to spend a day in multiple regions: perhaps you'll pass a morning at the Wild Center in Tupper Lake, grab lunch in Lake Placid, spend the evening at the theater in Westport, then stay the night in Keene Valley.

Although the first chapter, "Gateway Cities," includes travel information on two places that are outside the Blue Line, Saratoga Springs and Glens Falls are fascinating destinations in themselves. Because these cities have long been gateways to the great woods to the north, they deserve a place in this book. In this chapter you'll find descriptions of lodgings, restaurants, museums, and recreational opportunities available in both towns.

CASCADE FALLS, IN THE PIGEON LAKE WILDERNESS AREA COURTESY OF SHAUN ONDAK, WWW.SHAUNONDAK.COM

Throughout the book, many of the entries have phone numbers, websites, addresses (although many Adirondack hamlets are so rural, all that's available is the name of a street or route), and so forth. These facts have been checked as close to the book's publication date as possible, but businesses do change hands and change policies. It's always a good idea to call ahead.

For the same reason, you won't find specific prices listed for, say, restaurants or greens fees; descriptions for these should explain whether they're high-end or middle-of-the-road. A general price range is given for lodging—but keep in mind, prices often fluctuate according to season or other variables. And some rates include meals, which will be noted in the description.

LODGING PRICE CODES:

$	Up to $100 per couple
$$	$101–250 per couple
$$$	$251–400 per couple
$$$$	More than $400 per couple

WHAT'S WHERE IN THE ADIRONDACKS

Awhirlwind tour to see the Adirondacks can mean an awful lot of time spent in the car rather than getting to know a few nice places. So it may be best to carefully consider your tastes and concentrate your energy within a 40-mile area.

If you're a history buff and want to stroll through attractive, well-preserved towns and old forts, then head for the Champlain Valley, especially Ticonderoga, Crown Point, Westport, and Essex. Great restaurants and lovely bed & breakfast accommodations in Essex and Westport offer an excellent counterpoint to more rustic experiences. If you crave sweeping mountain vistas, aim your sights at the High Peaks, highlighting Keene Valley, Keene, and Lake Placid. The view from downtown Lake Placid, with chains of craggy peaks marching around the village, is unlike any other town in the park. If you like clean, island-dotted lakes, use Upper Saranac, Cranberry, Long, Blue Mountain, Indian, Raquette, Piseco, or Lake Pleasant as a base. For a terrific overview—literally—charter a floatplane from Long Lake or Inlet or take flight above the High Peaks from Lake Placid.

Recommended drives include NY 22 along Lake Champlain, NY 73 between Keene and Lake Placid, NY 30 between Long Lake and Lake Pleasant, and the Blue Ridge Road between Interstate 87 (the Northway) and Newcomb. Take a trip up the toll roads on Prospect or Whiteface Mountains; the views before you get to the summit are amazing. Incidentally, the Northway provides quite possibly the most scenic high-speed road experience in the Northeast.

Ads, Dacks, and Adirondacks

The word "Adirondack" reportedly comes from an Iroquois word that means "they eat bark," an insult referring to the Algonquin's allegedly lousy woodcraft skills. Though that can't be proven (neither their ineptitude nor the etymology), using romantic Native-sounding words has long been a favorite pastime of mapmakers, writers, and even politicians. What can be defined are some North Country specifics:

The Adirondack Park: Established in 1892, it covers 6 million acres of public and private land in a shield shape that includes much of the northern third of New York State. It's the largest state park in the nation. It's not all wilderness: everything within, from the summits of the highest peaks to the most remote bog to Main Street in Lake Placid, is in the park.

The Adirondack Forest Preserve: Established in 1885, the preserve is public land that makes up about 42 percent of the Adirondack Park, and is preserved as wilderness, wild forest, or primitive areas. It comprises many scattered parcels, not one contiguous unit, although some wilderness areas are vast enough to take days to cross on foot. In a nutshell, if you're on Forest Preserve land you're free to hike, hunt, fish, canoe, and do almost whatever else you want, although wilderness areas are off-limits to motorized vehicles (e.g., snowmobiles, ATVs, and motorboats). If you're not on public land, you're trespassing on somebody's property, unless you have

SAINT REGIS CANOE AREA COURTESY OF MARK BOWIE, WWW.MARKBOWIE.COM

permission to be there. Odd as it may seem to come across private land inside a state park, please respect it. If you want to go for a walk in the woods, look for trailheads with state Department of Environmental Conservation signs; they are on public land.

The Adirondack Mountains: The tallest summits—the celebrated High Peaks—occupy the northeast quarter of the Adirondack Park, but there are chains of mountains and scattered monadnocks throughout the region. They generally lie in parallel fault valleys, making a southwest–northeast diagonal across the park.

Transportation

In the earliest days of tourism, visitors were shuttled through the region on trains, stagecoaches and steamboats, but if you want to get around in the twenty-first-century Adirondacks, you'll need your own wheels. If you don't own a car, rent one before you get to the North Country. Even if you come here by some other means, once you arrive it can be difficult to do much without one. Public transportation is scarce and not always convenient. There are a handful of taxi companies in larger communities, such as Lake Placid, but popular ride-sharing services are just starting to move into the region—at press time, there are only two Uber drivers operating in the Lake Placid area.

The following information gives you the best routes for access to the Adirondacks and for getting around once you're here. We start with the most practical means of transportation—your car—and also provide details on bus, train, and air service. Routes that incorporate a Lake Champlain ferry crossing are also described.

BY CAR *Highways to Get You Here:* Major highways can get you to the perimeter of the Adirondack Park from all points.

- *From New York City*: Take I-87 north. This is the New York State (or Thomas E. Dewey) Thruway, a toll road, until Albany (Exit 24); then it becomes the toll-free Adirondack Northway (I-87). Principal exits off the Northway for the interior are: 14 and 15 for Saratoga Springs; 18 for Glens Falls; 21 for Lake George (roughly four hours from metro New York); 23 for Warrensburg and the central Adirondacks; 28 for Schroon Lake and Ticonderoga (about five hours from New York); and 30 for Lake Placid, Saranac Lake, and the High Peaks.

- *From Philadelphia and South*: Take the Northeast Extension of the Pennsylvania Turnpike and then I-81 north to Syracuse. From Syracuse take I-90 east to entry points such as Utica and Amsterdam, or I-81 farther north and then east on NY 3 at Watertown to reach the northern areas. Either way, it's not as far as you might think—you can reach the southwest edge of the park in about six hours from Philadelphia. Or you can take I-88 from Binghamton to Schenectady, go east two exits on I-90, and head north on I-87 from Albany; see above, "From New York City." And there's always the Garden State Parkway to the New York Thruway, then proceed as above.

- *From Buffalo, Cleveland, and West*: Take I-90 east to Syracuse, then proceed as directed above ("From Philadelphia"). From Buffalo to the edge of the park north of Utica is a little more than four hours.

- *From Toronto and Detroit*: Take NY 401 toward Montreal. Three toll bridges cross the Saint Lawrence River. The one that provides the most direct access not only to the edge of the park but also to such interior locations as Lake Placid and Blue Mountain Lake leaps from Prescott (Highway 16 exit) to Ogdensburg. On the US side, take NY 37 west a couple of miles to NY 68 south to Colton, and NY 56 into the park. From Toronto

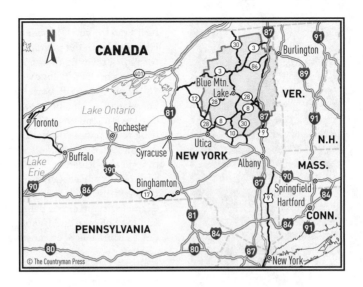

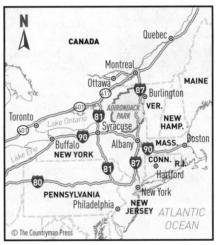

it's about five hours to the edge of the park and seven to the center. Travelers are required to present an enhanced driver's license or passport.

- *From Ottawa*: Take Highway 16 to the Prescott–Ogdensburg toll bridge and proceed as directed above ("From Toronto"). Allow two hours to the edge of the park, four to central points.
- *From Montreal*: Take Highway 15 south; this becomes I-87, the Adirondack Northway, at the border. Principal jumping-off exits for the interior

are 38 (Plattsburgh), only an hour (plus customs wait, which can be lengthy) from the outskirts of Montreal; and 34 (Keeseville), 20 minutes south of Exit 38.

- *From Boston*: Take the Massachusetts Pike, I-90, to I-87, then head north and follow the directions given under "From New York," above, to get past Albany. Or, take I-93 north to I-89, to one of the Lake Champlain ferry crossings described below. Via Albany, the Adirondack region is about four hours

WINTER DRIVING

Throughout the Adirondack Park, the state and county highway departments have plenty of snowplows that toil night and day to keep roads clear. The worst driving scenarios often occur when temperatures hovering at the freezing point cause a mixture of snow, rain, and sleet, with fog near lakes and low cold spots. Then it's best to consider your options: can you wait out the storm at your lodgings, or are you prepared to rest at a remote pullout if conditions deteriorate? Every winter traveler's car should carry a sleeping bag, a small shovel, a snow scraper, extra windshield-washing fluid, a powerful flashlight, and some candy or granola bars and bottled water, just in case you need to dig out of a snowbank or sit quietly beside the road for a few hours as the weather takes its course. Cell phone owners beware: coverage is spotty, so don't count on it.

from Boston; via the ferries it's closer to five, but the ferries are fun.

Highways to Get You Around Once You Get Here—North and South: Not surprisingly, four of the five north–south highways that traverse the Adirondacks do so in the narrow corridor between Lake Champlain and the mountains. This is where much of the region's population and many of its attractions are located, and it's also on a direct line between two concentrations of population: New York City and Montreal. These routes are:

- *NY 9N*, which rambles through lovely rolling countryside from Saratoga Springs northwest to Corinth and Lake Luzerne, then east to Lake George village, then up to Hague, and to Lake Champlain at Ticonderoga, where it meets:
- *NY 22*, which hugs Lake Champlain all the way from Whitehall up to Ticonderoga, where it joins 9N. The combined routes have expansive views of the lake on the east and of farmland in the valley beneath the High Peaks on the west, passing through Crown Point and Port Henry. At Westport, NY 22 follows the lake valley north to Willsboro, while 9N heads west to Elizabethtown, over Spruce Hill and on to Keene. This historic route passes through Upper Jay, Jay, and Au Sable Forks, paralleling the Ausable River, and connects again with NY 22 at Keeseville.
- *US 9* begins in the park just north of Glens Falls and skirts Schroon Lake and the Schroon and Boquet Rivers, but its route has been mostly supplanted by:
- *I-87*, the Adirondack Northway, an interstate highway named "America's Most Scenic Highway" in 1966–67.
- *NY 30*, the fifth north–south route, bisects the region from Gloversville via Speculator, Indian Lake, Blue Mountain Lake, Long Lake, Tupper Lake, and Paul Smiths to Malone. The remote and lightly populated western half of the region has no north–south highways.

East and West: Reflecting the reality that most travel in the Adirondacks always has been north–south, only three highways cross the entire region on the east–west axis, and two of them cover some of the same territory. These are:

- *NY 28*, which forms a semicircle from Warrensburg through North Creek, Indian Lake, Blue Mountain Lake, Inlet, Old Forge, and down to Utica.
- *NY 8*, which zigzags west from Hague, on Lake George, through Brant Lake, Chestertown, Johnsburg, Speculator, Lake Pleasant, Piseco, Hoffmeister, and southwest to Utica.
- *NY 3*, which crosses the northern part of the park from Plattsburgh, to Redford, Vermontville, Bloomingdale, Saranac Lake, Tupper Lake, Piercefield, Childwold, Cranberry Lake, Star Lake, and exits the Blue Line west to Watertown.

TRANSPORTATION

STAYING CONNECTED

With our increasingly wired lives, traveling to the Adirondacks can be a bit discombobulating: cell phone coverage is spotty—or even non-existent—and Wi-Fi hubs are hard to find. Make sure to plan accordingly.

One of the best ways to hop onto the information superhighway is at a local library—you can find one in most communities, and they all offer Wi-Fi. Another heads up: dialing the pizza joint down the road used to be a seven-digit process; now the area code (518 or 315) has to be tacked on for any calls to go through.

BY BUS Considering the size of the Adirondack region—you could fit Connecticut inside it—it's astonishing how little bus service exists. There's only one round-trip a day that's of any use, and once you get off the bus you're dependent on traveling by foot or finding sparse taxi service and even sparser rental car possibilities. If you do plan to use bus service, **Adirondack Trailways** (800-858-8555; www.trailwaysny.com) travels to various locations in the park (stops at diners and shops remind you you're not in urban America anymore): Keene Valley (Noon Mark Diner), Lake George (Lake George Hardware), Lake Placid (Olympic Authority), Paul Smith's College, Saranac Lake (Fusion Market), and Schroon Lake (Sunoco Gas Station). Also, bus tickets can be purchased at these hubs. Call ahead or visit your local terminal for the latest bus schedule since it changes season to season. In 2017, a one-way bus ticket from Port Authority, in Manhattan, to Lake Placid, was $69.

BY TRAIN **Amtrak** (800-872-7245; www.amtrak.com) operates one train a day each way between New York City and Montreal. The Adirondack leaves each city in the morning and reaches its destination the same evening (schedules are different on Saturdays and Sundays). The train closely follows the west shore of Lake Champlain for the better part of 90 scenic miles. The New York departure is from Penn Station. It makes stops in Saratoga Springs, Fort Edward, and the Adirondacks—Ticonderoga, Port Henry, Westport, and Port Kent—but how to get around once you are deposited at these places can be problematic. You may arrange, in advance, for shuttle service from the depot in Westport to Lake Placid by calling **Ground Force One** (518-523-4444; www.groundforce1.net). Train travel may not be what it once was, but compared to buses and puddle-jumper airplanes, this remains the most relaxing, visually engaging way to get to the Adirondacks. The trip is spectacular, involving tunnels, high trestles, rocky ledges 150 feet above the waters of Lake Champlain, and vistas of farm and forest, river, lake, and mountain that simply cannot be had any other way. In 2017, a one-way fare from Penn Station, in New York City, to Westport was $77.

Amtrak's Empire Service leaves New York's Penn Station several times a day and stops in Albany–Rensselaer, Schenectady, and Utica. One train a day from Boston hooks up with this route at Albany–Rensselaer. Coming from the west, Empire Service originates in Buffalo; Chicago–Boston/New York and Toronto–New York Amtrak trains also ply this route.

An Amtrak passenger train offers trips from Utica to Thendara/Old Forge, allowing at least semi-regular train service to the southwestern Adirondacks. Trains run primarily Thursdays and Saturdays, June through October. The ride takes approximately two-and-a-half hours; an adult round-trip fare in 2017 was $39.50. This route is not in Amtrak's database, so contact Adirondack Scenic Railroad's office (800-819-2291; www.adirondackrr.com) for schedule and fare information.

Tourist Trains: The **Adirondack Scenic Railroad (ASR)** operates a popular, short line from its Thendara station in spring through fall, with round-trip runs south along the Moose River to Otter Lake, and north to Carter Station. Look for special events (simulated train robberies, haunted histories, the Polar Express) and unique travel opportunities (mountain bikers and canoeists—and their respective gear—may use the train as part of their explorations). Fares in 2017 were between $16 and $39.50 for adults, depending on the trip. For fare and schedule information, call (315) 369-6290 or visit www.adirondackrr.com.

The **Saratoga and North Creek Railway** (877-726-7245; www.sncrr.com), which connects the Spa City to the central Adirondack town, revives a route that had been abandoned for half a century. North Creek's depot earned a place in history in September 1901 as the spot where Teddy Roosevelt, then vice president, learned that William McKinley had died in Buffalo, and that he was the next president of the United States (a museum in the station complex describes this event and showcases local history). The S&NCR runs Thursday through Monday, July through October; in 2017, Saratoga to North Creek round-trip fares started at $35.

BY FERRY Getting to the Adirondacks from the east generally means crossing Lake Champlain, the largest freshwater lake in America after the Great Lakes. You can do that via the Lake Champlain Bridge, which connects Crown Point, New York, and Addison, Vermont, but has a nice view that lasts for just 30 seconds. Why not savor the journey and take one of the Lake Champlain ferries? The views last for up to an hour and you don't have to steer. Three of the four crossings are operated by **Lake Champlain Transportation Company,** the oldest continuously running inland navigation company in America

(802-864-9804; www.ferries.com). Rates vary depending on type of vehicle, number and age of persons in it, and so forth; those shown were for car and one driver, one-way, in 2017. Credit cards are not accepted.

- *From Charlotte, Vermont, to Essex*: This may be the most scenic route, seeming to deliver you truly into the mountains. Crossing time is 20 minutes; trips run year-round, departing Charlotte starting at 6 or 7 AM, depending on the season. $10.25.
- *From Burlington, Vermont, to Port Kent*: This is almost as scenic, and delightful for its relaxing hour-long crossing of the widest part of the lake. Trips begin at 8 or 9 AM. and run several times a day from mid-May through the beginning of October. $30.
- *From Grand Isle, Vermont, north of Burlington, to Plattsburgh*: A bit north of the Adirondacks, this route provides a decent if long-distance view of them. It operates 24 hours a day year-round, blasting through ice packs in even the coldest snaps, generally every 20 minutes (every 40 minutes in the dead of night). Crossing time is 12 minutes. $10.25.
- *From Shoreham, Vermont, to Ticonderoga*: This crossing is a living museum. Following a route that's been in use since the British army arrived in the 1700s, it brings you to the foot of the promontory on which Fort Ticonderoga reposes. This is one of the few cable-guided ferries left in America: the cable is attached at each landing and a tugboat provides power. Crossing time is six minutes; the one-way fare is about $10 per car, and trips run from 7 AM to 5:45 PM from mid-May through late October, and until 6:45 PM July 1 through Labor Day. There's no set schedule; "We just go back and forth," says the captain. For more information: (802) 897-7999.

BIG-GAME CROSSING

Keep your eyes peeled for deer as you drive through the Adirondacks—not only to see them, which will be a pleasant memory of your trip, but also to avoid hitting them. Deer are most active in the late afternoon and evening, and particularly just after sunset, when they're also hardest to see. They often travel in pairs or small groups; if one crosses the road ahead of you, others are likely to follow. They're especially mobile during fall, for several reasons: that's their breeding season, they have to travel more to find food at this time of year, and hunters disrupt their daily routines. In winter they seek out plowed roads since the going is easier. Around Old Forge, especially NY 28 and the South Shore Road, deer are as common as squirrels all year.

One more thing: the instinctive reaction of a deer caught by car headlights is to freeze, not to scramble out of the way. It's up to you to miss. Your best bet: drive alertly, obey speed limits—and take those deer crossing signs seriously.

Deer aren't the only four-footed driving obstacles in the region—black bears have also been known to sprint across highways. And those MOOSE CROSSING signs that have been installed across the park, they're not just a tourist gimmick but a real warning of a potential hazard. The moose population has grown steadily, and sadly, car-moose encounters are becoming more common. Pay special attention in the fall, when 1,000-pound bulls can come crashing out of the forest directly into your lane, and at night, when your headlights may shine under their bodies without reflecting in their eyes.

BY AIR In all this vast territory there's only one commercial airport: **Adirondack Regional Airport** at Lake Clear (518-891-5157), about 15 minutes from Saranac Lake and 30 from Lake Placid. In 2017, it is served by the commuter line **Cape Air**, which has daily service to and from Boston to connect travelers with national and international airline services.

As these commuter airlines come and go, it's best to call first to make sure this one's still using Lake Clear. If you're calling another airport or a travel agent, ask about "Saranac Lake," not "Adirondack." Car rentals and driver services are available at the airport: **Hertz** (518-563-2051) and **Polar Express** (518-327-3331).

Cities just outside the Adirondacks that offer air service are Plattsburgh, Albany, Syracuse, Watertown, and Burlington, Vermont.

Private Airports: Private airports, ranging from a tarmac strip to a patch of grass in the woods, can be found scattered about the Adirondacks in such places as Schroon Lake, Ticonderoga,

and Westport. Consult a good map. The most significant is on the **outskirts of Lake Placid,** with a 4,200-foot runway, public lounge, and other facilities: (518) 523-2473. Another is at **Piseco** (518-548-3415). Better be prepared to be met at most of the others; taxi service and cars to rent are nowhere to be found in most cases, and it can be a hike to get to town.

Recreation

The Adirondack Park is the East's favorite outdoor playground, with terrain to suit people of any ability or fitness level.

ACCESSIBILITY For disabled New Yorkers, free passes to state-operated camping, swimming, and golf facilities, as well as historic sites, are available by applying to the **Office of Parks, Recreation and Historic Preservation** (518-474-0456).

The **John Dillon Park** (www.johndillonpark.org) is open to anyone with a disability, as well as his or her family, friends, and caregivers. You need a

FIRE TOWERS

There were once 57 fire towers within the borders of what we know as the Adirondack Park today. The very first was made of logs and was established on Mount Morris in Franklin County, in 1909; within a decade the total number of strategically placed fire lookouts had swelled to 52. At that time fires were rampant in this region, and spotters atop lookouts on peaks from one corner of the park to the other could report plumes of smoke before a raging inferno erupted.

It was the arrival of the light plane, coupled with rising costs to man the structures, that initiated the decline and eventual demise of the active fire towers. Many were torn down for safety or land-use reasons, but some towers still stand today. Recently, grassroots campaigns and volunteer workers have helped restore towers that remain, allowing hikers stunning views, but also serving as a reminder of the region's fiery past.

For those who need incentive, there's a **Fire Tower Challenge:** Climb 18 of the 23 designated mountains with fire towers in the Adirondacks (and all five in the Catskills) and you get a patch. Learn more about the challenge and read descriptions of the qualifying summits in *Views from on High: Fire Tower Trails in the Adirondacks and Catskills* by John Freeman (available at www.adk.org).

POKE-O-MOONSHINE MOUNTAIN'S FIRE TOWER COURTESY OF JOHNATHAN ESPER

RECREATION

permit, which you can get for free, and the lean-tos and trails are designed for people with disabilities. The park, with Grampus Lake and Handsome Pond, has more than 2 miles of nice trails with good surfaces for wheelchairs. Also, the **Department of Environmental Conservation**'s campground at **Scaroon Manor**, in Schroon Lake, has trails and campsites for those with mobility concerns (518-457-2500; www.dec.ny.gov). Contact the DEC about the universally accessible trails for people with mobility impairments at Ausable Marsh, Lampson Falls, Francis Lake, Moss Lake, and Silver Lake Bog. In Willsboro, an accessible 1.5-mile loop trail runs through The Nature

Conservancy's Boquet River Nature Preserve (www.nature.org/adirondacks). Find the trailhead behind the Paine Public Library on Main Street.

GUIDE SERVICES For all your hiking, biking, climbing, hunting, paddling, skiing, you-name-it needs, there's a guide. See the **New York State Outdoor Guides Association**'s website, www.nysoga.org, for a list of licensed Adirondack guides who can show you the adventure of a lifetime.

BICYCLING Road cyclists will discover that many state highways have wide, smooth shoulders. In April, road bikers might find that the snow banks are gone, but a slippery residue of sand remains on the road shoulders. You won't have to contend with much traffic in May and June or September and October, except on weekends, but main roads become busy with log trucks, sightseeing buses, and RVs throughout the summer.

Likewise, springtime backcountry cyclists might discover patches of snow in shady stretches of woods or muddy soup on sunnier trails. At the other end of the year, note that big-game season begins in October, and some of the best mountain-biking destinations are also popular hunting spots. Just a reminder: all-terrain bicycles are barred from Wilderness and Primitive Areas in the Adirondack Park.

Check www.bikeadirondacks.org for an online atlas. Be prepared for any long trips: check topographical as well as highway maps for significant hills on your proposed route. The most comprehensive guidebook for road cyclists is *25 Bicycle Tours in the Adirondacks: Road Adventures in the East's Largest Wilderness* by Bill McKibben, Sue Halpern, Barbara Lemmel, and Mitchell Hay. It describes loop trips in wonderful detail, with an eye toward scenic and historic destinations such as Willsboro

MOUNTAIN BIKE RULES OF THE TRAIL

- Ride on open trails only. Respect trail and road closures and avoid trespassing on private lands. Wilderness areas are closed to cycling.
- Leave no trace. Even on open trails, you should not ride under conditions where you will leave evidence of your passing. Practice low-impact cycling by staying on the trail and not creating any new ones. Pack out at least as much as you pack in.
- Control your bicycle. There is no excuse for excessive speed.
- Always yield the trail to hikers and others. Make your approach known well in advance; a friendly greeting or a bell works well.
- Never spook animals; give them extra room and time to adjust to your presence. Use special care when passing horseback riders.
- Plan ahead. Know your equipment, your ability, and the area in which you are riding, and prepare accordingly. Be self-sufficient; carry the necessary supplies and tools you may need.

—From the International Mountain Bicycling Association

AN ADIRONDACK LEAN-TO

Point, a thumb of land sticking into Lake Champlain, with great views coming and going. Another must-read is **Bicycling the Scenic Byways of the Adirondack North Country** (www.bikethebyways .org), sponsored by the Adirondack North Country Association. Remember: always carry plenty of water and a good tool kit. *And wear a helmet!*

BOATING Many Adirondack lakes have public launches for motor- and sailboats. Most are free, operated by the New York State Department of Environmental Conservation or villages; individual businesses may charge a nominal fee. You'll find these launch sites marked on regional road maps. State campgrounds often have boat ramps. If

LAY OF THE LANDS

State-owned forest preserve lands in the Adirondack Park are broken down into classifications that prescribe the kinds of uses allowed.

Wilderness, the most restrictive designation, is defined as "an area where the earth and its community of life are untrammeled by man—where man himself is a visitor and does not remain." Motorized vehicles, including snowmobiles, ATVs, floatplanes, and motorboats, are prohibited, as are mountain bikes.

Primitive Areas are either essentially wilderness in character or contain fragile resources that require wilderness management, but don't meet the criteria for Wilderness designation. They have the same restrictions on motorized vehicles and mountain bikes as Wilderness Areas.

Canoe Areas are where the watercourses or the number and proximity of lakes and ponds make possible a remote and unconfined type of water-oriented recreation in an essentially wilderness setting. They have the same restrictions on motorized vehicles and mountain bikes as Wilderness Areas.

Wild Forest Areas permit a somewhat higher degree of human use than the above designations while retaining an essentially wild character. They are open to snowmobile travel, mountain biking, and other recreation.

you have a reserved campsite, there's no extra charge to launch a boat, and if you'd like to make a short visit to Eighth Lake, for example, you pay the day-use fee. Marinas and boat liveries offer another chance for folks with trailers to get their boats in the water. Many more options are open to canoeists and kayakers who can portage their boats a short distance. The **New York State Boater's Guide** (www.nysparks.com) contains the rules and regulations for inland waters, and is available from offices of the New York Department of Transportation. See page 32 for information about invasive species and watercraft cleaning procedures.

Some statewide laws for pleasure craft:

- You must carry one personal flotation device for every passenger in your boat. Children under 12 are required to wear life jackets while on board.
- Any boat powered by a motor (even canoes with small motors) and operated mainly in New York State must be registered with the Department of Motor Vehicles.
- When traveling within 100 feet of shore, dock, pier, raft, float, or an

anchored boat, the speed limit is 5 mph. (Maximum daytime speed limits are 45 mph, and nighttime, 25 mph, although on many lakes with rocky shoals, or on water bodies that are also popular with nonmotorized craft, lower speeds are prudent.)

- Powerboats give way to canoes, sailboats, rowboats, kayaks, and anchored boats.
- The boat on your right has the right-of-way when being passed.
- Running lights must be used after dark.
- Boaters under 16 must be accompanied by an adult, or, if between 10 and 16 and unaccompanied, they must have a safety certificate from a New York State course.
- Boating under the influence of alcohol carries heavy fines and/or jail sentences.
- Littering and discharging marine-toilet wastes into waterways is prohibited.

CAMPING Camping is allowed year-round on state land, but you need a permit to stay more than three days in one backcountry spot or if you are camping with a group of more than six people. You may camp in the backcountry provided you pitch your tent at least 150 feet from any trail, stream, lake, or other water body. (See "low-impact camping," below.) Camping above an elevation of 4,000 feet is prohibited except in an emergency or in winter (December 15–April 30).

From Memorial Day through Labor Day, the Department of Environmental Conservation (518-402-9428; www .dec.ny.gov) operates public campgrounds, with 2017 rates ranging from $18 to $28 per night. Facilities at state campgrounds include a picnic table and grill at each site, water spigots for every ten sites or so, and lavatories. DEC public campgrounds do not supply water, electric, or sewer hookups for recreational vehicles. If you require these amenities, there are privately owned campgrounds in many communities. Along the Northville–Lake Placid Trail and on popular

JOY RIDE

For a chance to pedal your way around the park, sign up for Cycle Adirondacks (www.cycleadirondacks.com), an epic bike tour that covers more than 400 scenic miles and visits two dozen communities over the course of a week. It's a fully supported experience—gourmet meals and snacks, craft beer, even yoga and massages—that benefits Wildlife Conservation Society programs. Routes change every year; in 2017, rates started at $999.

canoe routes, you'll find lean-tos for camping. These three-sided log structures are an Adirondack icon.

Learn about particular campsites by visiting the DEC's website; reservations can be made for a site in the state campgrounds by contacting **Reserve America** (800-456-CAMP; www.reserveamerica

RECREATION

HAMLET TO HAMLET WITH CYCLE ADIRONDACKS COURTESY OF CYCLE ADIRONDACKS/PURE ADK

.com). Some campgrounds will take you on a first-come, first-served basis if space is available; before July 4 and after September 1, it's usually easy to find a nice site without a reservation.

LOW-IMPACT CAMPING Wilderness camping in the old days relied on techniques such as digging deep trenches around tents, cutting balsam boughs for backwoods beds, sawing armloads of firewood, and burying garbage and cans. For camp cleanup, we used to think nothing of washing dishes in the lake or scrubbing ourselves vigorously with soap as we cavorted in the shallows. All of these activities left a lasting mark on the woods and waters; today it's important to leave no trace of your visit.

Low-impact camping is perhaps easier than old-fashioned methods once you grasp the basics. Most of the skills are simply common sense: think of the cumulative effects of your actions when you set up camp, and you're on your way to becoming a responsible wilderness trekker.

Choose a site at least 150 feet away from the nearest hiking trail or water source, and try to select a place that will recover quickly after you leave. Separate your tent from your cooking area to avoid attracting animals and to distribute the impact of your stay. When you leave, tidy up. Be sure the spot is absolutely clean of any trash—even stuff we commonly regard as biodegradable, such as banana peels—and spread dirt or dead leaves around any trampled areas.

Use a portable stove for backcountry cooking rather than a campfire. (Use only dead and down wood in the Forest Preserve; cutting trees on state land is prohibited.) Plan your meals so that you don't have extra cooked food; if no one in the party can assume the role of "master of the Clean Plate Club," then pack out all of your leftovers. Wash your dishes and your body well away from streams and lakes, using a mild vegetable-based soap.

How to sh-t in the woods is something to consider; nothing kills that "Gee, isn't it terrific out here in the wilderness" feeling more than finding unmistakable evidence of other humans. Bring a shovel or trowel and bury that hazardous waste at least six inches down and 150 feet from the nearest water. Lean-tos and some backcountry campsites have privies; use them.

CANOEING AND KAYAKING The **Adirondack Canoe Map** shows several routes (518-576-9861; www.adirondack maps.com). *The Adirondack Paddler's Map*, a waterproof and tear-proof guide for multiday trips with enough details for navigating, includes trailheads, portages, and white-water ratings across the region.

The **Department of Environmental Conservation** (518-891-1200; www .dec.ny.gov) has pamphlets that describe canoe routes; ask for *Adirondack Canoe Routes* or the "official map and guide" of the area you wish to paddle. The excellent 24-page booklet *Adirondack Waterways Guide* is available at www .visitadirondacks.com. Always consult US Geological Survey topographic maps for the area you're traveling through.

When you're planning any trip, allow an extra day in case the weather doesn't cooperate. Remember that you're required to carry a life jacket for each person in the boat; lash an extra paddle in your canoe, too. Bring plenty of food and fuel, a backpacker stove, and rain gear. A poncho makes a good coverall for hiking, but you're far better off with a rain jacket and pants in a canoe, as a poncho can become tangled if you should dump the canoe. Always sign in at the trailhead registers when you begin your trip.

CLIMBING Plenty of steep, arduous rock walls can be found in the High Peaks. Possibilities for rock and ice climbers abound, from nontechnical scrambles up broad, smooth slides to gnarly 700-foot pitches in the 5.11+

NO-KILL FISHING

Angling for fun rather than for the frying pan is catching on across the country, especially in trout waters. If you'd like to match wits with a wild swimmer and then send it back to live another day, here are some tips for catch-and-release fishing:

- Use a barbless hook or take a barbed hook and bend down the barb with a pair of pliers.
- Be gentle landing your fish; some anglers line their nets with a soft cotton bag. When removing the hook, it's best not to handle the fish at all, as you can disturb the protective coating on the skin.
- If you have to touch the fish, wet your hands first, don't squeeze the body, and don't touch the gills.
- If you can, extract the hook without touching the fish: hold the hook's shank upside down and remove it. Usually, the creature will swim happily away.
- If your fish is tired, you can cradle it gently, facing upstream so that water flows through the gills, or if you're in a lake, move it back and forth slowly as a kind of artificial respiration.

difficulty range. See the High Peaks and Central chapters for the most popular rock- and ice-climbing areas in the park.

FISHING Begin your fishing education with the *New York State Freshwater Fishing Regulations Guide*, published by the Department of Environmental Conservation and available at DEC offices or www.dec.ny.gov, sporting goods stores, and tourist information centers. The free booklet details all the seasons and limits for various species. Everyone 16 and older who fishes in the Adirondacks must have a New York fishing license, which can be purchased at sporting goods stores and town offices. Nonresidents can get special five-day licenses; state residents 70 and older may get free licenses.

For information on special regulations and mercury levels, consult www.dec.ny.gov/outdoor/7917.html. *Adirondack Fishing: An Angler's Guide to Adirondack Lakes, Ponds, Rivers and Streams*, from the Adirondack Regional Tourism Council, has maps, game fish descriptions, and advice on techniques, and it is available in print or at www .fishadk.com.

HIKING AND BACKPACKING There are trails leading to pristine ponds,

roaring waterfalls, spectacular peaks, and hidden gorges; perhaps the toughest choice for an Adirondack visitor is selecting where to go.

On summer and fall weekends, the most popular trails in the High Peaks region resemble Times Square, but it's still possible to find solitude if you select the right destination. In some parts of the park, you can leave the trailhead and not see another person until you return to your car and look in the rearview mirror. There are also plenty of easy hikes of 2 to 5 miles that traverse beautiful terrain throughout the park.

Don't assume that just because the Adirondack Mountains don't reach the height of the Rockies, it's all easy strolling; trails can be steep and treacherous and weather is downright changeable. Wherever you choose to go, be prepared. Your pack should contain a flashlight, matches, extra food and water, map, compass, and extra clothes (wool or fleece for warmth; leave the cotton at home). At most trailheads, there's a register for signing in. Forest rangers rely on this data to estimate how much use a particular area receives; and, in the unlikely event that you get lost, the information about when you started, where you were planning to go, and whom you were with would be helpful to the search team.

RECREATION

TRAIL-SAFE

A few commonsense reminders could save your life:

1. Do your research—before your trip. Choose a trail that matches your fitness and experience levels, and check conditions ahead of time. The Department of Environmental Conservation posts a report of current trail and weather conditions in the Adirondacks on its website (www.dec.ny.gov) every Friday.
2. Note that conditions at the top of a mountain can differ significantly from those at the trailhead; snow can linger on peaks well into late spring some years, and it can reappear in early fall. Fog is also a concern; many unplanned overnight stays result from hikers becoming disoriented at a foggy summit.
3. Leave a detailed itinerary with someone who is not going on your trip, who can notify the forest rangers if you don't return on time.
4. Don't rely on your cell phone. Service is spotty in many parts of the Adirondacks, and batteries can die.
5. Though giardia is a legitimate concern when drinking untreated water (see page 32), in a survival situation, dehydration is the greater threat.

RECREATION

For neophyte hikers, the trails at the **Adirondack Interpretive Center** at Newcomb (518-582-2000) and the **Paul Smith's College Visitor Interpretive Center** (518-327-6241) are ingeniously designed to offer a wide range of nature in a relatively short distance, and you won't be too far from the building no matter how long you travel. You can join a guided trip to learn about wildflowers, mushrooms, trees, or birds.

The **Adirondack Mountain Club** (518-523-3441; www.adk.org) leads trips and gives map-and-compass, woodcraft, and low-impact camping workshops. Their comprehensive guidebook series covers seven different regions of the park, from the High Peaks to the Northville–Lake Placid Trail; these pocket-size paperbacks have plenty of detail. You can order them at www.adk.org or find them at most regional bookstores or outfitters.

HUNTING Native Americans, colonial scouts, and nineteenth-century travelers regarded the Adirondacks as happy hunting grounds. Today, wilderness, primitive, and wild forest areas are all open to hunting.

There are seasons for deer, black bear, snowshoe hare, coyote, bobcat, and other small mammals, plus ruffed grouse,

woodcock, wild turkey, and waterfowl. In general, big-game seasons begin with early bear (mid-September through mid-October); archery for deer or bear (late September through mid-October); muzzle-loading for deer or bear (one week in mid-October); and regular big-game season (third Saturday in October through the beginning of December). Bow and black-powder hunters may take antlerless deer; during regular season, it's bucks only in the Adirondack Park.

The booklets outlining game seasons are available at the Department of Environmental Conservation (www.dec.ny .gov) or by writing for them. Licenses can be purchased online, from sporting goods stores, town offices, or the DEC. Nonresidents may purchase 5-day licenses. If you have never had a New York State hunting license, you must show proof that you have attended a hunter-education course. Turkey hunting requires a special stamp from the DEC; waterfowl hunters must possess a Federal Migratory Bird Hunting Stamp.

Hunters—even if they have a brand-new, state-of-the-art GPS unit—should be proficient with map and compass. Global-positioning units don't always work well in thick forest, and batteries do wear out.

There are many Adirondack hunting guides, who can be found at the **New York State Outdoor Guides Association**'s site, www.nysoga.org.

CROSS-COUNTRY SKIING AND SNOWSHOEING The Adirondack Park is paradise for cross-country skiers. Most winters there's plenty of snow, especially in the higher elevations. A wide range of destinations entices skiers, from rugged expeditions in the High Peaks to gentle groomed paths suitable for novices, plus hundreds of miles of intermediate trails. Many of the marked hiking trails on state land are not only suitable for cross-country skiing or snowshoeing, they're actually better for winter recreation, as swampy areas are frozen, and ice-bound ponds and lakes can be easily crossed.

Designated wilderness and wild forest areas offer great ski touring on marked but ungroomed trails. The Adirondack Mountain Club's guidebook series includes information on backcountry skiing and snowshoeing. Another option for exploring the wild wintry woods is to hire a licensed guide.

Before setting out on any of these wilderness excursions, prepare your pack with quick-energy food; a thermos filled with hot tea or cocoa; extra hat, socks, and gloves; topo map and compass; matches; flashlight; and space blanket. Dress in layers of wool, polypropylene, or synthetic pile. Don't travel alone. Sign in at the trailhead register. Let friends know your destination and when you plan to return.

SNOWMOBILING Besides the Old Forge–Inlet area, many trail networks throughout the park cross private timberlands as well as the state forest preserve. Public lands designated as wild forest areas are open to snowmobiling; wilderness areas are not. The DEC's website, www.dec.ny.gov, has rules and regulations and links to sites with Adirondack snowmobile trails.

AN EPIC TREK

Parts of the Northville–Lake Placid Trail (NPT) are many miles from the nearest road; passing through the West Canada Lakes or Cold River areas, you might go several days with just the cry of the loon or the howl of the coyote for company. Going end-to-end on this long trail requires a minimum of 10 days (unless you're ultra trail runner Drew Haas, who in 2009 completed the NPT alone and unassisted in 60.5 hours). You also need a solid amount of backcountry knowledge, but you can pick shorter sections for three-day junkets. The Adirondack Mountain Club (www.adk.org) publishes a guidebook devoted to this popular route.

As with any winter pursuit, planning and preparation help make a successful outing. Know your machine; carry an emergency repair kit and understand how to use it. Be sure you have plenty of gas. Travel with friends in case of a breakdown or other surprise situation. Never ride at night unless you're familiar with the trail or are following an experienced leader. Avoid crossing frozen lakes and streams unless you are absolutely certain the ice is safe. Some town or county roads are designated trails; while on such a highway, keep right, observe the posted snowmobile speed limit—there are numerous fatalities each year due to excessive speed—and travel in single file.

Your basic pack should contain a topographic map and compass as well as a local trail map; survival kit with matches, flashlight, rope, space blanket, quick-energy food, and something warm to drink; and extra hat, socks, and mittens. Although a sip of brandy may give the illusion of warming you up, alcohol impairs circulation and can hasten hypothermia. And an arrest for snowmobiling under the influence carries with it severe penalties.

PATCH WORK

Becoming a 46er (see page 141) is the granddaddy of Adirondack challenges, but there are a wide variety of award programs tailored to outdoor enthusiasts of all abilities. Here are a few that are possible to tackle in a single (if ambitious) vacation:

LAKE GEORGE 12STER CHALLENGE

Climb a dozen peaks around Lake George—some 40 miles total and about 9,000 feet in elevation gain—and receive your accolades. Peaks, on both sides of the lake, include Sleeping Beauty, Black, Buck, Cat, Thomas and Erebus Mountains, plus the Tongue Range (www.lakegeorge12ster.com).

SARANAC LAKE 6ER

McKenzie, Ampersand, Haystack, Saint Regis, and Scarface Mountains, plus Mount Baker, are the sextet near Saranac Lake village that have attracted thousands of hikers since the challenge began in May 2013. The total elevation gain is more than 8,000 feet, with a total mileage of more than 30 (saranaclake6er.com).

TUPPER LAKE TRIAD

Mount Arab (2,545 feet), Coney Mountain (2,280 feet), and Goodman Mountain (2,178 feet) are the featured summits, all gentle enough for family outings (www.tupperlaketriad.com).

Flora and Fauna

VIRGIN TREES AND CHARISMATIC MEGAFAUNA The Adirondack forest primeval—which survives today in scattered tracts of old growth in remote wilderness areas such as the Five Ponds and West Canadas—varies according to elevation and soil. At the very tops of some mountains, only alpine shrubs and flowers grow, and below them are stunted trees known as **krummholz**, which can be hundreds of years old yet only a few feet high. Lower down, thick **spruce** and **fir** forests grow; on steep, inaccessible slopes some patches have remained undisturbed for centuries. **White pine** and spruce take over at an elevation of 2,500 feet or so, with mixed hardwood forests—**yellow birch, beech, sugar maple**, plus **eastern hemlock**—covering miles and miles of the central Adirondacks. The understory in this woodland is the classic Adirondack landscape, with beautiful ferns and wildflowers such as trillium, lady's slipper, and jack-in-the-pulpit.

There's a wide variety of wildlife ranging through the different habitats of woods and waters. **Small mammals** are numerous: varying hares, weasels, mink, raccoons, fisher, pine martens, otters, bobcats, porcupines, and red and gray foxes. **Coyotes**, with rich coats in shades of black, rust, and gray, can be seen in fall, winter, and spring, and their yips and yowls on a summer night can be thrilling to the backcountry camper's ears. **White-tailed deer** are seemingly everywhere, especially in the early spring before the fawns are born. **Black bears** have adapted remarkably well to life with humans, and run-ins are always a possibility. Whether you're deep in the High Peaks wilderness or at a campground in the heart of Old Forge, keep all food sources secure from bears—for their sake and yours. Bears that become conditioned to getting a free lunch may have to be euthanized by conservation officers.

TURKEYS ARE NOW COMMON IN THE CENTRAL ADIRONDACKS' MIXED HARDWOOD FOREST COURTESY OF ERIC DRESSER, WWW.ECDPHOTO.ADDR.COM

Loons, revered for their haunting songs, inhabit many larger Adirondack lakes and ponds. With luck you may see **ospreys, peregrine falcons,** or **bald**

LYNX ONCE WERE FOUND IN THE HIGH PEAKS AND OTHER RUGGED COUNTRYSIDE, PREYING ON SNOWSHOE HARES, BUT DISAPPEARED DUE TO HUNTING AND HABITAT CHANGES COURTESY OF ERIC DRESSER, WWW.ECDPHOTO.ADDR.COM

TALL TAILS?

Mountain lions and wolves were once thought to be a serious threat, but generous bounties paid out by counties (in the mid-1800s, some locales paid more for bounties in a year than they spent on schools) wiped out these populations. Still, questions linger—were gray wolves ever truly here at all, or were the smaller, reddish canines we call coyotes the historic Adirondack wolf?

Possible mountain lion sightings cause a lot of chatter around the region, though the Department of Environmental Conservation hadn't collected physical evidence of these elusive predators until December 2010, when a mountain lion was sighted in a Lake George backyard. His tracks led DEC personnel to a spot where hair samples were gathered for DNA analysis. In June of the following year, a 140-pound male cougar was killed by a car in Connecticut. It turned out to be the same animal, whose genetic markers indicated he had traveled from South Dakota.

eagles soaring on warm currents over a lakeshore or cliff. **Hawks** are fairly easy to spot; songbirds—especially **warblers**—are plentiful during warm weather; and at least ten varieties of **ducks** nest near the waterways of the park. In the fall, look up to see thousands of migrating **Canada** and **snow geese. Wild turkeys**—absent from the Adirondacks until the 1990s—are positively ubiquitous, especially along roadsides in the central Adirondacks.

More than 800 **moose** live here now, definitely restocking themselves and raising calves in the central Adirondacks and northwest lakes as well as other logged forests in the park. The best place to see moose is—no surprise—Moose River Recreation Area, where bulls can be seen in fall from woods roads. If you encounter one of these draft-horse–size guys, do not approach! They tend to be very cranky during rutting season.

PEREGRINE FALCON   COURTESY OF JEFF NADLER

Adirondack Icons

ADIRONDACK CHAIR With arms wide enough for a cocktail and a fat novel, a seat angle that's suitable for even the sorest back, and a name that shows its regional roots, the Adirondack chair just might be the most recognized symbol of our park.

The first Adirondack chair was created 113 years ago by Westport summer resident Thomas Lee, who sought comfortable outdoor seating for his family. Lee gave his design—and blessing—to his friend Harry Bunnell, who patented it and went on to manufacture the chairs until 1930. Bunnell's original Westport chair was made of wide planks—one for the back, one for the seat and one for each arm—not slats, like most designs you see today.

PACK BASKET Winslow Homer's 1875 painting *Two Guides* depicts legendary Keene Valley guide Orson Schofield "Old Mountain" Phelps and his colleague Harvey Holt in their High Peaks backyard, axes in hand, a pack basket fixed to Phelps's back. In those days a pack basket was the essential gear of the Adirondack guide—customizable, durable, with a curved back for comfort, a rounded "belly" to increase volume, and a flat

THE MOOSE POPULATION HAS GROWN STEADILY, AND SADLY, CAR AND MOOSE ENCOUNTERS ARE BECOMING MORE COMMON   COURTESY OF ERIC DRESSER, WWW.ECDPHOTO.ADDR.COM

HOW DO YOU SAY THAT?

Place names in the Adirondacks (ad-ih-RAHN-daks) can leave newcomers tongue-tied. Algonquin, Mohawk, French, Dutch, and English words have morphed over the years into a North Country patois that doesn't always follow the language of origin's usual rules of pronunciation. In some cases, like the Boquet River, in Essex County, even those who live along it can't agree. Is it bo-KETT? Bo-KWET? Just don't say "boo-KAY" and you'll fit in fine. Here is a guide to local pronunciation of some of the park's most mangled monikers:

- Athol (AY-thol)
- Ausable (ah-SAY-bull)
- Chateaugay (shad-a-GAY)
- Chazy (SHAY-zee)
- Couchsachraga (kook-sa-KRA-ga)
- Onchiota (on-shy-OH-ta)
- Piseco (pih-SEE-ko)

- Raquette (RACK-it)
- Sacandaga (sock-en-DOG-ah)
- Santanoni (san-ta-NO-nee)
- Schroon (SKROON)
- Tahawus (ta-HAWS)
- Thendara (then-DARE-ah)

bottom that allowed the pack to stand upright when placed on the ground or in a boat.

Inspired by Native American carrying vessels, pack baskets were traditionally made of splints pounded from black ash logs and finished with adjustable leather or canvas straps. The utilitarian design is timeless. Today, pack baskets are still used by trappers, hunters, paddlers, hikers, foragers, photographers—who all find these man-made icons every bit as functional, comfortable, and appropriate as their predecessors did to the task at hand.

LOON Imagine the soundtrack of an Adirondack lake on a summer evening: the crackle of a campfire, the slap of water against the shore, and the wails and yodels of a black and white, red-eyed loon, one of the most revered and protected creatures in the park.

Adult loons weigh up to 14 pounds and can stay underwater for as long as 15 minutes—their bones are solid, helpful for diving, but requiring a long runway for takeoff. Loons don't walk but rather slide on their bellies on land, and they nest close to water. They're believed to mate for life and are devoted parents known to take on boats to defend their offspring—fuzzy kitten-size chicks,

sometimes seen riding on their parents' backs.

LEAN-TO An overnight in one of these three-sided shelters is, some might say, the ultimate outdoor experience—the fresh mountain air, a dry place to sleep off the ground during inclement weather, a campfire meal shared on the deacon seat while feet dangle over the edge.

The lean-to we know today evolved from primitive wilderness structures built on the spot by guides in the mid-1800s using just their axes. They cut logs and limbs to make the shelter, then lined the floor with balsam branches to make a springy, fragrant bed for their hunting and fishing clients.

With the help of volunteer stewards, the Department of Environmental Conservation maintains approximately 185 round-log lean-tos on Adirondack state land, but you can also find ones with Persian rugs and well-stocked bars at several regional resorts.

GUIDEBOAT "Their little boats were their horses, and the lake their only path," wrote a visitor to Long Lake before the Civil War. In a region divided by mountains yet connected by waterways, the evolution of a signature watercraft was inevitable.

The Adirondack guideboat—crafted from cedar planks and spruce roots—is a double-ended rowboat graceful enough to slip through the water stealthily, light enough for one man to carry on his shoulders, yet strong enough to hold a guide, his sport and their harvest of fish and venison. These were in such demand that practically every lakeside town boasted its own makers, who refined the overall design to fit local needs, everything from 12-foot "raiders" for solo hunters to 22-foot "church boats" for folks on a Sunday outing.

Threats

GIARDIA The cool, clear water may seem like the ideal thirst-quencher, but please resist the temptation to drink freely from Adirondack lakes, rivers, ponds, and streams. Sadly, due to careless campers and occasional animal pollution, these wild waters may harbor a microscopic parasite known as *Giardia lamblia*, which can cause bloating, diarrhea, cramping, and vomiting. Giardiasis—also known as beaver fever—is easily diagnosed (with a stool sample) and treated (with quinacrine or Flagyl), but it's better to avoid the ailment in the first place. Practice good campsite sanitation. Treat all drinking water by boiling for 10 minutes, by using a specially designed Giardia-proof filter, or with chlorine or iodine tablets.

HIGH WATER/DROWNING Sadly, drownings happen too often in the Adirondacks. Always wear a personal flotation device (PFD) on the water, even in a tube or other flotation device. The Department of Environmental Conservation encourages people to use common sense when recreating in swift waters, especially post-rains, when streams and rivers swell. Seemingly innocuous swimming holes can be deadly. Never combine alcohol with aquatic activities.

INVASIVE SPECIES *Aquatic invasive species* are a major threat to Adirondack lakes, ponds, and rivers. Not native to this region and having no natural predators, invasive species spread uncontrollably, displace native plants and animals, and degrade habitat and deteriorate water quality and recreational opportunities. At least eight aquatic invasive plants are in Adirondacks waters. **Eurasian watermilfoil** (*Myriophyllum spicatum*), **curlyleaf pondweed** (*Potamogeton crispus*), **water chestnut** (*Trapa natans*), and **European frogbit** (*Hydrocharis morsus-ranae*) all form thick, impenetrable mats. Although native to Europe and Asia, these plants arrived in the United States as popular aquarium plants or ornamentals used in water gardens. Once released into the environment, they quickly spread. Plant fragments or seeds easily attach to recreational watercraft or cling to gear and are transported to new waterways.

Adirondack waters also harbor aquatic invasive animals. **Zebra mussel** (*Dreissena polymorpha*), **spiny waterflea** (*Bythotrephes cederstroemi*), and **Asian clam** (*Corbicula fluminea*) are invasive invertebrates from Europe and Asia. The primary pathways to the United States for these and other aquatic animal invaders are the ballast water of ocean-going vessels, the aquarium trade, and the live seafood market; once released, they, too, can attach to watercraft and gear or be transported in water in bait buckets or live wells.

Fortunately, two out of three Adirondack waters surveyed are still free of aquatic invasive species. A real opportunity exists to prevent widespread degradation. Individual actions make a difference. Check, clean, drain and dry all watercraft and gear before moving between waters, and dispose of unwanted bait in the trash. Report sightings of aquatic invaders to the **Adirondack Park Invasive Plant Program** at (518) 576-2082.

BUZZ OFF

Springtime in the Adirondacks can be lovely, but this earthly paradise has a squadron of tiny, persistent insects to keep humans from overwhelming the countryside: black-flies. Bug season is usually late May through June, although its duration depends on the weather. If you're planning an extended hike, golf outing, streamside fishing trip, or similar activity, you'll want to apply insect repellent, wear light-color clothing (blue, especially dark blue, seems to attract blackflies), and tuck in your pant legs and shirt. Avoid using perfume, shampoo, or scented hairspray—these products broadcast "free lunch!" to hungry little buggers.

There's a pharmacy of lotions and sprays that use varying amounts of DEET (diethyl-meta-toluamide) as the active ingredient, but note that products containing more than 25 percent DEET should not be applied to children's skin. DEET should not be used at all on infants.

Some Adirondackers prefer pine-tar–based bug dopes, such as Ole Woodsman, that also have the lasting aroma of authenticity; after a good dose of Ole Woodsman, your pillows and sheets will be scented, too. Lots of Adirondack shops sell homemade concoctions, including Shoo Fly by Pure Placid (pureplacid.com) and Bye Bye Black Fly made by Vermontviller Marge Glowa. If these fail, there are bug jackets and pants, veils, and even crusher-type hats with lightweight netting attached.

Terrestrial invasive species, from plants and pathogens to mammals, put ecosystems and the services they provide to human communities at risk. Not native to this region, invasive plants such as **Japanese knotweed** (*Fallopia japonica*), **purple loosestrife** (*Lythrum salicaria*), and **garlic mustard** (*Alliaria petiolata*) are prolific spreaders that form dense single-species stands along stream corridors, wetlands, and woodlands. More recent plant invaders such as **yellow iris** (*Iris pseudacorus*), **giant hogweed** (*Heracleum mantegazzianum*), and **swallow-wort vine** (*Cynanchum*) are now taking hold. Ornamental plantings are the primary source of terrestrial invasive plants. Roots, fragments, or seeds are also spread via roads or construction projects that create disturbed areas or use infected soils.

Tree-killing forest pests and pathogens are also of great concern because the rapid rate of introductions and spread may be faster than the speed at which forests can adapt. The **emerald ash borer** (*Agrilus planipennis*) attacks all species of ash, which comprise 7 percent of New York forests. **Asian longhorned beetle** (*Anoplophora glabripennis*) attacks a broader range of species, including maples and other hardwoods. Its distribution is limited in the United States, but if it spreads, it could devastate forests and the wood products industry.

Protect Adirondack woods and wildlands from terrestrial invasive species. Individual actions make a difference. Use local firewood. Never pick roadside wildflowers. Landscape with noninvasive plants. Clean shoes and gear upon leaving a natural area. Report sightings of terrestrial invaders to the **Adirondack Park Invasive Plant Program** (518-576-2082).

RABIES Rabies cases have been reported in all parts of the Adirondacks. The disease seems to be spread by raccoons, foxes, and skunks in upstate New York.

However, humans are not at great risk for rabies exposure, as contact with sick wildlings can be avoided. If you come across a wild animal acting unafraid or lying passively, by all means stay away

READ ALL ABOUT IT

Plenty of authors have been inspired by the Adirondacks, from Sylvia Plath, who chronicled her ski accident at Mount Pisgah in *The Bell Jar*, to Ian Fleming, who set *The Spy Who Loved Me* in a motor court near Lake George. For a taste of that inspiration before your own Adirondack idyll, try the following titles:

The book that started it all—the mad rush to the woods for a good dose of rest and relaxation—is *Adventures in the Wilderness: Or Camp-Life in the Adirondacks* (1869), by William H. H. Murray.

James Fenimore Cooper's classic French and Indian War novel, *The Last of the Mohicans* (1826), recounts a harrowing trip from what's now called Cooper's Cave, in Glens Falls, to Fort William Henry, in Lake George. Cooper visited Warrensburg and Lake George in 1824 to research his story and observe the landscape.

The Air We Breathe (2008), by Andrea Barrett, paints a fictional Saranac Lake when it was a haven for those suffering from tuberculosis.

Cloudsplitter (2011), by Russell Banks, is a riveting portrait of radical abolitionist John Brown, who had a farmstead near Lake Placid.

The Dirty Life: On Farming, Food, and Love (2010) charts author Kristin Kimball's journey from New York City to a Champlain Valley farm.

For a bit of the backstory on the mountains awaiting you, grab *Peaks and People of the Adirondacks* (1973), by Russell M. L. Carson.

E. L. Doctorow's *Loon Lake* (1980) gives a glimpse of life at an upscale Adirondack retreat during the 1930s.

Bill McKibben explores the landscape that spurred his environmental activism in *Wandering Home: A Long Walk Across America's Most Hopeful Landscape: Vermont's Champlain Valley and New York's Adirondacks* (2005).

THREATS

from it. If it bites you, seek medical attention immediately. And don't touch dead creatures you may find.

Dogs must be inoculated against rabies. Keep your pet under control when traveling through the woods.

TICKS Many cases of **Lyme disease** have been recorded in the Adirondacks, and hikers should take precautions against exposing themselves to deer ticks (*Ixodes scapularis*). The ticks can be found in deep woods, grassy meadows, backyards—everywhere. Dogs are also at risk; you can have your pet inoculated against Lyme disease.

You can minimize your exposure to ticks by wearing long pants (with cuffs tucked into your boots) and long-sleeve shirts, using a good insect repellent, and staying on the trail. If you wear light-color clothing, the ticks are easier to spot. Always check yourself and your kids after you've been in the woods.

Deer ticks are very tiny, no bigger than a sesame seed. They don't fly. If you find an eight-legged crawling creature on your body, it could be a spider, a wood tick (not a carrier of Lyme), or an arachnid locally called a "ked," which, despite its scary-looking, crab-like pincers, is harmless.

If you find a tick attached to your skin, pull it out steadily with a pair of

BLACKLEGGED OR DEER TICK COURTESY OF ADIRONDACK LIFE

tweezers or your fingers, grasping as close to the tick's mouth as you can. Save the creature in a jar—your doctor will probably want to see it. Apply a topical antiseptic to the bite.

If you see on your skin a clear area encircled by a red rash and are feeling flu-like symptoms, you may have contracted Lyme disease, though the bull's-eye rash doesn't always present. Visit your doctor or a medical center immediately for a Lyme test, but be aware that it takes several weeks after a bite for your body to show antibodies. Lyme symptoms mimic many other ailments, so it's difficult to get an accurate diagnosis; most medical practitioners will begin a course of antibiotics if they believe you've been exposed.

In 2017 researchers discovered ticks in the Adirondacks carrying the agent that causes human babesiosis, a malaria-like illness. It typically presents with fever, chills, sweats, fatigue, and anemia. If untreated, the infection can be very serious for the elderly and people with compromised immune systems.

Weddings

CENTRAL AND SOUTHWESTERN ADIRONDACKS More traditional houses of worship include the quaint **Big Moose Community Chapel** (315-357-2622) and historical **St. Williams on Long Point** (315-354-4265; www .stwilliamsonlongpoint .org), on

THE HIGH PEAKS IS A POPULAR WEDDING DESTINATION COURTESY OF MARK KURTZ, WWW.MARKKURTZPHOTOGRAPHY.COM

THE ADIRONDACK COCKTAIL

Recipe for an Adirondack, from A. S. Crockett's 1935 The Old Waldorf-Astoria Bar Book:

2 oz. gin
2 oz. orange juice

Pour the gin into an old-fashioned glass filled with ice. Top with orange juice.

Raquette Lake. Or go traditional Adirondack-style at a Great Camp: **Sagamore** (315-354-5311; www.greatcampsagamore .org), in Raquette Lake, was once the Vanderbilts' getaway. Old Forge's artsy **View** (315-369-6411; www.viewarts.org) makes for a modern setting, and at **Gore Mountain** (518-251-2411; www.gore mountain.com), in North Creek, you can ride the gondola up in warm or cold weather for high-altitude nuptials. For a nautical wedding, board **Old Forge Lake Cruises'** *Clearwater* (315-369-6473; www .oldforgelakecruises.com) or Raquette Lake Navigation Company's elegant *W. W. Durant* (315-354-5532; www.raquette lakenavigation.com), named after the nineteenth-century Great Camp builder.

NORTHWEST LAKES If you're seeking a traditional house of worship, consider the stone chapel **Saint John's in the Wilderness Episcopal Church** (518-891-3605), in Paul Smiths, or Tupper Lake's historical **Beth Joseph Synagogue** (518-359-3580). Sites that often accommodate receptions are Tupper Lake's slick natural history museum, the **Wild Center** (518-359-7800; www.wildcenter.org); President Calvin Coolidge's summer White House, **White Pine Camp** (518-327-3030; www .whitepinecamp.com), in Paul Smiths; and the **Lake Clear Lodge and Retreat** (518-891-1489; www.lodgeonlakeclear.com). And brides looking for exclusive, top-shelf luxury should consider **The Point** (518-891-5674; www.thepoint resort.com), on Upper Saranac Lake.

HIGH PEAKS AND NORTHERN ADIRONDACKS **Whiteface Mountain** (518-523-1655; www.whiteface.com) has a gondola that'll carry a wedding party into the clouds, and the High Peaks, depending on the size of your crew, make fine backdrops. **Heart Lake**, by Adirondak Loj (518-523-3441; www.adk.org), is a romantic spot. **Chapel Pond** in Keene is naturally beautiful, and some folks park their boats beneath Lake Placid's **Pulpit Rock**. There's also Jay's **covered bridge**, the **Mountain House** (www.mountain houseadirondacks.com) on Keene's East Hill—with dramatic views of High Peaks—and **Great Camp Santanoni**, in Newcomb, though that historic place comes with a 10-mile round-trip trek on foot, horse, or bike. For more traditional venues that can accommodate hundreds of guests, Lake Placid's **Crowne Plaza Golf Club** (518-523-2556; www.lake placidcp.com) has super views, **Lake Placid Lodge** (518-523-2700; www.lake placidlodge.com) is posh, **Mirror Lake Inn Resort & Spa** (518-523-2544; www .mirrorlakeinn.com; 77 Mirror Lake Drive) is classy, **Whiteface Club & Resort** (518-523-2551; www.whitefaceclubresort .com) has gorgeous gardens and lakeside charm; and **Whiteface Lodge** (518-523-0500; www.thewhitefacelodge. com) has every amenity you could ask for, including a bowling alley and movie theater.

LAKE GEORGE AND SOUTHEASTERN ADIRONDACKS Brant Lake's **Jimbo's Club at the Point** (518-494-4460; www .jimbosclub.com) can host hundreds in its rustic-style lodge. In Bolton Landing, the **Sagamore Resort** (518-644-9400; www.thesagamore.com) is the place for a classy event, with everything—spa, climbing wall, golf course, beach—on campus. Chestertown's luxurious **Fern Lodge** (518-494-7238; www.thefernlodge .com) can accommodate a small group— or elopements. People tie the knot on Lake George onboard one of the vessels operated by **Lake George Shoreline Cruises** (518-668-4644; www

.lakegeorgeshoreline.com) or **Lake George Steamboat Company** (518-668-5777; www.lakegeorgesteamboat.com). You can have an explosive affair (the cannon will blast after you exchange I dos) at **Fort William Henry Resort** (1-800-234-0267; www.fortwilliamhenry .com), a gathering at **Top of the World Golf Resort** with superior photo ops; a grand party with plenty of pomp and circumstance at the **Inn at Erlowest** (518-668-5928; www.innaterlowest.com), or, in Ticonderoga, at **The Barn at Lord Howe Valley** (518-321-4898; www.barnat lordhowevalley.com), an event with an "elegant rustic" vibe. If none of this says "I love you" in a memorable way, there's always **Elvis** (www.lakegeorgeelvisfest .com), who will officiate with panache.

HISTORY: THE PEOPLE'S PARK

Planning a trip to the Adirondacks in northern New York? Bring a road map, bring your bug spray, and by all means bring this book. But above all, bring your love of mystery and your capacity for wonder, for nothing is exactly as it seems here, and a taste for contradiction can only sweeten your encounter with a park bigger than the state of Vermont.

How did it come to pass that a vast swath of forest so relatively close to so many eastern cities was among the last in the lower 48 to gain the eye and expertise of the surveyor, cartographer, and lawmaker? Such marvelous proximity, and yet, for so long, so lightly valued and little known. So proudly venerable—yet so recent an addition to our pantheon of great parks. Like the proverbial girl next door who turns out to be a heart-stopping knockout, the Adirondack region has been, in terms of our appreciation of it, a very late bloomer. It took time for us to get wise to its rare beauty, time to learn to see and cherish the quiet treasure in our own backyard.

And maybe that's just as well, because the same forces that delayed a loving valuation of the region also stalled our rolling in and making an unholy hash of it (though the combined assault of such extractive industries as mining, logging, and tanning took a hard toll). Start with the Native Americans, for whom the Champlain Valley corridor

EARLY WARRENSBURG HOMESTEAD COURTESY OF TED COMSTOCK, SARANAC LAKE

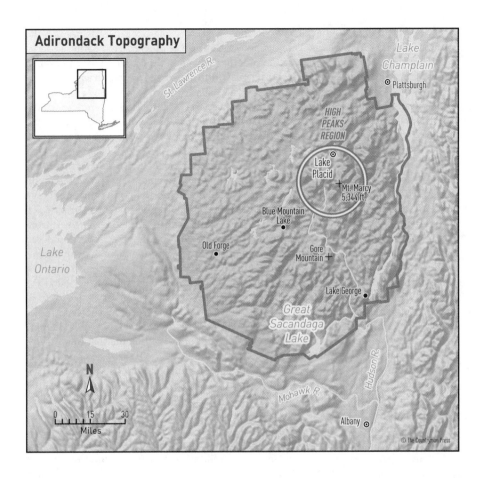

Adirondack Topography

Lake Champlain
Plattsburgh
St. Lawrence R.
HIGH PEAKS REGION
Lake Placid
+Mt. Marcy 5,344 ft.
Blue Mountain Lake
Lake Ontario
Old Forge
Gore Mountain +
Lake George
Great Sacandaga Lake
Hudson R.
N
Mohawk R.
0   15   30
Miles
Albany
© The Countryman Press

was long a borderland between hereditary enemies, the Iroquois and the Algonquin—or more particularly, the easternmost Iroquois tribe, the Mohawk, and from the other side of the lake, the Abenaki, westernmost of the wide-ranging Algonquin.

The Adirondack region was not a draw for European settlers in the seventeenth and eighteenth centuries, when a distant, long-lived imperial conflict pitted the British Crown against the soldiers of New France in one bloody raid and skirmish after another, culminating in the French and Indian War. In the Champlain Valley, in particular, much more was at stake than a show of military muscle. Each nation was as hot to lay claim to this commercially strategic thoroughfare as it was keen to edge the other out. This key waterway (comprising Lake Champlain and Lake George) was the conduit for the kind of abundant timber (including arrow-straight white pines that could mast a royal navy) that a wood-starved Europe hadn't seen for a century. It provided habitat and transport for enough furs to cloak all of "Gay Paree." Indeed, whosoever ruled these waters owned the markets that lined the royal purse. The upshot of this imperial conflict for the Adirondacks was inevitable. The eastern region on the west flank of Lake Champlain gained a reputation as, if not a full-blown war zone, at least a pretty darned dicey place to settle. And so, for the first two-thirds or so of the eighteenth century, settlers stayed away.

Or mostly. In 1730, soldier-farmers from New France colonized a settlement on the west side of Lake Champlain where the banks are close as pincers. Fort Saint Frederic, at present-day Crown Point, thrived for another 30 years, time enough for the French pioneers to raise families; build a trading post, mill, and chapel; and befriend the traveling bands of Native Americans. But in 1758, hearing of the imminent approach of British troops under the tireless Lord Jeffrey Amherst, the French homemakers of the region's first European enclave destroyed their Adirondack Roanoke and fled to Canada, leaving the charred remains to be rebuilt and reinvented as His Majesty's massive fort, Crown Point.

The French and Indian War also gave American and British soldiers their first glimpse of this virgin wilderness, and some of them liked what they saw well enough to come back at the conflict's end. Bands of Quakers found the region, too, and gave Quaker names to several early settlements in the southern and eastern Adirondacks, among them Wing's Falls, later called Glens Falls, the bustling mill town at the Adirondack park's southeastern edge. Laboring under the delusion that the underpopulated Adirondack region might somehow escape the ever-growing tension between native-born Americans grown restive under British rule and those loyal to the Crown, the peaceable Quakers were in for a rude surprise. Once again, during the American Revolution and for some years after, the eastern Adirondack corridor between Montreal and Saratoga emerged as a bloody frontier, and settlers hunkered down at their peril.

Among the ranks of the veterans who were nonetheless attracted to this dangerous frontier were many Scots, survivors of the Highlander regiments that fought with fabled valor at Lake George and Fort Ticonderoga. In the southern Adirondacks, Sir William Johnson, the high-living, Irish-born veteran and brilliant liaison between the Iroquois and the British Crown, bought himself a sweet chunk of real estate from the British-allied Mohawk and set about parlaying his riverside homestead into a wilderness fiefdom. (Proud local legends insist that the tireless Johnson sired 700 progeny, donned a kilt with his Scottish Highlander immigrant tenants, and reveled with the Mohawk braves who routinely camped and feasted on his baronial front lawns.) But the Johnson family was pro-British, and when William Johnson died and the patriotic fever of the Revolution took the Mohawk Valley by storm, his sons exiled themselves to Canada, their faithful Scottish tenants with them, and the old man's upstate kingdom was seized and broken up, never to be restored.

The Scotsman Sir Philip Skene sowed his fertile corner of the Adirondacks near today's Whitehall (formerly Skenesborough), with sawmills, iron forges, settlers, and his own small crew of African American slaves. Sir William Gilliland, a Scots-Irish immigrant, and like Skene and Johnson a veteran of His Majesty's Forces, set his dogged sights on the "howling wilderness" (his words) at the mouth of the Boquet River, near Willsboro (which he named for himself). Come the Revolution, the exiled Skene saw his shipyard seized, his slaves dispersed, and his pioneering iron forges used to fashion the cannonballs that stalled the British navy at the Battle of Valcour. Gilliland should have had better luck: he, at least, backed the winning party, even feeding three thousand shell-shocked American soldiers in weary retreat from a disastrous foray into Canada. But patriot or not, Gilliland's grand feudal ambitions were ill suited to the democratic temper of his times. Benedict Arnold (of all people!) charged Gilliland with treason: Gilliland went to jail, lost his holdings and his farms to marauding Loyalists, landed in debtors' prison, and wound up freezing to death in the Adirondack woods, leaving a handful of Adirondack villages to honor his good work with Gilliland family names.

To the names of Johnson, Gilliland, and Skene, add Alexander Macomb, brief owner in 1791 of almost 4 million Adirondack acres; add the Rhode Island merchant John

SEVENTEENTH- AND EIGHTEENTH-CENTURY IMPERIAL CONFLICTS SHAPED THE REGION—AND THE COUNTRY, AS SEEN IN THIS POSTCARD COMMEMORATING THE SURRENDER OF BURGOY COURTESY OF TED COMSTOCK, SARANAC LAKE

Brown, whose "tract" would encompass much of today's park before it reverted to New York State for taxes; add John Thurman, the New York City businessman who recruited Scottish pioneers to the region near the village that bears his name today. Their stories make such satisfying copy. The energetic Thurman: gored to death in his prime by a bull! The ever-hopeful Brown (who gave his ghostly, never-settled townships such names as Frugality, Sobriety, and Perseverance) lost his land agent, a son-in-law, to suicide, and his holdings to the state! The impecunious Macomb, who wound up in debtors' prison, half mad!

More enduring, if less flamboyantly dramatic, was the experience of the nameless pioneers who discovered the region in the half century or so after the Revolution, when a close-to-bankrupt New York State took over the Crown lands of the northern wilderness and sold upstate parcels by the thousands. Only then did the region see anything like a real influx of settlers, many of them veterans of the Continental Army. In they poured from the worked-over, exhausted hill farms of New England, and it wasn't long—maybe a decade, maybe two—before sod huts and log shanties donned neat suits of locally milled clapboard, and every crossroads settlement could boast an inn, tavern, and makeshift church. Historians call it the Yankee Migration, and Puritan-descended Yankees these land-starved settlers mostly were. But there were Hessians, too, and bands of Scots-Irish from northern Ireland, and once again Quakers trickling northward from the Hudson Valley; and, coming south after 1816, both French- and Anglo-Canadian homesteaders looking to make a fresh start after the quashing of the failed Canadian Rebellion.

Some came of their own accord, others in response to the propagandistic broadsides and handbills of land agents working for downstate speculators—speculators who had every reason to assume their settler-tenants would improve the value of their investment with each swing of the ax, even when they failed to pay rent or give over a portion of their crops. This time-honored colonial strategy had worked well enough elsewhere along the Eastern Seaboard. What went wrong up here? Why did one Adirondack empire after another fail to prosper?

It is true that many of these so-called harpy land barons would not live on or anywhere near their tracts, and not a few tenant farmers chafed under the high-handed, semifeudal expectations of their absentee landlords. But far more demoralizing than a long-distance landlord was the daily, blunt, implacable resistance of the terrain. If it wasn't the bitter thinness of the Adirondack soil (a few lush river valleys aside), it was the length and harshness of the winters, the stinginess of the growing season, the roughness of the topography, or the dread ferocity of predators—wolves and panthers, bugs and bears. Nor was the situation eased by the absence of transportation routes that might have eased the settlers' transition from subsistence to a market economy. What did it profit them to grow the sweetest hops, the fattest turnips, the reddest apples in their township, if they lacked a wagon route or railhead or boat landing to get their crops to market? To be sure, there were snug farming settlements in places as far-flung as Lake Placid and Lake Luzerne, but once other options were open (tourism, especially), agriculture as the prime force of the local economy quickly took a backseat.

The fact that the nineteenth-century Adirondack region was unvisited by marauding bands of horse-borne, painted Natives, or masked banditos, has made it hard for us to see it as a frontier territory every bit as dangerous and seemingly remote as the highlands of New Mexico or Arizona, but this is surely how it felt to the first lonely, forest-bound pioneers. As Adirondack cultural historian Philip Terrie has observed, "The only thing that distinguished the Adirondacks from western frontier regions was that exploitation of local riches—real or imaginary—did not involve the removal or slaughter of indigenous peoples."

Everybody knew the Adirondacks were no place for a farmer with any kind of means. Settlers moved there mostly when they couldn't afford better pickings elsewhere. But how many of these hopeful pioneers could guess at a glance that such fair-seeming country could make a poor man poorer still? Little wonder that so many from this first generation of Adirondack pioneers pushed on to greener pastures farther west when the Erie Canal opened for business in 1825, or hastened home to long-settled New England. At the same time, as the rough reality of the Adirondack climate and topography eroded the Jeffersonian dreamscape of a thousand well-tended, self-sufficient little farms, another kind of vision cast its own enduring spell—the view of the Adirondack woodlands not as a hindrance to a farmer's fortune but as a fortune in itself, rich as Croesus in the two crops that are the bane of any farmer's existence: tall trees and big rocks thickly seamed with iron ore.

It wasn't that these native crops weren't right there for the harvesting all along or that the colonists and the Native Americans before them were unmindful of them. But in 1700, what New Hampshire homesteader was thinking about the red spruce of the Adirondack interior? All the timber a colonist could hope for was right there in the back forty. It would take the depletion of the New England and southern New York forests to force a deeper move into northern New York, an advance that only quickened as innovations in the woods industries made it easier to get trees out. In the early 1800s, legislation that declared New York rivers public highways launched the great age of the Adirondack river drive. By midcentury, fast-running Adirondack rivers—the Saranac, the Grasse, the Schroon, the Hudson—were sometimes so densely shingled over with floating logs that a skilled river driver could hop from log to log for half a mile, with nary a glimpse of the water roiling beneath.

By 1850, New York State led the nation in timber production. Tiny sawmills that once catered to the basic needs of pioneers now shipped and sledded their product north to Canada or south to Albany. The feudal land baron was supplanted by the capitalist lumber baron, and the homesteader once as game to burn a tree as look at it now added skilled logger or river driver to his résumé. Every tree, it seemed, had its use: white pine and red spruce for ships' masts and house construction, hardwood for charcoal, hemlock for the bark whose tannin-rich liquor was essential in the curing of leather, a particularly vital Adirondack industry from 1860 to 1880. In the last two decades of the nineteenth century, the shift from rags to wood pulp in the papermaking industry brought a whole new world of trees into the loggers' line of fire. Pulp-grinding machinery didn't care how straight or true or old or long the wood it used was. Cellulose fiber did the trick, and trees as skinny as three inches round were fair game.

As for that other bumper Adirondack crop, iron ore, it, too, owned a hearty appetite for vast stands of wood. Ore was so abundant in the northeastern Adirondacks you could see it plainly in the outcrops along Lake Champlain, and so famously pure, some of it, you could work it fresh from the seam. More than 200 forges operated in the nineteenth-century Adirondacks, almost half of them along the iron-russet banks of two Adirondack rivers, the Ausable, and the Saranac. Of the scores of remote hamlets that owed their founding to these charcoal-hungry forges, many are now ghost towns or little more than a cluster of leafy sinkholes in the woods, but in 1850, New York State led the nation in iron ore production. The lumber barons who had overtaken the "harpy land barons" were now joined in their pursuit of wood by mining magnates, whose prolific crews of woodchoppers and colliers (charcoal makers) kept their forges bright with burning charcoal. Thanks to those mining magnates, the Adirondack forest suffered its first clear-cut. Indeed, it was the mining industry, much more than lumbering, that did so much to load the quills of illustrators whose before-and-after engravings of the Adirondacks (virgin, then denuded) in such magazines as *Harper's* and *Frank Leslie's Illustrated Weekly*, spurred an outraged readership to support the notion of an Adirondack forest preserve. Consider: It took two and a quarter cords of wood to make 100 bushels of charcoal, and up to 500 bushels of charcoal to generate a ton of Adirondack ore. The hills were alive with the sound of crashing hardwoods.

As industrialization stepped up the demand for the extractive products of the northern New York wilderness—tanbark, logs, pulpwood, ore—settlers found plenty of pickup work to buttress the meager output from their hardscrabble farms. And a good thing, too: the flexible, seasonally responsive diversification of the Adirondack home economy—a potato farm in the summer, a logging gig in the winter, a little hauling, a little millwork, a job guiding city fishermen to favorite streams—was the key to survival, and this tradition defines the Adirondack lifestyle even now.

But when local hands proved too few to meet the labor needs of fast-growing mining towns, tannery hamlets, and logging camps, another source of labor was introduced: immigrants and migratory workers. To an extent, different industries generated different ethnic enclaves. Irish immigrants, for example, were often drawn to tannery towns. French Canadians worked in the woods, Italians on the railroad tracks, Poles and Lithuanians in the mines. But no single ethnic group monopolized any single industry to the exclusion of any other. Saint Regis Mohawk Indians worked on river drives and in Adirondack tanneries as well. In Lyon Mountain, Witherbee, or Mineville, Eastern European miners worked cheek by jowl with Italians, Spaniards, Irish laborers, and African Americans; indeed, the first iron miners in the Adirondacks were the land baron Philip Skene's black slaves. The logging camp at Wanakena featured a Swedish sauna, and up near Chazy an encampment of Italian stonemasons built themselves a hive-shaped bread oven in the woods.

Because these rough-hewn, company-built settlements rose and dispersed with the success and decline of the industries that founded them, their story has excited little notice among Adirondack historians. If anything, the Adirondack region has enjoyed a certain nativist reputation as a demographic land apart, free and clear of "outsiders,"

OLD ROCKS, NEW MOUNTAINS

The rocks beneath Adirondack peaks and valleys were formed from sediments laid down in shallow seas some 1.3 billion years ago. Although that sounds like a tranquil enough beginning, the intervening millennia between the Grenville period and modern times was a chaotic riot of rumpling, folding, shearing, compressing, cracking, and colliding. Himalaya-like peaks rose, then were beaten down by weather and wave; the land was then stretched and cloven as continents crashed into one another. The metamorphic rocks we walk on today, atop Mount Marcy or even along a southern Adirondack stream, were once buried 15 to 20 miles beneath the surface.

Today's mountain ranges, though, were ultimately shaped by the scraping action of a mile-thick glacier 10,000-plus years ago. This moving wall of ice took the jagged peaks down to their hardest bedrock, deposited sand as sinuous eskers, and left behind giant boulders—erratics—as calling cards. The Adirondack Mountains are rising still, reaching up at a rate of 2 to 3 millimeters a year, about the length of Lincoln's nose on a penny, thanks to a hot spot deep within the Earth.

From the high points of land, hundreds of rivers drain north into the Saint Lawrence River, east to Lake Champlain, and south to the Hudson and Mohawk Valleys. Lakes often fill the ancient fault valleys, in diagonal lines between the mountains.

THE ADIRONDACK MOUNTAINS ARE RISING AT A RATE OF 2 TO 3 MILLIMETERS A YEAR, ABOUT THE LENGTH OF LINCOLN'S NOSE ON A PENNY COURTESY OF JOHNATHAN ESPER, WWW.WILDER NESSPHOTOGRAPHS.COM

the monolithic stronghold of the Yankee pioneer. But northern New York was never exempt from the demographic trends that salted so much of rural America with ethnic enclaves during the great age of industrialization. If a migratory lifestyle deprived many of these immigrant communities of a place in the written historical record, you can still trace the evidence of an ethnic presence in the tongue-twisting nomenclature of early headstones, the sunken remains of one-time railroad tracks, the French or Irish street names in Adirondack towns.

Not every nineteenth-century Adirondack railroad spur bore carloads full of hemlock bark or iron ore, pulpwood, or massive logs. Some were built specifically to ferry a special cargo *to* the woods: the sightseers and "city sports" for whom, from 1870 to 1910 or so, a visit to the distant Adirondacks held all the exotic cachet of an African safari. The burgeoning resort scene was an inevitable extension of the "Grand Tour" of the North Country that already encompassed tony Saratoga Springs and elegant Lake George. And where railroad sleepers left off, stagecoaches and steamboats picked up—another source of seasonal employment for enterprising locals, some some of whom would parlay modest stagecoach routes into backwoods transportation empires.

This new, bourgeois resort clientele expected rather different lodgings than the circuit riders and traveling peddlers who preceded them, and Adirondack hostelries made haste to adjust. The proverbial backcountry tavern with its rough pallets in the attic begat the North Country inn, which in turn begat the double-balconied hotel, with uniformed black waiters, Irish cooks, and a ready stable of picturesque, authentically gruff Adirondack guides. More socially positioned visitors were lucky enough to enjoy an invitation to one of the Adirondack Great Camps, private compounds sometimes as built up as small towns. Here, guests were plied with the bubbliest champagne, the mildest Cuban stogies, and the most delicious six-course feasts that the ruthlessly gotten gains of the Gilded Age could buy.

Wilderness no longer had to justify itself as a means to an agricultural or industrial end; it was increasingly an end in itself, restorative for spirit, soul, and body, especially those bodies in the early grip of tuberculosis. Lots of rest and good clean air—that pretty much summed up the homely prescription of Dr. Edward Livingston Trudeau, the great champion of the "Adirondack cure," and that's what a 6-week stint in the screened-in porch of a Saranac Lake village cure cottage delivered. In this hill-bound hamlet, there were, in addition to Trudeau's well-known sanatorium, cure cottages for Lower East Side tenement girls, for Cuban aristocrats, for show business mavens, and for Hungarian aesthetes. Robert Louis Stevenson did a turn at Saranac Lake. So did baseball star Christy Mathewson and the gangster "Legs" Diamond. You sat, you ate, you rested, you got bored out of your mind. But as often as not, you did get better. And if you didn't, your problem was you found the Adirondacks too late to do you good.

What happened when the tourists and the travelers collided with the worked-over, roughed-up landscape of the Adirondack industrialist and his heavy-booted teams of loggers, tanners, river drivers, and mill workers? No matter how pristine the eventual destination, the view from the stagecoach or sleeper window almost certainly exposed the Adirondack adventurer to the occasional glimpse of clear-cut hillsides and tangled slash. Sometimes it seemed the more prolific the newly converted admirers of the region, the faster it was changing—and not for the better. Was it an accident that in the same year (1864) an anonymous editorial in the *New York Times* suggested that the Adirondack region be preserved as a "Central Park for the world" and George Perkins Marsh published his seminal book, *Man and Nature*, on the delicate relationship between a healthy forest and a secure watershed?

Cut too much, Marsh argued, and you set the scene for a tidal wave of muddy runoff and unleash the threat of flood and drought. Too much cutting can even make the

PRESIDENTS IN RESIDENCE

Although we can't claim that George Washington slept here, the father of our country was certainly aware of the vital importance of fortifications at Ticonderoga and Crown Point along Lake Champlain's western shore. Thomas Jefferson and James Madison visited Lake George in 1791 on a summer reconnoiter to Vermont that doubled as a vacation; Jefferson, a seasoned world traveler, described the lake as the most beautiful he'd ever seen.

In 1817, James Monroe skirted the wild edge of what would become the Adirondack Park during a trip from Champlain to Sackets Harbor, on the Saint Lawrence River.

Andrew Jackson, who served in Congress from 1827 to 1829, was a close friend of Richard Keese II, after whom the village of Keeseville is named. Jackson ("Old Hickory") went north to see Keese, and in honor of the occasion, a hickory sapling was sought to plant in the front yard of the homestead. But no hickories could be found for miles around, so a bitter walnut was substituted. It thrived.

Chester A. Arthur stayed at Mart Moody's Mount Morris House, near Tupper Lake, in 1869, and slept on the floor like everyone else. When he was president, in 1881, Arthur named the guide and innkeeper postmaster of a new settlement named—surprisingly enough—Moody.

Grover Cleveland also knew Moody as a guide. While hunting near Big Wolf Pond, Cleveland reportedly said to him, "There's no wolves, here, darn it! But—there ain't a hundred pencils here, either, goin' every minute to take down everything I say." The president returned to the Adirondacks for his honeymoon, and also stayed at posh places in and around Lake Placid.

Benjamin Harrison visited his vice-presidential candidate Whitelaw Reid at Loon Lake during the 1892 campaign, and he whistle-stopped in Crown Point, Lyon Mountain, Blooming-dale, and Saranac Lake. Along the way, he was feted with band concerts and pageants and given gifts of iron ore and wildflower arrangements. In 1895, Harrison built a rustic log camp named Berkeley Lodge on Second Lake, near Old Forge.

William McKinley made a special trip here to John Brown's grave in 1897, but it was his assassination that led to one of the most exciting footnotes in Adirondack history. Theodore Roosevelt, who first came to the mountains as a teenager in 1871, was climbing Mount Marcy when news of McKinley's imminent demise was cabled north. A guide scrambled up the peak to tell TR, who made it down in record time. Three relays of teams and wagons whisked him in the murk of night from the Tahawus Club to North Creek, and Roosevelt learned in the North Creek railroad station that he had become the 26th president on September 14, 1901.

Calvin Coolidge established a summer White House at White Pine Camp, on Osgood Pond, in 1926. This was at the height of Prohibition; silent Cal's place was a mere stone's throw away from Gabriels, a hotbed of bootleg activity.

climate change and diminish rainfall, which in turn would damage agricultural production. No more rain: no more farms, no more food—worst-case scenario, no more people. In New York State specifically, as surveyor Verplanck Colvin pointed out, a ravaged watershed in the north could mean lower water levels for the Hudson River and the Erie Canal—a disaster for commercial and transportation interests and for downstate politicians. A healthy watershed was also a safeguard against waterborne disease, a concern of no small moment to the epidemic-leery voters of metropolitan New York.

Although it would take a few more decades to gather steam enough to win the necessary political support, here was a perfectly utilitarian rationale for the founding of a preserve. No early advocate ever argued for the Adirondack Park in aesthetic terms alone. It helped that the region was gorgeous, but it was health and public safety, not good looks and recreation, that won the day in 1885 with the creation of the Adirondack Forest Preserve, then almost 700,000 acres scattered across 11 counties. Five years later, the state began to consolidate its holdings with additional purchases, and

Franklin D. Roosevelt was no stranger to the North Country. He officiated at the opening of the 1932 Winter Olympics, dedicated the Whiteface Veterans Memorial Highway in 1935, and celebrated the fiftieth anniversary of the Forest Preserve in Lake Placid that same year.

Bill Clinton's August 2000 visit to Lake Placid included golf and plenty of fresh air, but what locals remember is how a young woman flashed the commander in chief as he waited for a cone at Ben & Jerry's ice cream shop on Main Street.

George W. Bush came to Wilmington to promote his "Clear Skies" initiative in April 2002. Heavy snows, perhaps laden with noxious chemicals described in the initiative, forced the speeches from a beach on the Ausable River to the lodge at Whiteface Mountain.

BERKELEY LODGE, ON SECOND LAKE, THE SUMMER COTTAGE OF FORMER PRESIDENT BENJAMIN HARRISON COURTESY OF TED COMSTOCK, SARANAC LAKE

the expectation was expressed that someday all the land within the penciled "Blue Line" that outlined the edges of this new park would comprise "One Grand, Unbroken Domain."

In 1892, the Adirondack Park was officially defined. Three years after that, a new state constitution declared these Forest Preserve lands should be "forever kept as wild forest lands." Private land could still be logged, but state land was off-limits, allowed to grow up and fall down without interference from humans. It was, notes historian Philip Terrie, a provision that made the Adirondack Forest Preserve "one of the best protected landscapes in the world." And enacted not a day too soon: late-nineteenth-century innovations in pulp making meant that virtually all the woods were fair game for the lumber magnates, and between 1890 and 1910, the very years the park was birthed, logging activity on privately held lands within the park actually peaked. Of course, the more frenetic the pace of logging, the faster the non-state-owned forest was depleted, and as shortages occurred, many lumber companies began to move their logging operations elsewhere, to tree-cloaked Quebec, for instance, or to the temperate South.

And what was moving in about this time, sputtering exhaust and spitting gravel and scaring horses half to death? Infernal combustion. Automobiles were rare enough in the Adirondack region in the early 1900s, but within a generation roads were snaking between passes. In their dusty wake followed not only carloads of vacationers but trailheads that met the roads and led hikers to remote summits; roadside auto courts, housekeeping cabins, and filling stations; and roadside attractions with music, dancing, and even dancing bears.

Was it the end of the Adirondack Park or the beginning? Certainly the age of the automobile spelled the death of the Adirondacks' vaunted isolation and mystique. You didn't need to come for a season anymore. From the necklace of midsize cities that outline the Adirondack region (Glens Falls, Plattsburgh, Ogdensburg, Watertown, Amsterdam, Gloversville, Massena, Malone), you could do it in a day. Or chug up from Albany or even Brooklyn for a nice long weekend: pack the trunk with tent and camping gear, throw the kids in back under a blanket, check the oil, kick the tires—you're off. No 2-week stay at one hotel; you could play connect-the-dots between lakeside campgrounds under the towering white pines, cook your own chow over an open fire instead of dealing with a stuck-up waiter in a uniform at some swank hotel. You didn't need to hire a guide; a good map and one of those new wood-canvas canoes could do you just as well.

Roads democratized the Adirondack experience as no paper legislation ever could, and with the ease of access, the reputation of the region as a recreational nirvana grew by leaps and bounds. Small towns reeling under the recent loss or exodus of the extractive industries rebounded with a plethora of services aimed squarely at the car-borne tourist: diners, supper clubs (maybe, during Prohibition, with a speakeasy in back), motels, and souvenir shops. As the century wore on, those small-town storefronts increasingly included the recreational outfitter and the real estate office. Nothing like the completion of a superhighway, the "Northway," or Interstate 87, in 1967, to whet the appetite of city dwellers keen to build their Adirondack getaway.

Indeed, so rapid was the proliferation of Adirondack second homes in the 1960s, and so potentially damaging was their impact on the landscape, that Governor Nelson Rockefeller appointed a commission that recommended a new agency just to oversee land use and development. Thus was spawned the controversial Adirondack Park Agency (APA) in 1974. Many are the local objections to the APA's unwieldy bureaucratic mandate (to guide development on public and private lands), but on one thing its critics can almost all wholeheartedly agree: the establishment more than a hundred years ago of the Adirondack Park was a miracle of timing, foresight, and good luck. It could not have happened any sooner, and it certainly could not have happened since. Love the park for its variety and beauty, and you won't be disappointed, but love it for its hidden history as well—the lost loggers, the vanished tannery towns, the boarded-over mine shafts, the stagecoaches, the peddlers, and the wedding cake hotels—and your love and understanding of it can only be enhanced.

—*Amy Godine*

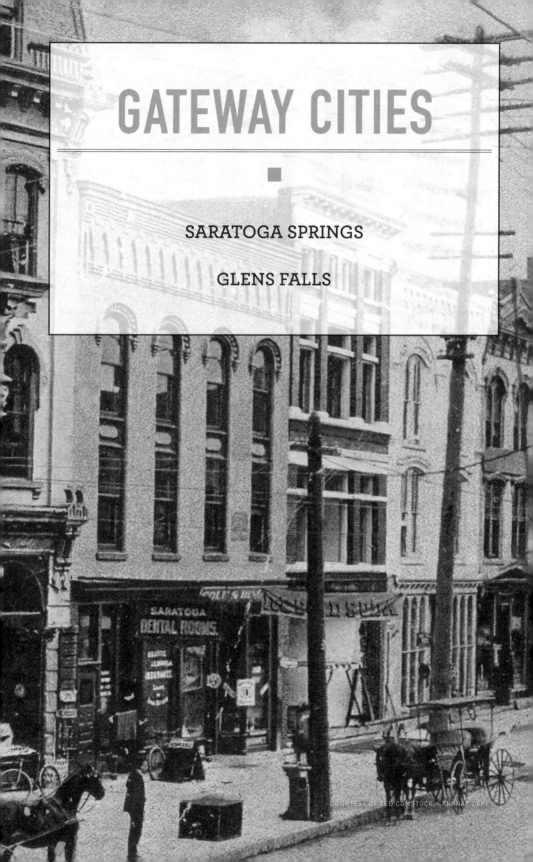

GATEWAY CITIES

■

SARATOGA SPRINGS

GLENS FALLS

COURTESY OF TED COMSTOCK, SARANAC LAKE

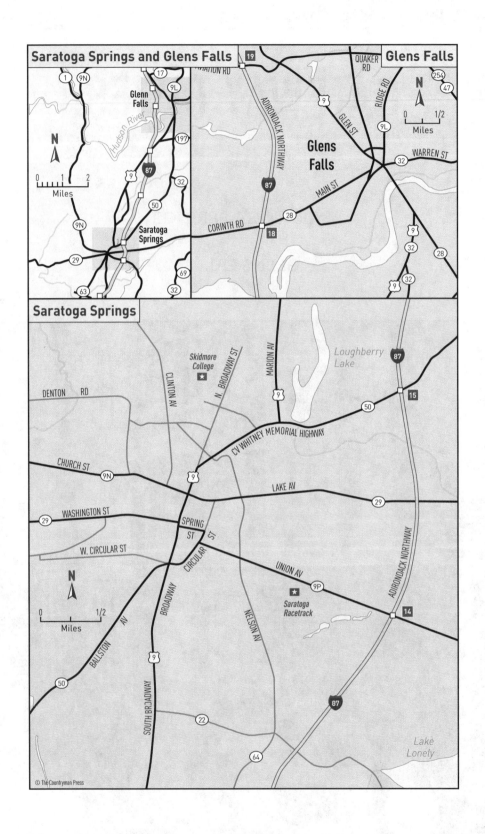

SARATOGA SPRINGS

lthough neither Saratoga Springs nor Glens Falls is in the Adirondack Park, that fact is merely technical for people from downstate heading north on I-87. After the three-hour push out of metropolitan New York and up the Hudson Valley, the exit signs for Saratoga and Glens Falls signal that you're in the homestretch.

Once in a blue moon the urge may overtake an Adirondacker to swap the warble of a loon for the strains of Yo-Yo Ma—and then it's off to Saratoga, which every summer serves up an arts and music calendar that leaves no day unfilled. This is the Adirondack region's favorite getaway, a retreat of high culture, fine dining, and matchless Victorian architecture. You can use Saratoga as a springboard to explore the North Country, or for its own hospitable, hedonistic self. Just peel off the Northway (I-87) at exits 13, 14, or 15, and as fast as you can say "I got the horse right here," you're there.

From the beginning, Saratoga—Mohawk for "place of the rapid water"—has enjoyed a reputation as a bold exception to every imaginable rule. In the colonial era, when New York's wild country was a war zone for rival bands of Native Americans, Saratoga, home to scores of cherished therapeutic springs, was off-limits, an oasis of tranquility. Two centuries later, Prohibition-era gangsters honored a summer truce while ensconced in sumptuous Saratoga digs.

In the nineteenth century and into the next, Saratoga was the first stop on the Grand Tour of the Northern Wilderness, which introduced Gilded Age excursionists to the wonders of Ausable Chasm and Lake George. Halfway between Manhattan and Montreal, here was founded the oldest running thoroughbred racetrack in the country; here constructed the nation's biggest hotel, the Grand Union. And here was built a perfect stunner of a casino that the *New York Times* called "the finest hell on earth."

The grand piazzas have given way to street-side cafes, and Canfield Casino is now a respectable historical museum, but you can still play the odds at the world's prettiest racetrack—or skip the horseplay completely. In the 6-week "season," Saratoga Springs is as good-times crazy as ever.

Nowadays, Saratoga's dozen-plus open-sided spring pavilions no longer draw dapper men and wide-hatted women waiting for a dipper boy to dole out a dram. Hydrotherapy fell from favor more than a half-century ago, and with it the tradition of the two- or 3-week "cure," a regimen of porch sitting, park promenading, mud soaking, and ritualized sipping of spring water reputed to be good for everything from eyestrain to arthritis. But Saratogians swear by the stuff; pick up a map at the Urban Cultural Park on Broadway and treat yourself to a walking tour of the downtown springs. Although the mud baths are gone, you can still savor the romance of an old-time spa in the porcelain tubs at the **Roosevelt Baths and Spa** (1-800-452-7275; www.gideonputnam.com) in Saratoga Spa State Park and at other sip-and-soak options around town.

Broadway is a draw in its own right. Bracketed on the north by Victorian mansions and the woodsy campus of Skidmore College, and on the south by the Spa State Park, this is the street that gives Saratoga Springs its architectural spine. The 1953 demolition of the landmark Grand Union Hotel was a wake-up call for preservation. Boarded-up Victorian storefronts and office buildings emerged from a deep sleep with smart new paint jobs and a market-savvy agenda. Ethnic restaurants joined the steak-and-spuds standbys. An infusion of hip venues—a classy wine bar, an artisanal bakeshop, a gourmet food purveyor, brewpubs, and a city arts center—revived half-dead facades. With the coming of chain stores, the Parisian-profile Broadway is gone, but it is still hands-down the sprightliest downtown around.

Then, when Broadway stales, stroll the side streets. Franklin Square, west of Broadway, is crammed with architectural gems—some fixed-up, some in seedy disrepair. To Broadway's east are Phila Street and Caroline Street, both chockablock with offbeat shops and restaurants.

On Phila is the modest entrance to the legendary **Caffè Lena,** (518-583-0022; www .caffelena.org; 47 Phila Street), the longest-running coffeehouse in the country, a funky upstairs 1960s throwback serving up good folk music most every night. Bob Dylan, Dave Van Ronk, Arlo Guthrie, Greg Brown, Odetta, Rick Danko, and Emmylou Harris have played here. In 2016 the nonprofit institution began a $2 million renovation of its nineteenth-century building to double the performance space, upgrade the lights and sound, and make it handicap-accessible.

Keep walking and you come to Circular Street, the heart of Saratoga's venerable Victorian district. Follow Circular to Union Avenue, lined with graceful homes, one top-flight museum of horse racing, and the fabled thoroughbred track itself.

✳ To See and Do

ARTS AND HISTORICAL CENTERS If you like your history but museum captions make your eyes water, head to the **Saratoga Springs Heritage Area Visitor Center** (518-587-3241; www.saratogaspringsvisitorcenter.com; 297 Broadway) across from Congress Park. Built in the Beaux-Arts style in 1915 as a trolley station, the "VC" is the best place to load up on news of current events and walking tour brochures on Saratoga's historic districts, one of which includes a tour of its elegant old springs. Of the three Depression-era spa complexes developed by then governor Franklin D. Roosevelt, only the Lincoln Bath still brings the old-time fizz. The Spa Park itself is as

YADDO'S GARDENS MAKE A PLEASANT PICNIC SPOT COURTESY OF TED COMSTOCK, SARANAC LAKE

SARATOGA'S NATIONAL MUSEUM OF DANCE IS THE ONLY MUSEUM IN THE COUNTRY DEVOTED TO AMERICAN PROFESSIONAL DANCE COURTESY OF THE NATIONAL MUSEUM OF DANCE

serene and restorative as ever, even if day guests know it less for its constellation of mineral springs than for a lovely 18-hole championship golf course, a posh hotel (the Gideon Putnam), and a great open-sided concert arena, the Saratoga Performing Arts Center, set like a moonstone in a grove of pines. The local volunteers are well informed and helpful; the location is as central as it gets.

Catercorner to the "VC" at the corner of Broadway and Spring is a building that resembles nothing more than the old city library, which it was. Today it houses the handsome **Saratoga County Arts Council at the Arts Center** (518-584-4132; www .saratoga-arts.org; 320 Broadway), home to a flourishing arts council and a roomy art gallery whose monthly exhibitions range from equine art to the hippest of video installations.

The public lawn and rose garden at **Yaddo** (518-584-0746; www.yaddo.org), a famous art colony, are lovely places to picnic.

Exhibitions about social history in Saratoga County are featured at the **Saratoga County Historical Society at Brookside** (518-885-4000; www.brooksidemuseum.org; 6 Charlton Street, Ballston Spa). In a modest Georgian clapboard building thought to be the oldest hotel in the nation are a handful of galleries and exhibitions. Ballston Spa is also home to the **National Bottle Museum** (518-885-7589; www.nationalbottlemuseum .org; 76 Milton Avenue) in an old downtown commercial building. Arrayed here are thousands of hand-blown bottles, the tools that made them, and the stories of the eighteenth- and nineteenth-century settlements that manufactured New York's glassware for generations. The Bottle Museum also features a diorama of an 1880s glass furnace and hosts an annual antique bottle show in Saratoga Springs.

MUSEUMS **Children's Museum at Saratoga** (518-584-5540; www.childrensmuseum atsaratoga.org; 69 Caroline Street) is a hands-on children's museum that will work your youngsters, ages seven and under, into a frenzy. A gaily colored mockup of a generalized downtown offers stations to play postal worker, storekeeper, short-order cook, and firefighter (slide down the pole, pull on the boots, climb on the fire truck, and you're off). Another floor features stations for making giant bubbles, climbing into a tree house, and learning how to make music in a motion-activated mini bandstand. Kids love serving up orders in the 1950s diner and practicing their hammering skills in the construction zone. Admission: $8 adults; children 12 months and under free.

The **Historical Society of Saratoga Springs** (518-584-6920; www.saratogahistory .org; Canfield Casino, Congress Park) is a calm oasis in the middle of busy Congress Park. The city-managed Canfield Casino boasts a top-floor Victorian house museum, a permanent and in-depth exhibition on the history of Saratoga Springs, a revolving gallery (often focusing on some offbeat aspect of local history), and the architectural landmark, the casino itself. Gambling was outlawed when the casino fell into the hands of the city in 1911, and the building was overtaken by springs sippers and tea parties. But you can admire the old chips, roulette wheel, and cards in the "High Stakes Room," and even rent the glorious grand old place for a wedding party or a bash. Admission: $6 adults; $5 seniors; children under 12 months free.

The **National Museum of Dance** (518-584-2225; www.dancemuseum.org; 99 South Broadway at the Saratoga Spa State Park) occupies the former Washington Bath House, an Arts and Crafts–style structure built in 1918. The museum—overseen by the Saratoga Performing Arts Center and located in the Saratoga Spa State Park—is the only one in the country devoted expressly to American professional dance. A permanent Hall of Fame honors the abiding genius of Fred Astaire, Bill "Bojangles" Robinson, Ted Shawn, Martha Graham, Alvin Ailey, Jerome Robbins, and Gregory Hines, plus dozens

SEE GORGEOUS JOCKEY SILKS, GLEAMING TROPHIES, AND A FIRST-RATE EQUINE ART COLLECTION AT THE NATIONAL MUSEUM OF RACING AND HALL OF FAME ON UNION AVENUE COURTESY OF THE NATIONAL MUSEUM OF RACING AND HALL OF FAME

of others. The interactive children's wing allows future dancers to try on costumes and perform on a miniature stage. Open late May through mid-October. Admission: $6.50 adults; $5 students and seniors; $3 children.

National Museum of Racing and Hall of Fame (518-584-0400; www.racingmuseum .org; 191 Union Avenue) is the place to go when your luck flags at the track and celebrity spotting loses its allure. You don't have to love or even like horse racing to be seduced by the interactive exhibits, the life-size starting gate with hidden soundtrack (hoofbeats drumming, the crowd roaring), the gorgeous jockeys' silks, gleaming trophies, first-rate equine art collection, and the Racing Hall of Fame. New in 2017 is a cutting-edge racehorse simulator that puts you in the saddle in a race against five other horses. Admission: $10 adults; $5 seniors and students; members and children under 5 free.

New York State Military Museum (518-581-5100; 61 Lake Avenue) is located in a nineteenth-century armory and houses the records and stories of New York State's military forces and veterans. Some 10,000 artifacts from the Revolutionary War to World War II to contemporary conflicts have a permanent home here—everything from uniforms to weapons to flags (there are more than one thousand state battle flags in this collection, more than half from the Civil War). Soldiers' experiences are captured in the Veterans Research Center, the museum's two-thousand-volume library, which has endless photographs (more than 2,300 images from the Civil War), scrapbooks, maps, and letters. Appointments are recommended for the research center.

Saratoga Automobile Museum (518-587-1935; www.saratogaautomuseum.org; 110 Avenue of the Pines at Saratoga Spa State Park), in the handsome old bottling plant in the heart of the Spa Park, is a flashy place. Vintage car buffs and youthful gearheads alike throng to the colorful installations. The permanent exhibition "East of Detroit" features the automobile industry in New York State; another hall explores the world of racing. The cars displayed at the museum change constantly. In summer, lawn shows bring hot rods, famous motorcycles (one ridden by Audrey Hepburn, another owned by Elvis), and all sorts of international models to the museum. Admission: $8.50 adults; $6 seniors and students; $4 ages 6–16 years old; children under 6 free.

The Frances Young Tang Teaching Museum and Art Gallery (518-580-8080; www .skidmore.edu/tang; 815 North Broadway) brings a touch of edginess to Saratoga. This Skidmore College museum can look like a giant foundering ship or a streamlined Incan monument. Exhibitions, which are always changing, are provocatively interdisciplinary and designed to make you think. The UpBeat on the Roof summer evening music series is very cool.

FAMILY FUN A few years back, die-hard historic preservationists protested the introduction of an Illions carousel in Frederick Law Olmsted's historic Congress Park. Now that it's installed, complaints are few. The carousel runs weekend afternoons from late spring into fall—rides cost just $1—and it's a stunner. So, for that matter, is **Congress Park**, famous with the stroller set for its ducks, ponds, and pretty fountains.

The **Saratoga Spa State Park** (518-584-2535; www.saratogaspastatepark.org; US 9) on the outskirts of town makes a big splash with its two vintage outdoor pools: the big shallow Peerless is pretty much for children only; the Victoria Pool is very nice for adults. A tree-shaded, somewhat unkempt but still hugely popular wading pool in the **East Side Recreation Field** on Lake Avenue (NY 29) keeps the toddlers cool in summer, and there are jungle gyms and sand boxes and swings for all (518-587-3550).

The **Bog Meadow Brook Nature Trail**, 3 miles from downtown, is a level, easy hike (518-587-5554). Another way to get some exercise: bring a bike and sample Saratoga's growing tangle of bike loops.

Family-friendly events include evening bandstand concerts in Congress Park and tailgate picnics at the **Saratoga Polo Grounds** (518-584-8108; www.saratoga polo.com; Bloomfield Road). Around the middle of July the **Saratoga County Fair** (518-885-9701; www.saratogacountyfair.org) comes to Ballston Spa.

A great family movie option is the old-time **Malta Drive-In Theater** (518-587-6077; www.maltadrivein.com) just south of town on US 9. And last, but by no means least, in summer there is the **horse track** (518-584-6200; www.saratogaracetrack.com; 267 Union Avenue). As far as children go, forget the races—it's the paddock that brings the news. Small wiry men in giant polka dots, plus huge horses with swishy tails!

✳ Lodging

Accommodations in Saratoga Springs range from bare bones to celestial, in keeping with the wildly diverse ways and means of summer throngs. Modest but serviceable motels line US 9 along the north and south exurbs of Saratoga Springs. Chains, with restaurants, conference centers, indoor pools, and parking—the **Saratoga Hilton** ($$; 518-584-4000; www.saratogahilton .com; 534 Broadway), and **Holiday Inn** ($$; 518-584-4550; www.saratogahi .com; 232 Broadway)—anchor both ends of Broadway, with a plain but honest hometown standby, the **Saratoga Downtowner Motel** ($; 518-584-6160; www .saratogadowntowner.com; 413 Broadway), pinning down the middle.

Whatever the class or quality of lodging, from a Depression-era housekeeping cottage to a palatial suite at the **Batcheller Mansion Inn**, one rule abides for all—when the track is open, rates go up. Waaaaayyyy up.

The **Adelphi Hotel** (www.theadelphi hotel.com; 365 Broadway) was once the haunt of gangster types, but it's now a favorite of the New York City Ballet during its annual summer residency at the Saratoga Performing Arts Center, and the undisputed jewel in the crown of Saratoga's elite hotels. Flanking Broadway at Caroline, it is the only surviving grand hotel from the Gilded Age. At press time, the hotel was nearing the end of an extensive renovation that promises to make it even swankier. $$$$.

Batcheller Mansion Inn (518-584-7012 or 1-800-616-7012; www .batchellermansioninn.com; 20 Circular Street) is the ultimate for fans of Victorian Gothic design—your stay at this luxurious inn with its stunning mansard roof, clamshell arches, and dome-capped minaret will make you think you went to historic conservation heaven. This over-the-top B&B was the first residence in the United States to be patented (the minaret was inspired by the original owner's appointment as magistrate to Cairo under President Ulysses Grant). Rooms range from simply elegant to outright decadent, with canopy beds, double Jacuzzis, billiard tables, and, in the library, a large-screen TV, should Saratoga's nightlife fail to divert. $$$.

Saratoga Arms (518-584-1775; www .saratogaarms.com; 497 Broadway) is only a stone's throw from the heart of downtown. If the Adelphi is a giddy debutante, the 16-room Saratoga Arms is the oh-so-suave bachelor—quiet, eminently tasteful, scrupulously private, and set up with every boutique treat (including, according to the London *Financial Times*, "the best coffee this side of the Hudson River"). Meticulously restored, down to the antique wicker on the porch, this concierge hotel on the north end of Broadway is a getaway within a getaway. $$$.

Union Avenue, the elegant thoroughfare that runs from the artists' retreat Yaddo past the thoroughbred racetrack to Congress Park, is where you'll find **Union Gables** (518-584-1558; www .uniongables.com; 55 Union Avenue), a grand Queen Anne stalwart designed by R. Newton Bresee. In the early 1990s it underwent a massive restoration and emerged a sparkling pet-friendly B&B with all the trimmings: hot tub, exercise room, bikes for guests, and a refrigerator in every lavish room. While some are themed (the Adirondack-style room features branches for curtain rods), most hew faithfully to Saratoga's high-Victorian style. There are 13 rooms in the main house, each with a distinctive "personality," plus additional guest rooms in an adjacent carriage house, a pondside cottage, and a separate Victorian house. $$$.

✳ Where to Eat

Saratoga Springs has always been a city with an outsized appetite. High-roller Diamond Jim Brady could pack away four-dozen oysters, six lobsters, a whopping steak, and a dozen crabs at a sitting. You can still chow your way through a brace of country or Victorian themed steak-and-salad joints, or find yourself an all-you-can-eat Chinese or Mexican buffet.

But you can also eat well. Very well. And spend a lot of money doing it—which Saratogians and a lot of other northern New Yorkers are evidently prepared to do. But humbler spots abound as well—down-home diners and night-owl getaways, ethnic takeout joints, and pizza parlors galore.

DINING OUT **Chianti Il Ristorante** (518-580-0025; www.chiantiristorante.com; 18 Division Street) serves Northern Italian cuisine that's as exuberant as the ochre-heavy, mural-rich decor. A nice range of pasta selections, rich risottos, and grilled meats fills the menu, with nightly specials. Good red wine, too, and lots of it. No pretense here, just lots of fun.

Druthers Brewing Company's beer garden is a fine place to spend a warm summer afternoon or evening working your way through the craft-beer selection (518-306-5272; www.druthersbrewing .com; 381 Broadway). The food menu tends toward comfort foods like loaded mac-and-cheese, wood-fired pizzas, and burgers that verge on the obscene (the Ugly Burger comes topped with gorgonzola, bacon, beer cheese, caramelized onions, onion rings and a fried egg). Don't worry—there's a veggie burger, shrimp tacos or a kale Caesar salad to satisfy the lighter eaters.

Hattie's (518-584-4790; hatties restaurant.com; 45 Phila Street) is probably the only spot in the North Country where you'll find soul food. The owners of this Depression-vintage downtown icon are determined to maintain Hattie Mosley's beloved legacy of solid Southern and New Orleans–style fare. On hot nights, grab a table in the patio out back. You can't lose with the tried-and-true deep-fried chicken, mac and cheese (with andouille sausage or chicken), or spicy jambalaya.

Karavalli (518-580-1144; www .karavallisaratoga.com; 47 Caroline Street) is a find. It has a superb Indian buffet, varied dinners, and a hopping takeout business. Karavalli's weekend brunch is popular with locals.

HATTIE'S COMFORT FOOD IS A FAVORITE AMONG LOCALS COURTESY OF HEATHER BOHM-TALLMAN

OFF TO THE RACES

During the 40-day track season, from mid-July to Labor Day, the population of Saratoga Springs triples—and prices, traffic, and the wearing of extravagant hats proliferate right along with it. But even if you have no interest in gambling, it's worth visiting the historic racetrack at least once, if only for a glimpse of the uniquely Saratogian scene.

Saratoga held its first thoroughbred meet a month after the Battle of Gettysburg, in 1863, making its racetrack the oldest thoroughbred track in the United States. Some of the equine celebrities that have raced here include Secretariat, Seattle Slew, Man O' War and American Pharaoh. Scenes from the movies *Seabiscuit* and *The Horse Whisperer*, among others, were filmed at the track, and Carly Simon fans will recall it was mentioned in the song "You're So Vain."

To get the full track experience, start your morning with the breakfast buffet served on the porch of the clubhouse, where you can watch the horses work out from 7 to 9:30 AM every race day except Travers Day and Labor Day. From there you can take a walking tour or a tram to visit the historic stable area. Or head across the street to the Oklahoma Training Track, where you can view the morning workout from the new Whitney Viewing Stand, modeled after the 1892 judges' stand.

The gates open for race viewing at 11 AM weekdays and 10:30 AM on weekends, with no racing on Tuesdays. Most days, racing starts at 1 PM. Picnicking is allowed in the backyard grounds area, but tables go quickly—many people stake out a spot at breakfast, leaving a cooler or tablecloth on the table to hold their place. There are also a few reserved picnic tables. You can reserve viewing seats in the grandstand or clubhouse, or take your chances with general admission. Proper attire (no short shorts or tank tops) is required in the clubhouse, and some areas, such as box seats, call for spiffier duds—suits or sport jackets for men, dresses or slacks for women. Fancy hats—from the elegant to the outrageous—are *de riguer*; a hat contest is an annual tradition.

The season is bookended by celebrations—the Hats Off to Saratoga Music Festival kicks off opening weekend, and the Final Stretch Music Festival brings it to a close. The biggest race day by far is the Travers Stakes, held on the last Saturday in August, when three-year-old thoroughbreds compete for a $1.25 million purse.

For another interesting perspective on horse-racing culture, check out one of the Fasig-Tipton horse auctions (www.fasigtipton.com) at the Humphrey S. Finney Pavilion.

For racetrack information call (718) 641-4700 or visit www.nyra.com/saratoga.

HOOF-POUNDING ACTION AT THE SARATOGA RACETRACK COURTESY OF ADAM COGLIANESE, NEW YORK RACING ASSOCIATION

The Wine Bar (518-584-8777; www
.thewinebarofsaratoga.com; 417 Broadway), is an establishment with a full,
creative menu—light plates, entrées,
gourmet cheeses, and homemade desserts—served on two floors and, in summer, on the patio. The bar itself is still an
elegant spot with live piano music and an
endless wine list, but do venture to the
dining room for dishes like yuzu crudo,
free-form ravioli or wild boar with peach
chutney. And ask about the Wine Bar's
overnight suite for a luxury getaway.

CASUAL BITES For a quick and easy
morning fix, a poppy-seed bagel with lox
and a cream cheese schmear at **Uncom-
mon Grounds Coffee & Tea** (518-581-
0656; www.uncommongrounds.com; 402
Broadway) is a winner every time. Many
other spreads, toppings, and bagel flavors
are available as well. Early-rising city
workers pack no-nonsense **Compton's**
(518-584-9632; 457 Broadway) for the
swiftest and most reliable foursquare
breakfast on Broadway. Another town
favorite, the cozy **Country Corner Café**
(518-583-7889; 25 Church Street) draws a
Skidmore crowd with its Green Mountain
coffee, berry pancakes, and orange juice
in jelly jars. If you're visiting during the
race season, breakfast at **Saratoga Racetrack** (888-516-6972; www.saratoga
racetrack.com) is a longstanding tradition. Get there early because clubhouse
tables fill up fast, starting at 7 AM, or bring
your own basket with juice and muffins
and climb the bleachers to a long view. A
free tram ride takes you to the barns.

Good, solid, fail-safe lunches are
available at all of the above, but if
you're after something more original,
try **Ravenous** (518-581-0560; www
.ravenouscrepes.com; 21 Phila Street) for
savory crepes and crisp pommes frites;
Duo Modern Japanese Cuisine (518-580-
8881; www.duo-japanese.com; 175 South
Broadway) serves tasty lunches to stay
or to go.

The elegant **Mouzon House** (518-226-
0014; www.mouzonhouse.net; 1 York
Street) makes mostly Creole-infused cuisine. The wine list is nice, and High Rock
Park is just a stroll away.

The **Local Pub and Teahouse** (518-
587-7256; www.thelocalpubandteahouse
.com; 142 Grand Avenue) has sandwichy
eats and beer and tea that people love.
In summer head to **PJ's** for barbecue and
pecan pie (518-583-7427; www.pjsbarbqsa
.com; 1 Kaydeross Avenue West). A local
favorite for bistro fare, **Sperry's** (518-
584-9618; www.sperrysrestaurant.com;
30½ Caroline Street) is really tasty and
as reliable as Big Ben.

A wide range of delicious takeout food
may be found at neighborhood joints
such as **Spring Street Deli & Pizzeria**
(518-584-0994; www.springstreetdeli
.net; 132 Spring Street). For a family-run
Italian deli, go to **Roma Foods** (518-587-
6004; romafoods.com; 222 Washington
Street). The **Bread Basket Bakery** (518-
587-4233; www.saratogabreadbasket
.com; 65 Spring Street) is where regulars
line up for muffins, scones, bear claws,
and a great array of sandwich breads.
Mrs. London's Bakery and Café (518-581-
1652; www.mrslondonsbakery.com; 464
Broadway) offers nothing but the real
deal: Valrhona chocolate, Plugrá butter,
and the purest of biodynamic grains. The
prices are not for the fainthearted, but
hard-core pastry lovers won't care. You
won't find a better double-berry charlotte, cherry clafouti, or Ricard-flavored
Gâteau Basque north of New York City,
and the hot chocolate is divine.

Skidmore students line up late-night
for doughboys—a carbo-licious local
concoction of spiced chicken, cheese
and scallions baked in pizza dough—
from **Esperanto** (518-587-4236; www
.esperantosaratoga.com; 4 Caroline
Street).

❋ Entertainment

Rumor has it that the dimly lit, moody,
40-seat jazz-scored **9 Maple Avenue**
(518-583-2582; www.9mapleavenue

.com) has the largest selection of single-malt Scotch in New York State and a martini menu longer than your arm. **The Parting Glass** (518-583-1916; www.partingglasspub.com; 40–42 Lake Avenue) is for the Guinness-loving, dart-and-penny-whistle crowd and acoustic music fans, and live jazz is the draw at the atmospheric **One Caroline Street Bistro** (518-587-2026; www.onecaroline.com). Here, the bar is always busy, and the waiters bearing plates of hearty food move with skill between the close-set tables.

Saratoga Performing Arts Center (518-587-9330; www.spac.org; Saratoga Spa State Park, Hall of Springs, 108 Avenue of the Pines) is the summer home of the New York City Ballet, the Philadelphia Orchestra, the Saratoga Chamber Music Festival, and Freihofer's Jazz Festival. The **Homemade Theater** (518-587-4427; www.homemadetheater.org) and Opera Saratoga sojourn in Spa Little Theater, also in Spa Park. On the packed schedule, the opera and ballet go first (more or less through July). When Philly claims the stage you might expect to see the likes of Yo-Yo Ma, Sarah Chang,

Lang Lang, and Joshua Bell. SPAC is touted for its outdoor sound, so if you'd sooner watch the stars than the conductor's back, buy a lawn ticket and bring a blanket to the big grassy slope in front of the amphitheater, along with binoculars and bug spray. In August, pop and rock events, such as performances by the Allman Brothers, Lucinda Williams, Bruce Springsteen, and Phish fill the place.

SPAC and other venues around town host dynamite annual events. Some of the best include the **Saratoga Food & Wine Festival**, the many free readings from the **Writers Institute at Skidmore College** (regular guests include novelist Russell Banks and former Poet Laureate Robert Pinsky), the big-ticket **Travers Stakes** in late August (dress sharp, bet big, lose nice), the **Saratoga Native American Festival**, and the **Nutcracker Tea Party**.

The **Saratoga Shakespeare Company** (518-209-5514; www.saratogashakespeare.com), made up of professional directors, designers, and actors, puts on free productions in Congress Park in July.

CROWDS GATHER FOR ORCHESTRAL CONCERTS, BALLET PERFORMANCES, AND ROCK SHOWS AT THE SARATOGA PERFORMING ARTS CENTER COURTESY OF CHRIS LEE

GLENS FALLS

Glens Falls was named "Hometown U.S.A." by the editors of *Look* magazine in 1944 and, 19 years later it was voted America's "most typical town" by Swedish National Television. The little city is a true child of the Adirondacks, a hard-working, four-square mill town.

Saratoga may own bragging rights as the "Turning Point of the American Revolution" (a distinction, it must be noted, claimed by several other towns with famous battlefields), but when it comes to really regional history, the story of the Adirondacks, surely Glens Falls commands center stage. Quakers founded the settlement in 1763, built a sawmill, ran a tavern, lost their shirts, and saw their homes go up in smoke during the Revolutionary War, their pacifism provoking the suspicion of Loyalist and Patriot alike. After the Revolution, the settlement bounced back, buoyed by an influx of pioneers from New England and Warren County's emerging lumber industry and bolstered by the adoption of the fast-running Schroon and Hudson Rivers as highways for the log drives. Glens Falls earned a century of industrial fame and quiet fortune thanks to logging and papermaking. The Hudson, which winds through Glens Falls from west to east, gave rise as well to a smoky necklace of long-lived mills and factories—lime kilns, canal boat operators, foundries, cement mills, collar factories, railroad spurs, and, looming over all, the pulp and paper mills whose chimney-borne emissions give the city a fragrance all its own.

Finch, Pruyn & Company, for nearly 150 years the major employer in town as well as a major Adirondack landowner, drove the local economy, philanthropy, and even recreation, through its 160,000 acres of woodland.

The city is far from all business. One of the finest little art museums in New York, the Hyde Collection, flourishes here on the high banks of the Hudson, as do several other museums.

Today, in Glens Falls's center, old storefronts have been revitalized as toy stores, bookshops, a coffee roaster, gift galleries, and interesting restaurants. The former Woolworth's is now home to the Adirondack Theatre Festival.

✳ To See

GALLERIES, LIBRARIES, AND MUSEUMS **Chapman Historical Museum** (518-793-2826; www.chapmanmuseum.org; 348 Glen Street), part classic nineteenth-century house museum, also offers a temporary exhibition gallery and space dedicated strictly to the work of the Adirondacks' best-known late-nineteenth-century photographer, Seneca Ray Stoddard (1843–1917). In the mid- and late nineteenth century, the Adirondack region attracted hordes of painters and photographers. No shutterbug could match the range and detail of Stoddard's vision of this changing landscape with its log drives and rough-hewn towns on the one hand, its posh lakeside resorts and scenery-seeking swells on the other. Scrutinize Stoddard's photographs at the Chapman and you come away with a fair idea of the industrial and cultural currents that helped sweep Glens Falls into its age of prosperity and growth.

Crandall Public Library (518-792-6508; www.crandalllibrary.org; 251 Glen Street) is a true anchor for downtown, with excellent book, DVD, and periodical selections, a helpful staff, and a full roster of events, from film to lectures. Folklorist Todd DeGarmo curates exhibitions in a vest-pocket gallery at Crandall. Sample exhibits have explored the drawings of Navajo children, the photographs of Alan Lomax, and crafts of the colonial era. At the museum the **Center for Folklife, History and Cultural Programs** (518-792-3360), an archival resource for regional historians, is open Monday through Saturday, and also hosts great readings, workshops, and performances.

The Hyde Collection Art Museum (518-792-1761; www.hydecollection.org; 161 Warren Street) is the city's pride and joy—the inspired notion of Charlotte Pruyn, daughter of lumber magnate Samuel Pruyn, and Charlotte's art-loving husband, Louis Fiske Hyde. Mentored by the savvy likes of Bernard Berenson, the world-traveling, fast-learning Hydes amassed an art collection that continues to delight visitors for its diversity and taste. Here, in the Hydes' former home (an Italian Renaissance–Revival mansion overlooking the mill that made the family fortune) are paintings by Rembrandt, Degas, Seurat, Rubens, El Greco, and Botticelli, as well as American masters Eakins, Hassam, Ryder, and Whistler. In 1952, 18 years after her husband's death, Charlotte Hyde bequeathed the art collection to Glens Falls. The museum opened in 1963, adding a stylish wing for temporary exhibitions in 1989 and later undergoing a massive restoration and expansion project. In 2017, after a local couple bequeathed its collection of modern and contemporary art, the museum unveiled the new 1,500-square-foot Feibes & Schmitt Gallery to showcase works by Ellsworth Kelly, Robert Rauschenberg, Dorothy Dehner (who spent her early career in Bolton Landing), Sol LeWitt, and other major artists of the last century.

The museum features a fine collection of old and modern masters—works by Rembrandt, Homer, Leonardo, Degas, Eakins, Rubens, Van Gogh—in its lovingly furnished

THE HYDE FEATURES A FINE COLLECTION OF OLD AND MODERN MASTERS COURTESY OF THE HYDE COLLECTION ART MUSEUM

and restored 1912 Italian palazzo home and adjoining arts complex. Recent temporary exhibitions include "Degas and Music," a collection of impressionist Edgar Degas's work; "The Hydes and Rembrandt"; and "Georgia O'Keeffe's Lake George Paintings," exploring the artist's early landscape works. The Hyde's Helen Froehlich Auditorium hosts lectures and performances; studios and classrooms provide space for art workshops for adults and children. The museum is also the backdrop for the de Blasiis series—chamber music that includes such groups as the Biava String Quartet, with performances inside the house in an enclosed patio with soaring windows and tile floors.

Lower Adirondack Regional Arts Council (518-798-1144; www.larac.org; 7 Lapham Place) features Adirondack artisans and artists in this organization's gallery. LARAC offers workshops, plus its summer craft fair in the city park by Crandall Library.

The **Shirt Factory** (518-793-9309 or 518-824-1290; www.shirtfactorygf.com; Lawrence and Cooper Streets) is an arts and healing center in a former clothing manufacturing facility. The historic four-story brick structure's renovated, light-filled studios are leased by more than 50 artists and a dozen healing-related businesses.

✳ To Do

Runners, dog walkers, and bicyclists can get a blast of fresh air, New York engineering history, and a 7-mile workout on a graded path that runs the length of the **Feeder Canal Park**, from the feeder dam 2 miles southwest of Glens Falls to five massive combines in Fort Edward. In 1822, a canal was dug from the Hudson River to "feed" the Champlain Canal some miles off. The surviving locks at the Five Combines Historic Lock Area in Fort Edward are the only ones in New York State that date from the time of the Erie Canal. Kayakers and canoeists can put in at small launch areas at either end of the canal—it's a mellow, easy ride for little kids.

The Feeder Canal Park also marks the southern tip of a 12-mile **Warren County Bikeway** that traces a scenic stretch of the old Delaware & Hudson line to fetch up in Lake George's Battlefield Park. Bikers should figure on a one- to two-hour ride each way. **Rick's Bike Shop** (518-793-8986; www.ricksbikeshop.com; 368 Ridge Road, Queensbury) offers a great selection of sports equipment and information, catering to road cyclists, backcountry bikers, and even winter bikers who install spikes on their tires.

For scenic flights, if you want to float on air, call **Adirondack Balloon Flights** (518-793-6342; www.adkballoonflights.com).

Typical of perhaps a half dozen Adirondack towns, Glens Falls has ski slopes of its own, **West Mountain Ski Center** (518-636-3699; www.westmtn.net; 59 West Mountain Road). It's small, family-operated, mere minutes from downtown, and with more than 20 trails, there's a slope for every skier and snowboarder's speed and style. Another just source of civic pride are the Crandall Park **International Ski Trails** in Cole's Woods (518-615-0446), 7 groomed kilometers of wooded trails lighted for night skiing and free to all, right within the city limits. The **Inside Edge** (518-793-5676; www.insideedgeskiandbike.com; 643 Upper Glen Street, Queensbury) provides downhill and cross-country ski sales and rentals; it's the best local source for racing supplies.

There are plenty of golf courses in Glens Falls and the surrounding area, including **Sunnyside Par 3 Golf Course** (518-792-0148; www.sunnysidepar3.com; 168 Sunnyside Road, Queensbury), and **Bay Meadows Golf Club** (518-792-1650; www.baymeadowsgolf .com; 31 Cronin Road, Queensbury).

For more family fun, Glens Falls is within a few minutes' drive of many outdoor amusement parks and roadside attractions. **Six Flags The Great Escape & Splashwater**

Kingdom (518-792-3500; www.sixflags.com/greatescape), in Queensbury—more than 100 rides strong—is the biggest fun park of its kind in northern New York State. It's open spring through fall, but if you're looking for year-round fun, check out the new adjoining **Six Flags Great Escape Lodge and Indoor Water Park** (518-824-6060; www.sixflagsgreatescapelodge.com), a great place for you and the kids to chase away the winter blahs.

✳ Lodging

Because it is not itself a tourist destination, Glens Falls doesn't have many cozy bed & breakfasts. Motels abound off Exit 19 on I-87 at Aviation Mall and along US 9 heading north and south out of Glens Falls, where such chains as **Econo Lodge** ($$; 518-793-3700; 543 Aviation Road, Queensbury) and **Ramada Queensbury/ Lake George** ($$; 518-793-7701; 1 Abbey Lane, Queensbury) are available.

Inside the city proper, lodging choices winnow down to a fine few, each with comfortable rooms at sensible rates that—along with Saratoga room rates— shoot up in the "high season" of August.

Glens Falls Inn (518-743-9365; www.glensfallsinn.com; 25 Sherman Avenue) has brass beds and nice quilts among scrupulously selected period features that characterize this sunny bed & breakfast in a 100-plus-year-old Victorian home. The inn has five guest rooms with private baths, plus a roomy apartment suite. $$.

The newest bed & breakfast in town, **The Bell House Inn** (518-745-0200; www.thebellhouseinn.com; 153 Bay Street), inhabits a renovated Victorian with an interesting backstory: legend has it the builder added a bell-shaped tower to this and two other Glens Falls houses in honor of his three school-teacher daughters. Each of the four rooms is tastefully decorated, with flat-screen television and a large private bath with tub and shower. $$.

The **Queensbury Hotel** (518-792-1121; thequeensburyhotel.com; 88 Ridge Street) is the belle of the ball—if there *were* a ball, if the ballroom that once pulsed to the beat of Benny Goodman and Guy Lombardo hadn't changed to a reception room years ago. This historic 125-room full-service hotel in the heart of town is the darling of conventioneers and visiting politicos and stars. Ronald Reagan stayed at the Queensbury, as did Bobby Kennedy, ZZ Top, Ozzy Osborne, Bob Dylan, and Phish. The Who also stayed here, in splendid anonymity, working out the kinks of a North American tour.

The Queensbury was built in 1924, when 100 local businessmen, bolstered by substantial start-up gifts from Finch, Pruyn, and Glens Falls Insurance, joined forces to get a hotel built in the heart of their beloved boomtown. Today it remains a fine place to stay, handy to downtown with requisite shop and lounge, pool and Jacuzzi, restaurant, salon, and exercise room. $$$.

✳ Where to Eat

DINING OUT **Bistro Tallulah** (518-793-2004; bistrotallulah.com; 26 Ridge Street) is a chic downtown bistro that would seem at home in a larger city. Its superb New Orleans–style fare can be ordered as small or full portions. Some highlights are the Southern buttermilk fried chicken with smoked cheddar grits, cochon de lait, and the chocolate bourbon pecan torte.

After closing a popular upscale bistro in Saratoga Springs and a stint on the Food Network show *Dinner Impossible*, chef David Britton became a partner in the hip **Downtown City Tavern** (518-480-3500; www.downtowncitytavern.com; 21 Elm Street), where the menu offers creative wood-fired pizzas, wings, grinders, and other casual fare, plus boozy milkshakes.

Rebecca Newell-Butters and Steve Butters, the husband and wife chef-owners of **Morgan & Co.** (518-409-8060; www.morganrestaurant.com; 65 Ridge Street), have both appeared on TV—she was a winner of the cooking game-show *Chopped* in 2009; his comical appearance on the Food Network's *Sweet Genius* led to a cameo on *The Soup*. In 2014 the couple renovated a charming historic mansion into a stylish restaurant with an eclectic menu. Starters range from Moroccan "cigars"—lamb spring rolls with harissa—to poutine; main dishes include grilled pork chops with cranberry apple stuffing and seafood bouillabaisse. In summer there's seating on the elegant porch, often with live music.

Siam Thai Sushi (518-792-6111; www .siamthaisushi.com; 14 Maple Street) serves delicious curry dishes and other Thai specialties, and the sushi is a fine treat for a place so far from the Big Apple.

CASUAL BITES Poopie's? Dirty John's? These beloved places reflect the owners' nicknames and not failed hygiene. The nickname thing is part and parcel of Glens Falls' mill town roots—where lunch counters are like Cheers, without beers.

Order ice cream or a frosty one at **Cooper's Cave Ale Company** (518-792-0007; www.cooperscaveale.com; 2 Sagamore Street)—the root beer is excellent. Find more suds at **Davidson Brothers Brewing Company** (518-743-9026; www .davidsonbrothers.com; 184 Glen Street) in a historic exposed-brick building with a courtyard for outdoor dining. Onion rings on a stick are the perfect accompaniment to a cold beer. **Gourmet Café** (518-761-0864; www.downtowngourmet .com; 185 Glen Street) has soups, salads, sandwiches, ample options for vegetarians and the gluten-averse, and outdoor seating. Check out **New Way Lunch** (518-792-9803; 21 South Street), famous for its Dirty John's hot dogs with meat sauce—also known as Dirt Dogs. **Poopie**

DiManno's Lunch Inc. (518-792-6155; 54 Lawrence Street) has the best breakfasts. Since World War II, it's been run by the DiManno family, who serve huge portions, scrumptious slabs of ham, and attitude at no charge; vegetarians and the easily offended should consider going elsewhere. **Rock Hill Bakehouse** (518-615-0777; www.rockhillbakehouse.com; 19 Exchange Street), near the hospital, serves lunch: smoked turkey and cranberry sandwiches with cheese, Black forest ham, roast beef, all on signature Rock Hill breads. The chowders, minestrone, and beef barley soups are worth trying, too, plus good coffee and sweets.

In Queensbury, **Silo Country Store** (518-798-1900; 537 Aviation Road) is an atmospheric place—poke around the old barn for knick-knacks after enjoying hearty sandwiches, soups, and salads.

✳ Entertainment

Adirondack Theatre Festival (518-480-4878; www.atfestival.org; Charles R. Wood Theater, 207 Glen Street) was launched more than two decades ago. Founders of the company were involved with the original production of the Broadway hit *Rent*, and bring real sophistication to their shows, performed in a theater that was converted from an old Woolworth's department store (see listing below). The season begins in June, with five or six shows, children's workshops, and new play readings.

Charles R. Wood Theater (518-480-4878; www.woodtheater.org; 207 Glen Street) has 30,000 square feet of space for performances, rehearsals, meetings, and receptions. The place's namesake, the late Charles R. Wood, was the founder of Storytown, now The Great Escape, and a driving force in funding community-based projects and organizations—his foundation played a major role in shaping an old Woolworth's into this modern theater. You'll see it all here: the Adirondack Theater Festival in summer, and an assortment of acts, troupes, and galas throughout the rest of the year.

Glens Falls Community Theatre (518-792-1740; www.gfcommunitytheatre .org) is an old-fashioned family-friendly theater that serves up hearty rations of drawing-room mysteries, vintage dramas, musicals, and revues—community-supported and community-staffed all the way.

Glens Falls Symphony Orchestra (518-793-1348; www.gfso.org; 7 Lapham Place) performs a repertoire that ranges from Bach's *St. Matthew Passion* to commissioned pieces by the resident composer at Union College. A high-school chorus augments offerings during the holiday season, and every Fourth of July, the orchestra gives a free performance at City Park; fireworks follow. The symphony plays at a variety of venues in the area, including Glens Falls High School and Skidmore College's Zankel Music Center.

❊ Special Events

Adirondack Balloon Festival (518-222-4593; www.adirondackballoonfest.org) is a famed four-day hot-air balloon event in mid-September that attracts folks from all over the world. This is a big draw and if you aim to catch it up close and personal, make your way to the Warren County Airport by dawn's early light.

Taste of the North Country (www .glensfallstaste.com), a downtown food fair that draws 40-plus restaurateurs of every description, happens every September in City Park.

The Chronicle Book Fair (518-792-1126; Queensbury Hotel, 88 Ridge Street, Glens Falls) is a gathering of dozens of authors, publishers, and members of nonprofit groups who sign books, discuss writing, and give various workshops and kids' activities.

CENTRAL AND SOUTHWESTERN ADIRONDACKS

COURTESY OF JOHNATHAN ESPER, WWW.WILDERNESSPHOTOGRAPHY.COM

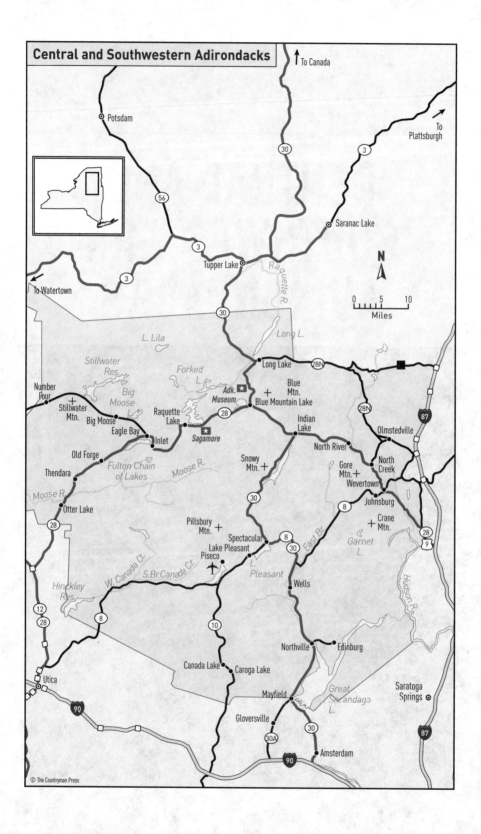

CENTRAL AND SOUTHWESTERN ADIRONDACKS

Old Forge's Fulton Chain is a family-friendly natural waterpark, Blue Mountain Lake has the venerable Adirondack Experience, and North Creek draws white-water rafters part of the year and skiers the other. Yet this region is still one of the most tangled, untrammeled chunks of the Adirondack Park, with a wealth of less crowded peaks and sprawling systems of trails for hiking, biking, skiing, and snowmobiling. And for those looking to really get away from it all, tracts such as the Moose River Plains mean a getaway with just you and, well, the moose.

✳ To See

Lakes and woods define the central Adirondacks, and the same elements shape iconic architecture in Great Camps, such as **Sagamore** and **Santanoni**, as well as the lively cultural scene. Community arts centers are bustling in every season with theater, classes, exhibitions, and concerts, but summertime is the star, when one-of-a-kind views become a stunning backdrop for alfresco paint-outs, plays and music. Whatever the time of year, no visit is complete without a day at **Adirondack Experience**, a museum celebrating the region's roots in state-of-the-art style.

ARCHITECTURE AND HISTORIC BUILDINGS For rustic architecture, a boat tour of Raquette Lake on the **W. W. Durant** (315-354-5532; www.raquettelakenavigation .com), a replica of an old steamboat, allows glimpses of Great Camps such as Pine Knot (the first rustic camp designed by William West Durant), Camp Echo, and Bluff Point (the former Collier estate). **Adirondack Architectural Heritage** (518-834-9328; www.aarch.org) offers tours of the icons of Adirondack style, including Camp Santanoni, a National Historic Landmark in Newcomb, and historic resorts around Big Moose Lake.

THE ARCHITECTURE OF GREAT CAMP SANTANONI, IN NEWCOMB, IS CLASSIC ADIRONDACK COURTESY OF NANCIE BATTAGLIA

ARTS CENTERS **Adirondack Lakes Center for the Arts** (518-352-7715; www .adirondackarts.org; NY 28, Blue Mountain Lake), a multi-arts center, has brought a full palette of programs to Blue Mountain Lake—population 150 (give or take)—for more than four decades, offering workshops, concerts and a Summer Theatre Festival that travels to venues around the park.

GILDED PLAYGROUND

Great Camp Sagamore (315-354-5311; www.greatcampsagamore.org; Sagamore Road, off NY 28, Raquette Lake), a massive rustic lodge along the lines of a Swiss chalet, was built by Adirondack entrepreneur William West Durant in 1897, and then sold to Alfred G. Vanderbilt Sr. in 1901. Even though the Vanderbilts spent much of their time elsewhere, Sagamore was a self-sufficient village in the heart of the wilderness, with its own farm and a crew of craftsmen to supply furniture, hardware, and boats. Today, the millionaires' complex—main lodge, dining hall, rustic guest cottages, casino/playhouse, open-air bowling alley, and boathouse—and the artisans' barns, carriage house, workshops, and blacksmith shop are open to the public for two-hour tours.

Sagamore is a National Historic Landmark in a gorgeous setting on Sagamore Lake, 4 miles off the main state highway on a rough dirt road. Besides tours, the Great Camp sponsors workshops and conferences, is available for overnight accommodations, has a small gift shop and cafe, and can be hired for special events such as wedding receptions and family reunions. The Sagamore was the backdrop for scenes from director Robert DeNiro's 2006 film *The Good Shepherd*, starring Angelina Jolie and Matt Damon, and often appears as the iconic Great Camp in mainstream publications.

Call ahead for walking tour schedule. Admission: $16 adults, $14 seniors and military, $8 school-aged children, preschoolers are free. Open Memorial Day through Columbus Day.

Sacandaga Valley Arts Network (518-863-8047; www.svanarts.org; Northville) provides the south-central Adirondacks with a lineup of gallery shows and workshops, as well as a summertime concert series at Northville Park.

Tannery Pond Center (518-251-2505; www.tannerypondcenter.org; 228 Main Street, North Creek) hosts lectures, concerts, and performances in its 150-seat auditorium, and houses a gallery featuring the work of regional artists.

View (315-601-9728; www.viewarts.org; 3273 Route 28, Old Forge) is the region's premier arts destination, a beautiful 28,000-square-foot LEED-certified facility

VIEW, OLD FORGE'S STUNNING ARTS CENTER COURTESY OF VIEW

THE NEW, INTERACTIVE ADIRONDACK EXPERIENCE, IN BLUE MOUNTAIN LAKE COURTESY OF DUNCAN R. MILLAR

with a state-of-the-art theater, slick gallery spaces, and workshop studios. Annual events include the Adirondacks National Exhibition of Watercolors (August–October), the Old Forge Plein Air Paint Out (September), and a packed performance schedule.

CINEMA The community-run **Indian Lake Theater** (518-648-5950; www.indian laketheater.org, Main Street) brings mainstream and indie films, as well as a variety of musical performances. In Old Forge, the **Strand Theatre** (315-369-2792; www .strandoldforge.com; Route 28) is a beautiful vintage cinema with three screens.

MUSEUMS The **Adirondack Experience** (518-352-7311; www.theadkx.org; 9097 Route 30, Blue Mountain Lake) is the new name of the Adirondack Museum, a cultural icon. Simply put, no visit to the Adirondacks is complete without visiting the place. Perched on the side of Blue Mountain and overlooking the island-studded lake, this is a major outdoor museum that is user-friendly, scholarly, beautiful, amusing, and superlative in every way. Not surprisingly, the place has been described by the *New York Times* as "the best museum of its kind in the world."

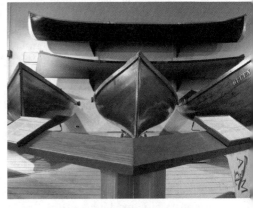

THE ADIRONDACK EXPERIENCE, IN BLUE MOUNTAIN LAKE, IS A MUST-SEE FOR ALL PARK VISITORS COURTESY OF THE ADIRONDACK EXPERIENCE, BLUE MOUNTAIN LAKE

The museum's theme is interpreting man's relationship to the Adirondacks,

Adirondack photography graces coffee-table books, wall calendars, and the pages of popular regional magazines such as *Adirondack Life*. The Adirondack Park is such a photography mecca that photographer John Radigan established the Adirondack Photography Institute (518-478-8592; www.adkpi.org), which provides workshops on a range of topics. Workshops happen at various venues within the Blue Line and are taught by an A-list staff of expert regional photographers.

and it does so in 20-plus exhibit buildings, including a new nineteen-thousand-square-foot interactive exhibit space where visitors can break up a virtual logjam, captain an Adirondack guideboat, and meet colorful characters from the region's past. Though this immersive experience is a big draw, all the old favorites are still here, such as the cabin of Adirondack hermit Noah John Rondeau, a nineteenth-century log hotel, and even a fire tower to climb.

The museum comes alive with craft demonstrations, music, and storytelling on selected days. The early 1800s are revisited every summer during the popular American Mountain Men event, when interpreters in period dress show off their survival skills. And the Rustic Furniture Fair in September showcases 50-plus builders so that visitors can decide how to begin their own Adirondack collections.

Open daily late May through early October, though workshops and lectures continue year-round. Admission is $20 adults, $12 children under 17, free for ages 5 and under, discounts available for seniors.

The outdoor museum complex near Caroga Lake, the **Caroga Historical Museum** (www.carogamuseum.org; London Bridge Road), re-creates pioneer life in the southern Adirondacks in a farmstead, schoolhouse, and country store.

And in Old Forge, the **Town of Webb Historical Association** (315-369-3838; Main Street) has exhibits on railroads, resorts, rustic furniture, and early industries in its **Goodsell Museum**, which is open year-round.

MUSIC Although art centers such as **View** (315-601-9728; www.viewarts.org; 3273 Route 28), in Old Forge, and **Tannery Pond Center** (518-251-2505; www.tannerypondcenter .org; 228 Main Street), in North Creek, offer concerts throughout the winter, lineups around here really heat up when the weather does too. Most communities have summer concert series in unforgettable settings, including the **Caroga Lake Music Festival** (www.carogalakemusicfestival.org); **Friends of Music Summer Concert Series** (518-624-2056; www.mylonglake.com), in Long Lake; **Inlet Concert Series** (315-357-5501; www.inletny.com), on Fourth Lake; **Music by the River** (518-251-2612; on Facebook), in North Creek; **Music on the Trail** (518-624-3077; www.mylonglake.com), in Long Lake; **Thursday Evenings on the Lake** (315-354-4265; www.stwilliamsonlongpoint.org), in Raquette Lake; **Sacandaga Valley Art Network's Summer Concert Series** (518-863-8047; www.svanarts.org), in Northville; and the **Saturday Series** (518-352-7715; www .adirondackarts.org), in Blue Mountain Lake.

SEASONAL EVENTS **Old Forge Winter Carnival** (315-369-6983; www.oldforgeny .com), in February, has torchlight skiing, cardboard-sled races, a snow-sculpture contest, parade, and fireworks.

Frozen Fire and Lights (315-357-5501; www.adirondackexperience.com), in Inlet, which happens in February, starts off with sledding, ice skating, snowshoeing, and cross-country skiing at Fern Park during the day, and wraps up with a bonfire, hot cider and fireworks at Arrowhead Park.

Old Forge marks **Father's Day Weekend** (315-369-6983; www.oldforgeny .com) with a classic car show as well as frog-jumping and ugly-tie contests.

Long Lake hosts an old-fashioned **July 4th Celebration** (518-624-3077; www .mylonglake.com), including music, bed races, a scavenger hunt, fireworks, sack races, and an egg toss.

Raquette Lake's **Durant Days** (518-624-3077; www.mylonglake.com) is a three-day celebration of Great Camp architecture in August, offering tours of landmarks around the lake, as well as concerts, cruises, and a boat parade.

ADIRONDACK POET

Poet Jeanne Robert Foster, born Julia Elizabeth Oliver, grew up in grinding poverty in Johnsburg and went on to be an editor of the *Transatlantic Review*. Her circle of friends included Ezra Pound, T. S. Eliot, and John Butler Yeats, father of the Irish poet. Her poetry and prose memories of her youth were published in *Adirondack Portraits: A Piece of Time*. Foster is buried in Chestertown, as is John Butler Yeats.

Adirondack Authors' Fair at Hoss's Country Corner (518-624-2451; www.hosss countrycorner.com), in Long Lake, is a great opportunity to meet and greet regional writers, held under a huge tent on the second Tuesday in August.

Antiques Show & Sale at the **Adirondack Experience** (518-352-7311; www.theadkx .org), in September, and the **Adirondack Mountains Antiques Show** (518-648-5112; www.indian-lake.com), which runs concurrently in Indian Lake, draw dealers and buyers from all over.

Teddy Roosevelt Weekend (518-582-3211; www.newcombny.com), in Newcomb, celebrates Teddy Roosevelt's wild ride from the High Peaks to the presidency in September, with historical programs, tours, and sporting contests.

Great Adirondack Moose Festival (518-548-3076; www.indian-lake.com), in Indian Lake, is a September weekend of music, guided hikes, children's activities, and scat-counting and moose-calling contests.

THEATER The Adirondack Lakes Center for the Arts (518-352-7715; www.adirondack arts.org), based in Blue Mountain Lake, presents a **Shakespeare in the Parks** tour that visits open-air venues around the region.

✳ To Do

The central Adirondack region is defined by water, with interconnected lakes and swift rivers. It's also defined by snow, with the most impressive cover in places like Old Forge, North River, and Long Lake. Mountain snobs may look down their noses at the peaks here, though some—like Snowy—are higher than some of the vaunted 46 High Peaks. In every season there are challenging adventures, such as white-water rafting or backcountry skiing and trout fishing on pristine ponds. Every outdoorsperson has a favorite spot, from the fire tower on Pillsbury Mountain to the lean-to on Cascade Pond. And there's more public land in this part of the Adirondack Park than in any other.

BEACHES There are plenty of swimming spots throughout this region—most state campgrounds and cabin colonies include one—but here are a few of the standouts:

VINTAGE WATERCRAFT

In 1843, John Todd visited the lonely settlers in Long Lake and wrote, "Their little boats were their horses, and the lake their only path." Traditional wooden boats, especially the guideboat—a narrow wooden crafts, pointed at both ends and propelled by oars, that was favored by early Adirondack guides for its portability and gear-carrying capacity—performed a major role in nineteenth-century work and play. At several affairs across the park, you can get a taste of this era, and enjoy beautifully restored guideboats, canoes, sailboats, and even classic powerboats.

In July the Fulton Chain Rendezvous of the Antique and Classic Boat Society (315-369-6983; www.oldforgeny.com) welcomes exhibitors and members, with a dockside show at the Old Forge waterfront, and a grand parade—everything from old Fay & Bowens and Chris-Crafts, to HackerCrafts and Gar Woods—through the channel that marks the beginning of the eight lakes.

GUIDEBOATS PLAYED A MAJOR ROLE IN NINETEENTH-CENTURY WORK AND PLAY COURTESY OF TED COMSTOCK, SARANAC LAKE

For the budding buccaneer, the place to be is at Inlet's **Arrowhead Park** (315-357-5501; Route 28), on the banks of Fourth Lake. The midsize beach offers a pirate-ship playscape that's perfect for pillaging parties, lots of sand to build—and destroy—enemy forts, and a fishing dock to replenish rations. Plus Northern Lights, a gelato mecca, is a short walk away.

With rope swings, a slide, and a trampoline waiting to jettison the willing into about 11 feet of bracing water, the **Long Lake Town Beach** (518-624-3077; Route 30) is custom-made for teens. But this pretty little tract has thrill rides for the younger set, too: rocking animals and a slope just right for running, or tumbling, down to the shore.

The **North Hudson Town Beach** (518-532-9811; Route 9) fronting 150 feet of the Schroon River is often overlooked. The water is cold—even by North Country standards—but the place's peaceful, private-beach vibe is worth a few goosebumps. Depth depends on the year and season, but it's often shallow enough for preschoolers to navigate and, off the far bank, deep enough for older kids to cannonball.

The **Village of Speculator Public Beach** (518-548-7354; Route 30) on Lake Pleasant, right in the middle of downtown, is the total package. Sure, it has clear water, sparkling sand, and a stunning view. But it's also a stone's throw from a playground, boat launch, hiking and mountain-biking trails, and ice-cream stands.

BIKING As mountain biking continues to grow in popularity, the Inlet–Old Forge area has emerged as a center for the sport. (Just a reminder: all-terrain bicycles are barred from wilderness and primitive areas in the Adirondack Park.) Old Forge welcomes pedalers to explore its extensive snowmobile trails; see www.oldforgeny.com for a map. There are also 50 kilometers of trails at **McCauley Mountain** ski center (315-369-3225; www.mccauleyny.com; McCauley Mountain Road, Old Forge), though without lift service. Inlet has **Fern Park**, with 25 miles of loops, and it's perched on the edge of the **Moose River Recreation Area**, laced with old logging roads and fantastic trails. Check out www.adirondackexperience.com for a list of trails and maps.

The **Speculator Loop** mountain-biking trail system is actually two loops—running 14 and 7 miles. There's a trailhead at the town ball field; pick up a map at the Speculator Chamber of Commerce (518-548-4521; www.speculatorchamber.com).

Lift-serviced biking is available at New York State–owned ski area **Gore Mountain** (518-251-2411; www.goremountain.com; Peaceful Valley Road, North Creek). Some ski trails—as you'd suspect—are gnarly, scary, bumpy rides, but there are traverse routes and woods roads, too. A favorite of Neil Auty's, of the **Bike Works** (518-762-1342), just outside the Blue Line in Johnstown, is the intermediate 5-or-so-mile loop alongside Nine Corner Lake, north of Route 29A near Canada Lake. Ted Christodaro, of bike and flower shop combo **Pedals & Petals** (315-357-3281; 176 Route 28), in Inlet, recommends the area's surrounding snowmobile network, which doubles as mountain-bike trails,

THE INLET-OLD FORGE AREA HAS EMERGED AS A MOUNTAIN BIKING CENTER

Here's a sampling of iconic outdoor adventures for this region:

1. Paddle the **North Branch of the Moose River**, an 11-mile family-friendly ride between Old Forge and Rondaxe with plenty of options for swimming and fishing along the way. This is a summertime trip—water levels are too high in spring.
2. Ski, bike, or hike 5 miles into one of the wonders of Adirondack architecture, **Camp Santanoni**, in Newcomb. You can even hitch a ride on a horse-drawn wagon (518-639-5534; newcombefarmwagonrides@gmail.com). Bonus: There's a beautiful lake at the end of the trail—and you can stash a canoe on the wagon.
3. Trek to **Kunjamuk Cave**, near Speculator, rumored to be an old hideout of Adirondack hermit and all-around colorful character French Louie.
4. Hike 3 miles in to spectacular **OK Slip Falls**, in the Hudson Gorge Wilderness Area—or sign up for a guided hike to the falls and a rafting trip out on the Hudson River with Square Eddy Expeditions (518-251-5200, www.squareeddy.com).
5. Climb 2 moderate miles to the restored fire tower on **Goodnow Mountain**, in Newcomb, and take in a sweeping view of the High Peaks.

but also the quiet dirt Uncas Road from Eagle Bay to Raquette Lake, with a side trip to Sucker Brook. Find more of his recommendations and maps at www.pedalsandpetals .com. And on the second Saturday in June, hard-core bikers can compete in the **Black Fly Challenge** (www.blackflychallenge.com), a grueling 40-mile mountain-bike race through the Moose River Plains, between Inlet and Indian Lake.

Road cyclists will discover that many state highways have wide, smooth shoulders. You won't have to contend with much traffic in May and June or September and October, except on weekends, but main roads become busy with log trucks, sightseeing buses, and RVs throughout the summer. Find ideas for routes at www.bikethebyways.org.

THE NARROWS BETWEEN THIRD AND FOURTH LAKES COURTESY OF TED COMSTOCK, SARANAC LAKE

OSGOOD POND IS A SERENE PLACE FOR A PADDLE   COURTESY OF JOHN DIGIACOMO, WWW.PLACIDTIMESPHOTOGRAPHY.COM

Be prepared for any long trips: check topographical as well as highway maps for significant hills on your proposed route. Always carry plenty of water, a compass, and a good tool kit. Remember, there's no cell-phone service here. *And wear a helmet!*

BOAT TOURS If you'd prefer not to be your own helmsman, board a cruise vessel. Prices vary widely depending on the length of the tour and what kind of frills come with it (music, dancing, champagne). Most boats can be chartered for special events; some captains are licensed to perform weddings. The season generally runs from early May through October; always call ahead for a reservation.

Dunn's Boat Service (315-357-3532; www.dunnsboats.com; 1500 Big Moose Road, Eagle Bay) gives tours of the setting of *An American Tragedy* aboard *Grace*, a beautiful inboard.

Norridgewock III (315-376-6200; www.beaverriver.com; 150 Norridgewock Lake Road, Eagle Bay) takes visitors on tours and offers water-taxi service on Stillwater Reservoir, which allows access to remote Beaver River.

Old Forge Lake Cruises (315-369-6473; www.oldforgecruises.com; 116 Steamboat Landing, Old Forge) has a narrated 28-mile cruise on the Fulton Chain of Lakes, following a historic steamboat route.

Raquette Lake Navigation Co. (315-354-5532; www.raquettelakenavigation.com; Pier I, Raquette Lake) does lunch, brunch, and dinner cruises—by reservation only—aboard the posh *W. W. Durant*.

CANOEING AND KAYAKING The Adirondack Park offers some of the best canoeing and kayaking in the Northeast. For thrill seekers, there's serious white water (with rapids up to Class V) on the **Upper Hudson**, the **Moose**, portions of the **Schroon**, and other rivers. For flat water fans, there are long trips linking lakes, such as the 44-mile route from **Long Lake to Tupper Lake**; the 35-mile trip from **Old Forge to Blue Mountain Lake**; the 25-mile trip from **Osgood Pond to Lake Kushaqua**; or the Old Forge to Lake Champlain stretch of the 740-mile **Northern Forest Canoe Trail**, which begins in Old Forge and ends in northern Maine. There's even a 3-day race, the **Adirondack Canoe Classic,** or "**Ninety-Miler,**" which covers 90 miles of water in a long diagonal from the Fulton Chain of Lakes to Saranac Lake village.

And if you're eager to try canoeing but just aren't sure of your abilities, there are plenty of places where you can get lessons in flat-water or white-water techniques. Old Forge's **Paddlefest** (315-369-6672; www.mountainmanoutdoors.com), in mid-May, has demonstrations and more than 100 different boats to try. For lessons, hire a guide for one-on-one sessions. Other good resources are **Beaver Brook Outfitters** (888-454-8433; www.beaverbrook.net; 3921 Route 28, North Creek), **Blue Mountain Outfitters** (518-352-7306; 144 Main Street, Blue Mountain Lake), **Haderondah Company** (315-369-3868; 3011 Main Street, Old Forge), **Mountainman Outdoor Supply Company** (315-369-6672; www.mountainmanoutdoors.com; Route 28, Old Forge), and **Tickner's Canoes** (315-369-6286; www.ticknerscanoe.com; 117 Riverside Lane, Old Forge).

CLIMBING The High Peaks isn't the only great place to rock climb—challenging routes abound in this region of the park. Among the sweet spots are **Shanty Cliffs, Crane Mountain**; newly developed crags near Caroga Lake, such as **McMartin, Lost T,** and the **Annex**; plus classics including **Nine Corner Lake**—a mega-bouldering area—and **Good Luck Mountain**, home of **Mystery Achievement, Deck of Cards,** and **Medicine Man.** A go-to climbing guidebook for the region is *Adirondack Rock* (Adirondack Rock Press; second edition, 2014) by Jeremy Haas and Jim Lawyer.

FAMILY FUN Looking for something that doesn't involve hiking boots or paddles? You won't have to break a sweat to do the following:

Adirondack Scenic Railroad (315-369-6290; www.adirondackrr.com; Route 28, Thendara) runs one-and-a-half- to two-hour excursions out of Thendara. Inquire about bike-and-rail or canoe-and-rail combinations. Special events include train robberies, haunted history rides, a hobo day, and more. Open May through November.

Barton Garnet Mine Tours (518-251-2706; www.garnetminetours.com; Barton Mines Road, North River) happen in garnet central. Take a tour of Barton's open-pit mines, collect rocks, then browse the specimens in the mineral shop. Open June through Columbus Day.

Calypso's Cove (315-369-6145; www.calypsoscove.com; 3183 Route 28, Old Forge) has an arcade, bumper boats, batting cages, rock-climbing wall, zip line, mini golf, and go-karts—plenty of entertainment for the entire family. Open Memorial Day through Labor Day.

Enchanted Forest/Water Safari (315-369-6145; www.watersafari.com; 3183 Route 28, Old Forge), New York's largest water theme park, is a blast for teenagers and younger kids. Open daily June through Labor Day.

Gore Mountain Scenic Gondola Rides (518-251-2411; www.goremountain.com; Peaceful Valley Road, North Creek) take you up high for primo foliage viewing. Open late summer and fall weekends.

McCauley Mountain Scenic Chairlift Ride (315-369-3225; www.mccauleyny.com; McCauley Mountain Road, Old Forge), with a view of the Fulton Chain of Lakes, is open Monday through Sunday late June through Labor Day, and weekends Labor Day through Columbus Day. No credit cards.

Natural Stone Bridge and Caves (518-494-2283; www.stonebridgeandcaves.com; 535 Stone Bridge Road, Pottersville), a 1,000-acre property, is a stunning natural attraction. Walk into three caves, peer into others, or follow trails through the woods. Open late May through Columbus Day. Adventure tours—be prepared to get wet and dirty!—may be available in July and August, depending on water levels. Open winter weekends for self-guided snowshoe treks on 14 miles of trails.

Saratoga & North Creek Railway (877-726-7245; www.sncrr.com; 3 Railroad Place, North Creek) revives a route that had been abandoned for a century by connecting the Spa City to North Creek, a two-hour trip with a stop in Hadley. Trains run Thursday through Sunday, July to Columbus Day.

GOLF Savor the green rolling hills, craggy peaks, deep blue lakes, and bracing air—the Adirondacks do recall Scotland's landscape just a wee bit. Once upon a time, there were even more golf courses than are open today, links that were attached to grand hotels and exclusive private clubs. The courses in this region include:

Brantingham Golf Club (315-348-8861; Brantingham Road, Brantingham Lake). Eighteen holes, par-71, 5,300 yards.

Cedar River Golf Club (518-648-5906; www.cedarrivergolf.com; 6689 Route 30, Indian Lake). Nine holes, par-36, 2,700 yards.

Inlet Golf Course and Country Club (315-357-3503; 300 Route 28, Inlet). Eighteen holes, par-72, 6,000 yards.

Lake Pleasant Golf Course (518-548-7071; 2537 Route 8, Lake Pleasant). Nine holes, par-35, 2,900 yards.

Nick Stoner Golf Course (518-835-4220; 1803 Route 10, Caroga Lake). Eighteen holes, par-70, 5,800 yards.

Sacandaga Golf Club (518-863-4887; 126 Pine Avenue, Northville). Nine holes, par-36, 3,000 yards.

Thendara Golf Club (315-369-3136; www.thendaragolfclub.com; 151 Fifth Street, Thendara). Eighteen holes, par-72, 6,000 yards.

ICE SKATING Many towns offer lighted rinks with warming huts; check with tourist offices for hours. **Long Lake's Geiger Arena Adirondack Skating Rink** (518-627-3031) is one of the better ones, and it's conveniently located on Route 30. At **Indian Lake**, the town has built a small rink (518-648-5828) at the foot of the ski hill, off Route 30. There's free indoor skating at the **Fern Park Pavilion**, in Inlet (315-357-5501); **Old Forge** has ice-skating at the intersection of Upper Joy Tract Road and Railroad Avenue, at the site of the old town highway garage.

Paul Bunyan at the Enchanted Forest

ENCHANTED FOREST/WATER SAFARI, NEW YORK'S LARGEST WATER THEME PARK, IS AN OLD FORGE INSTITUTION COURTESY OF TED COMSTOCK, SARANAC LAKE

UP FOR INTERPRETATION

The Adirondack Interpretive Center (518-582-2000; www.esf.edu/aic; 5922 Route 28N, Newcomb), part of the State University of New York College of Environmental Science and Forestry, offers opportunities for hiking, paddling, and learning about flora and fauna on 236 beautiful acres in the heart of the Adirondack Park. Programs include primitive skills workshops, guided canoe excursions, mushroom forays, and a full calendar of lectures.

CANOE AND GUIDE BOAT EXCURSION ON RICH LAKE AT SUNY-ESF'S NEWCOMB CAMPUS COURTESY OF THE ADIRONDACK INTERPRETIVE CENTER

KIDS' CAMPS Famous folks spent their summers at Adirondack kids' camps: Arlo Guthrie and his mother, a dance instructor, enjoyed many seasons at **Raquette Lake Camp** (315-354-4382; www.raquettelakecamp.com), and Demi Moore and Bruce Willis enrolled their kids at **Long Lake Camp for the Arts** (914-693-7111; www.longlakecamp .com). Another popular one in this region is **Adirondack Woodcraft Camps** (315-369-6031; www.woodcraftcamps.com), in Old Forge.

If you're in the Adirondacks during July or August, and would like to visit a particular camp with your prospective happy camper, call ahead. Or check out www.acacamps .org for camps accredited by the American Camping Association.

RACES AND SEASONAL SPORTING EVENTS **Raquette Lake Winter Carnival** (518-624-3077; www.mylonglake.com) has a ladies' fry-pan toss, snowshoe relay, snow dodgeball, tug-o-war, plus crosscut and chain-saw competitions, in February.

Hudson River Whitewater Derby (518-251-2005; www.whitewaterderby.com; North River, North Creek and Riparius), held on the first weekend in May, includes canoe and kayak slalom races and a Not-So-Whitewater Race on Saturday, and the Whitewater Derby Downriver races on Sunday.

Adirondack Paddlefest (315-369-6672; www.adirondackpaddlefest.com; Old Forge) is a popular canoe, kayak, and stand-up paddleboard weekend with demos, clinics, and hundreds of boats to test paddle, in mid-May.

Black Fly Challenge (315-357-3281; www.blackflychallenge.com), in June, is a 40-mile mountain-bike race through the Moose River Plains.

Adirondack Birding Festival (518-548-3076; www.adirondackexperience.com) includes birding outings and lectures throughout Hamilton County, in June.

Piseco Lake Triathlon (518-548-4521; www.speculatorchamber.com) is a 0.5-mile swim, 11.5-mile bike, and 3-mile run, in July.

Race the Train (www.adirondackrunners.org; North Creek/Riparius), in August, is a 8.4-mile run along the Upper Hudson River Railroad.

Adirondack Canoe Classic (518-891-2744; www.macscanoe.com), sponsored by the Saranac Lake Chamber of Commerce, is a 90-mile, three-day canoe race from Old Forge to Saranac Lake village, in early September.

SEAPLANES Seaplane services are equipped to take canoeists, fishermen, and hunters into ponds and lakes. Among the few fixed-wheel and seaplane private charters in this region are **Helms Aero Service** (518-624-3931; Town Beach, Long Lake) and **Payne's Air Service** (315-357-3971; 431 Route 28, Inlet). Always call ahead for a reservation.

CROSS-COUNTRY SKIING Many of the designated wilderness and wild forest areas offer great ski touring on marked but ungroomed trails. State campgrounds—closed to vehicles from November through May—offer quiet, woodsy, snow-covered roads with gentle grades. **Lake Durant**, near Blue Mountain Lake, and **Lake Eaton**, near Long Lake, are popular with local skiers and usually have set tracks. Locals also love the work of the Siamese Pond Trail Improvement Society, which has revived seemingly endless miles of a spectacular cross-country-ski-trail network in the 114,000-acre **Siamese Ponds Wilderness Area.**

Before setting out on any of these wilderness excursions, prepare your pack with quick-energy food; a thermos filled with hot tea or cocoa; extra hat, socks, and gloves; topo map and compass; matches; flashlight; and space blanket. Dress in layers of wool or synthetic fabrics. Don't travel alone. Sign in at the trailhead register. Let friends know your destination and when you plan to return. Cell phones don't work in this part of the park.

Besides wilderness trails and informal town ski trails, there are also some excellent cross-country-ski areas with meticulously groomed tracks and rental equipment.

Fern Park Recreation Area (315-357-5501; 9 Loomis Road, Inlet). Twenty-two kilometers of groomed trails, night skiing.

Garnet Hill Ski Center (518-251-2150; www.garnet-hill.com; 39 Garnet Hill Road, North River). Fifty-five kilometers of groomed trails, connects with trails in Siamese Ponds Wilderness Area, rentals, lessons, ski shop, food, lodging.

Gore Mountain's Nordic Center (518-251-2411; www.goremountain.com; North Creek Ski Bowl) is an exciting addition to this ski hub, providing an inviting venue for cross-country ski races. The 5 kilometers of new trails offer something for all abilities, and much of the network is supported with snowmaking and lights.

Lapland Lake Nordic Vacation Center (518-863-4974; www.laplandlake.com; 139 Lapland Lake Road, Northville). Founded by former 1960 Olympic cross-country-ski team member Olavi Hirvonen. Fifty kilometers of groomed trails, rentals, lessons, ski shop, food, lodging.

McCauley Mountain (315-369-3225; www.mccauleyny.com; McCauley Mountain Road, Old Forge). Twenty kilometers of groomed trails at downhill area, plus skiing at Thendara Golf Club, rentals, lessons, food.

Speculator Trails (518-548-4521). Check out www.adrkmts.com for a variety of free, southern Adirondack trails.

DOWNHILL SKIING AND SNOWBOARDING Skiing has been a part of Adirondack life since the 1930s. Weekend ski trains brought thousands of folks to Old Forge and North Creek. In North Creek they could "ride up and slide down." The "ride up" was in school buses equipped with wooden ski racks mounted on the outside, and the "slide down" was on twisty trails carved out of the forest near Barton Mines, across from the present-day slopes on Gore Mountain.

Today the Olympic Regional Development Authority (ORDA) runs Gore Mountain. Also in this region is nice little McCauley, where the emphasis is on family fun rather than on the trendiest gear. Indian Lake runs a free downhill area for residents and guests. Of course, you won't find human-made snow there, and you'll have to remember dormant skills for managing a Poma lift or a rope tow, but you can have a blast with the kids and beat the crowds.

GROOMED CROSS-COUNTRY SKI TRAILS CAN BE FOUND ACROSS THIS REGION—AT GORE, LAPLAND LAKE, AND GARNET HILL COURTESY OF ORDA/DAVE SCHMIDT

Gore Mountain Ski Resort (518-251-2411; www.goremountain.com; 711 Peaceful Valley Road, North Creek) is the cradle of North Country alpine skiing and the home of state-owned Gore Mountain, which opened in 1964. Since 1984, Gore has been managed by ORDA, which also manages Whiteface Mountain.

Gore, with its 2,537-foot vertical drop, 108 trails, seven freestyle areas, and 27 glades—the longest ones in the East—has trails for all levels of skiers and riders: wide-open cruising runs, but also double black diamonds such as The Rumor and Lies. The high-speed eight-passenger gondola is a godsend on frigid days, while another nine chairs and four surface lifts deliver people up the slopes. In 2012, 160 tower guns for snowmaking—using water from the Hudson River—were added, allowing fine skiing during a lackluster winter.

North Creek's original Ski Bowl has been revitalized, offering family-friendly slopes, a terrain park with half-pipe, and a top-notch Nordic Center. Gore Mountain's Interconnect links the Ski Bowl to Gore Mountain proper. The mountain has four lodges, excellent snow sports

633: -SKI HILL AND TOW, OLD FORGE, N.Y., ADIRONDACK MTS.

PHOTO BY WEEDMARK

OLD FORGE SKI HILL AND TOW COURTESY OF TED COMSTOCK, SARANAC LAKE

instruction, and day care. A free ski shuttle runs from Main Street on weekends and holidays. Weekend lift tickets are $75 adults, $58 teens, $40 kids; ages 6 and under are free daily.

McCauley Mountain (315-369-3225; www.mccauleyny.com; McCauley Mountain Road, Old Forge) is where Hank Kashiwa, the international racing star and ski designer, learned his first snowplow turns; his brilliant career is something folks in Old Forge still talk about. Actually, the Town of Webb school has produced several US Olympic ski-team members, thanks to good coaches and the welcoming intermediate slopes at the local hill.

This little mountain has 21 trails, a lift, and four tows—plus a terrain park for snowboarders—and heaps of natural snow. Helmers and Olympic, both of which have snowmaking, are the most difficult runs. Intermediates can sample Upper God's Land, a ridge trail; Sky Ride, a wide route serviced by the double chair; or the gentle, sweeping Challenger. You'll find all the amenities at McCauley: a ski school, rentals, food, and drink. Weekend and holiday lift tickets: $30 adults, $25 students and seniors, under five free. Discounts on weekdays, closed Tuesdays.

SNOWMOBILING A hub of snowmobile activity is **Old Forge**, which provides 500-plus miles of groomed, packed trails. Folks around here like calling it the "Snowmobile Capital of the East." Trails in Old Forge spread out like a river with numerous tributaries. You can connect with the Inlet trails to the east, or the Independence River Wild Forest and Big Moose trails to the north, and Forestport and Boonville routes to the south. These trails meet still other trails, so that you can continue farther east from Inlet to Indian Lake or Speculator, and then from Speculator to Wells, or you can go from Inlet to Raquette Lake, and then on to Long Lake and Newcomb. Confused? Permits, safety course information, events, clubs, trail maps, trail conditions, dealers and rentals, and everything else you need to know can be found at www.snowmobileoldforgeny.com.

Besides the Old Forge–Inlet area, many trail networks throughout the park cross private timberlands as well as the state forest preserve. Public lands designated as wild forest areas are open to snowmobiling; wilderness areas are not. The DEC's www .dec.ny.gov has rules and regulations and links to sites with Adirondack snowmobile trails. For maps of local trails, contact **Long Lake Parks, Recreation and Tourism Department** (518-624-3077; www.mylonglake.com), **Indian Lake Chamber of Commerce** (518-648-5112; www.indian-lake.com), Inlet Information Office (315-557-5501; www.inletny.com), and **Adirondacks Speculator Region Chamber of Commerce** (518-548-4521; www.speculatorchamber.com). For Indian Lake trail conditions, go to www .ilsnow.com.

As with any winter pursuit, planning and preparation help make a successful outing. Know your machine; carry an emergency repair kit and understand how to use it. Be sure you have plenty of gas. Travel with friends in case of a breakdown or other surprise situations. Never ride at night unless you're familiar with the trail or are following an experienced leader. Avoid crossing frozen lakes and streams unless you are absolutely certain the ice is safe—warmer winters have dramatically shortened ice-in/ice-out spans. Some town or county roads are designated trails; while on such a highway, keep right, observe the posted snowmobile speed limit—there are numerous fatalities each year due to excessive speed—and travel in single file.

Your basic pack should contain a topographic map and compass as well as a local trail map; survival kit with matches, flashlight, rope, space blanket, quick-energy food, and something warm to drink; extra hat, socks, and mittens. Although a sip of brandy may give the illusion of warming you up, alcohol impairs circulation and can hasten hypothermia. And an arrest for snowmobiling under the influence carries severe penalties.

WATERFALLS Some of the park's cascades are spectacularly high, including T Lake, which is taller than Niagara; others, such as Buttermilk Falls, are just a quick walk from the car. You can visit **Auger Falls** on the Sacandaga River in Wells, **Buttermilk**

OLD FORGE IS OFTEN CALLED THE "SNOWMOBILE CAPITAL OF THE EAST" COURTESY OF NANCIE BATTAGLIA

COURTESY OF TED COMSTOCK, SARANAC LAKE

Falls on the Raquette River in Long Lake, **Cascade Lake Inlet** falls in Bog Moose, **Falls Brook** in Minerva, **OK Slip Falls** in Indian Lake (with the highest vertical drop in the Adirondacks), and remote, steep, and dangerous **T Lake Falls** in Piseco. Russell Dunn's *Adirondack Waterfall Guide: New York's Cool Cascades* (Black Dome Press, 2003) is a good resource.

WHITE-WATER RAFTING The wild, remote **Upper Hudson River** provides some of the East's most exhilarating white water: nearly 17 miles of continuous Class III to IV+ rapids. From 1860 to 1950, river drivers sent logs downstream every spring to sawmills and pulp mills, and they followed along behind the churning, tumbling timber in rowboats to pry logjams loose. Since the mid-1970s, the Hudson's power has been rediscovered for recreational purposes, with numerous rafting companies making the trip from the Indian River, just south of Indian Lake, to North River.

Reliable water levels are provided by a dam release below Lake Abanakee, courtesy of the town of Indian Lake. Releases begin about April 1 and last through fall.

Although you don't need white-water paddling experience to enjoy a trip down the Hudson, you do need to be in good physical condition, and a competent swimmer. (Nobody under age 18 is permitted to raft when the water is at its highest—or on Class V waters such as the Moose River.) The outfitters supply you with wetsuit, paddle, life jacket, and helmet; they also shuttle you to the put-in and give on-shore instructions in safety and paddling techniques, and most serve lunch. Rafters should bring polypropylene thermals to wear under the suits; wool hats, gloves, and socks; sneakers; and dry, warm clothing for after the trip. (Springtime Adirondack air can be chilly, and the water temperature is truly frigid.)

A licensed guide steers each raft and directs the crew. It's a good idea to research Adirondack rafting companies before booking a trip. Recent troubles on the river— unlicensed guides, among other problems—have spotlighted this sport's dangers. This

THE BIG BLOWDOWN

Sixteen-year-old Richard "Bud" Brownell was scoping the woods around Russian Lake, near Big Moose Lake, on the last day of hunting season, November 25, 1950. He had split from a hunting party when a hurricane crashed in "from the east around noon, felling huge trees that had survived for centuries," according to *Big Moose Lake in the Adirondacks: the Story of the Lake, the Land and the People*. Brownell crouched "alone under a large tree for what seemed like an eternity while the (100-mile-per-hour) wind howled and trees all around were snapping like matchsticks, flying through the air." Later that day, the young hunter was reunited with his party, though it took them hours to make their way through the jumbled trees to safety. Scenes like this played out from the High Peaks to Herkimer County, with some hunters and hikers barricaded for days behind the blowdown.

Networks of roads were impassable, telephone and power lines were wiped out, dozens of public campsites and private residences were destroyed. And the forest was ravaged: Barbara McMartin, in *The Great Forest of the Adirondacks*, reported that the blowdown "affected 420,000 acres and was said to have caused a loss that ranged from a quarter of the trees to the entire forest cover. The loss was estimated at 2 million cords of softwood and 40 million board feet of hardwood. The Cold River country between Seward and Santanoni experienced the greatest destruction, followed closely by the Moose River Plains," and private lands of more than a quarter-million acres were also wrecked.

Hikers would have to wait five years until trails could be cleared to scale more than a half dozen High Peaks. Even Article XIV of the state constitution, which protects the Forest Preserve, had to be circumvented to allow lumberjacks in to clean up the mess. Otherwise the fallen timber posed a fire hazard: One spark and the entire park could be torched. Most of the cleanup was finished by 1956, though you can still find blowdown across the region.

trip is not for passive passengers; you're expected to paddle—sometimes hard and fast—as the guide instructs. The trip is only hard and strenuous in spring or during high water from, for example, a tropical storm. The **Hudson Gorge** is an all-day adventure, containing four to five hours of strenuous exercise, with the 2017 price, depending on the season, of about $90 per person.

Several rafting companies also offer short, fun trips on the **Sacandaga River** near Lake Luzerne. These junkets float 3.5 miles and last, from start to finish, about two hours. Dam releases make the stream navigable all summer. On the other end of the spectrum is the **Moose River** from McKeever to Fowlerville Falls; this is a 14-mile beast absolutely for experienced white-water paddlers only. The Moose is runnable after spring ice-out.

Among the Adirondack white-water rafting companies are: **Adirondac Rafting Company** (518-523-1635; www.lakeplacidrafting.com; Lake Placid), **Adirondack Adventures** (518-251-2802; www.adkadventures.com; North River), **Adirondack River Outfitters Adventures** (800-525-7238; www.aroadventures.com; Old Forge), **Adventure Sports Rafting Company** (1-800-648-5812; www.adventuresportsrafting.com; Indian Lake), **Beaver Brook Outfitters** (888-454-8433; www.beaverbrook.net; Wevertown), **North Creek Rafting Company** (800-989-RAFT; www.northcreekrafting.com; North Creek), **Sacandaga Outdoor Center** (866-696-RAFT; www.4soc.com; Hadley), **Square Eddy Expeditions** (518-251-5200; www.squareeddy.com; North Creek), **Whitewater Challengers** (800-443-8554; www.whitewaterchallengers.com; North River), and **Wild Waters Outdoor Center** (800-867-2335; www.wildwaters.net; Warrensburg and Lake Luzerne).

WILDERNESS AREAS These portions of the Forest Preserve are 10,000 acres or larger and contain little evidence of modern times. Wilderness areas are open to hiking, cross-country skiing, hunting, fishing, and other similar pursuits, but seaplanes may not land on wilderness ponds, nor are motorized vehicles welcome. Following are Adirondack wilderness areas in the Central and Southwestern region:

Blue Ridge. 46,000 acres, south of Blue Mountain Lake. Contains several miles of the Northville–Lake Placid Trail for hiking and cross-country skiing. Cascade, Stephens, Wilson, Mitchell, and other trout ponds.

Five Ponds. 101,000 acres, between Cranberry Lake and Stillwater Reservoir. Numerous ponds, canoeing on the Oswegatchie River, many acres of old-growth forest, some hiking trails. This area receives little use.

Ha De Ron Dah. 27,000 acres, west of Old Forge. Small ponds and lakes, hiking and cross-country-ski trails around Big Otter Lake. This area receives little use.

Hoffman Notch. 36,000 acres, between Minerva and the Blue Ridge Road. Ponds and trout streams, a few hiking trails. This area is used mostly by fishermen and hunters.

Nehasane Primitive Area. 6,000 acres, lovely Lake Lila, near Long Lake.

Pepperbox. 15,000 acres, north of Stillwater Reservoir. Few trails, difficult access, mostly wetlands, excellent wildlife habitat.

Pigeon Lake. 50,000 acres, northeast of Big Moose Lake. Numerous lakes, ponds, and streams. trails for hiking and cross-country skiing.

Siamese Ponds. 114,000 acres, between North River and Speculator. Canoeing on Thirteenth Lake. Sacandaga River and numerous trout ponds. Trails for hiking and cross-country skiing.

HIGH-ALTITUDE SKIING COURTESY OF ORDA

UNCLASSIFIED

The 20,758-acre Boreas Ponds tract was purchased by New York State in 2016, though its permanent classification—as a Wilderness, Wild Forest or Primitive area—hasn't been finalized as of press time. Even so, this gateway to the High Peaks, a paddling paradise with spectacular views, is now open to the public. See www.dec.ny.gov for more information.

Silver Lake. 105,000 acres, between Piseco and Wells. Silver, Mud, and Rock Lakes. Southern end of the Northville–Lake Placid Trail. This area receives little use.

West Canada Lakes. 157,000 acres, west of Speculator. Cedar, Spruce, West Canada Lakes, and 160 other bodies of water. Portions of the Northville–Lake Placid Trail and other hiking trails. One of the largest roadless areas in the Northeast.

William C. Whitney. 15,000 acres, between Long and Tupper Lakes. Little Tupper Lake and Rock Pond for excellent paddling and camping, miles of woods roads for cross-country skiing, several remote ponds.

WILD FOREST AREAS Wild forest areas are open to snowmobile travel, mountain biking, and other recreation. The areas in this region are:

Black River. Between Otter Lake and Wilmurt. Ponds and streams.

Blue Mountain. Northeast of Blue Mountain Lake. Contains part of the Northville–Lake Placid Trail. Tirrell Pond. Views from Blue Mountain.

Ferris Lake. Between Piseco and Stratford. Dirt roads for mountain biking and driving through by car. Numerous ponds and streams.

Independence River. South of Stillwater Reservoir. Dirt roads. Independence River. Snowmobile trails. Beaver ponds.

Jessup River. Between the south end of Indian Lake and Speculator. Miami and Jessup Rivers, and Lewey Lake. Views from Pillsbury Mountain. Trails for snowmobiling, hiking, and mountain biking.

Moose River Plains. Between Indian Lake and Inlet. Dirt roads. Numerous ponds and streams. Cedar River and Cedar River Flow. Primitive car-camping sites. Snowmobile trails. If you want to see moose, this is the place.

Sargent Ponds. Between Raquette Lake and Long Lake. Trout ponds. Hiking trails. Canoe route between Raquette Lake and Blue Mountain Lake.

Shaker Mountain. East of Canada Lake. Dirt roads. Hiking, cross-country skiing and mountain-biking routes.

Vanderwhacker Mountain. Northwest of Minerva. Fishing on the Boreas River. Views from Vanderwhacker Mountain.

✳ Lodging

Highlights for this region, particularly its iconic rustic lodges, follow, but this is housekeeping cabin central. Meaning, from Memorial Day through Columbus Day, affordable little waterside cottages with kitchenettes abound—perfect backdrops for an Adirondack vacation. Most need to be booked way ahead and some don't accept credit cards. But all offer a quintessential Adirondack vacation.

BIG MOOSE LAKE

Big Moose Inn (315-357-2042; www .bigmooseinn.com; 1510 Big Moose Road, Eagle Bay), a turn-of-the-century backwoods lodge, ranks tops among spots locals recommend to visiting friends and family. The place is rustic, but comfy,

ADIRONDACK HERMIT

Noah John Rondeau, the "Mayor of Cold River," as he called himself, lived near a tributary of Long Lake in the 1930s and '40s. Noah John was popular among hikers, who trekked deep in the woods for an audience with the eccentric hermit at his handmade "village," which included two semi-log cabins with hard-packed floors—one dubbed "Town Hall"—and three teepee-like stacks of tree-length firewood. After the great blowdown of 1950 destroyed his camp, Rondeau didn't return to the woods. But the charismatic character—hardly hermitlike—soaked up the spotlight as a featured exhibit at the 1947 National Sportsmens Show in New York City, and as part of the Saranac Lake Winter Carnival parade, waving to the crowd as he rode a farm sleigh pulled by a tractor. Today you can see his Town Hall on display at the Adirondack Experience, in Blue Mountain Lake.

FAMOUS HERMIT AND "MAYOR OF COLD RIVER CITY" NOAH JOHN RONDEAU COURTESY OF HOLLY WOLFF

and there's a popular on-site restaurant and tavern (see page 96). Twelve of its 16 rooms have water views. Unlike other accommodations around here, the inn is an all-season draw: in late spring you can paddle and fish on Big Moose Lake, in summertime you can hike around Pigeon Lake Wilderness Area or visit nearby towns Inlet and Old Forge, in fall you can take in the foliage or hunt, and when snow comes, there's snowmobiling or cross-country skiing practically right to the front door. Closed in April and November. $$.

Covewood Lodge (315-357-3041; www .covewoodlodge.com; 120 Covewood Lodge Road, Eagle Bay), one of the all-time great woodsy Adirondack retreats, was built as a hotel back in the days when guests stayed all summer long. Along the shoreline and in the trees are 18 housekeeping cottages. Big Moose Laker Earl Covey built the 1924 rustic lodge and iconic stone fireplace (his charming chapel just down the road is a

must-see). There's no cell coverage here, and you won't find TVs on the property, but Covewood offers sailboat, kayak, canoe, paddleboard, and motorboat rentals. The Covewood Kids' Program provides daily activities for young guests. Because families return year after year, book at least six months ahead. Open May through October. $$.

The Waldheim (315-357-2353; www .thewaldheim.com; 502 Martin Road, Eagle Bay), built in 1904 by E. J. Martin from trees cut on the property, has been run by the same family for more than a century. Its 17 cottages, some constructed of vertical half logs and twiggy accents, have names such as "Cozy," "Comfort," and "Heart's Content," and each has a fireplace. The secluded 300-acre property is adjacent to state land—guests can hike, canoe, swim, and fish; arrangements can be made to have a seaplane pick you up at the dock for a scenic flight. Rates include three full meals a day, which are served in a gracious, high-ceilinged dining room. Open June through Columbus Day. No credit cards. $$$.

BLUE MOUNTAIN LAKE

The Hedges (518-352-7325; www .thehedges.com; 1 Hedges Road) was built in the early 1880s by Colonel Hiram Duryea, a Civil War veteran and millionaire industrialist. The iconic Adirondack camp caters to both couples and families, with adults-only guest rooms—all with private baths—in its three lodges and a necklace of cabins that sleep up to eight. There's a sandy swimming beach, as well as access to canoes, kayaks, rowboats, a clay tennis court, and the library. The Birch Room, with museum-quality rustic detail, is worth a visit. Meals are served in the dining room lodge, where there's a full bar, and a lean-to is the venue for nightly campfires. Off-site—about 35 miles down the road—the historic Lodge at Twitchell Lake can accommodate larger groups by the week. Open May through October. Book a stay at least a year in advance. No credit cards. $$$.

Hemlock Hall (518-352-7706; www .hemlockhall.com; Maple Lodge Road), another old-school lakeside hostelry, was carefully restored in the 1950s. There are guest rooms in the main lodge with shared and private baths, plus motel units and one- or two-room cottages. The tower suite in the main lodge has its own screened porch, several of the lodge rooms have lake views, and you can rent the top floor of the boathouse. Breakfast and dinner, served family-style, are included in the room charges; alcoholic beverages are not permitted in the dining room. On the waterfront, there's a diving float, as well as canoes, kayaks, rowboats and a Sunfish sailboat. Open mid-June through mid-October. No credit cards. $$.

INDIAN LAKE/SABAEL

Timberlock (518-648-5494; www .timberlock.com; Route 30) hasn't changed much since it welcomed its first guests in 1899—the common buildings and the guests' log cabins are still equipped with gaslights and woodstoves.

THE HEDGES, IN BLUE MOUNTAIN LAKE, IS CLASSIC NINETEENTH-CENTURY ADIRONDACK LODGING COURTESY OF TED COMSTOCK, SARANAC LAKE

WORDSWOMAN

Anne LaBastille, 1933–2011, was best known for her 1976 book *Woodswoman*, about roughing it solo in the Adirondack wilds. The young divorcée lived in a handmade cabin on Twitchell Lake, near Big Moose, and wrote as breezily about swinging an ax as she did about skinnydipping—she made woodcraft sexy during a time when Boy Scouts and lumberjacks dominated the scene. LaBastille, who was a wildlife ecologist and Adirondack advocate, empowered women who wanted to ditch their traditional roles, and she went on to pen many more books and articles for publications such as *National Geographic*, *Adirondack Life*, and *Backpacker*. Her log cabin is now on permanent display at Adirondack Experience, the Museum on Blue Mountain Lake.

WOODSWOMAN ANNE LABASTILLE'S CABIN IS ON DISPLAY AT THE ADIRONDACK EXPERIENCE IN BLUE MOUNTAIN LAKE COURTESY OF DUNCAN R. MILLAR

The atmosphere here is rustic and relaxed, yet the resort offers a variety of activities and amenities, such as tennis courts, horses for guided trail rides, a sandy beach, boats to sail, paddle, or row on Indian Lake, and trails on the property for hiking and birding. Sixteen "family cottages" have full baths, screened porches, and lake views, and there are some small cabins without baths. Rates include three meals a day (in the open-air dining porch) and use of all the facilities and activities except horseback riding. There are no neighbors within miles, and your wake-up call in the morning may well be a loon's yodel from the lake. Open mid-June through mid-September. $$$.

INLET

The Woods Inn (315-357-5300; www .thewoodsinn.com; 148 Route 28) was built by Fred Hess in 1894 and purchased four years later by Philo Wood, who renamed it the Wood Hotel. Much has changed in more than a century, but thanks to a massive restoration, this place is operating as the grand inn it once was. Guests can choose between 21 rooms in the inn, all with private baths, some with balconies and mountain and lake views; one nearby cottage with a kitchenette; or three Adirondack Guide Tents, throwbacks to nineteenth- and early-twentieth-century luxury platform tents. The tents are comfortably furnished and have electric lights and adjacent bathhouses. A restaurant and tavern are also on-site. Closed in April, available for private events in November and December. $$.

JOHNSBURG

Camp Orenda (518-251-5001; www .camporenda.com; 90 Armstrong Road) transports guests back to the Gilded Age with its six posh platform tents nestled in the forest. This is camping without all the bother: your bed is already made and gourmet meals—cooked in cast-iron skillets over an open wood flame—appear three times a day. Nearby, there are ample opportunities for hiking, biking, swimming, paddling, and more. Open Memorial Day through mid-October. $$$.

NORTH CREEK

The Alpine Lodge (518-251-2451; www .adirondackalpinelodge.com; 264 Main Street) has a charming Adirondack vibe in its 14 guest rooms and four kitchen suites. There's something here for everyone: families can mix and match adjoining rooms, or couples can cozy up in a more romantic space, complete with fireplace and back porch. The setting is equally charming—restaurants, bars, and boutiques are out the front door, and a shuttle can get you to Gore Mountain Ski Area or to the Hudson for a white-water adventure. $$.

The **Copperfield Inn Resort** (518-251-2200; www.copperfieldinn.com; 307 Main Street), shuttered for years, is now revived as an inn with all the amenities you'd expect at a ski resort—31 big rooms; health and fitness center; sauna; tennis court; conference facilities; pub and dining room; and shuttle bus to the slopes. The Copperfield's rooms and shared space aren't done up in Adirondack style, but it's hard to beat the location. $$.

NORTH RIVER

Garnet Hill Lodge (518-251-2444; www .garnet-hill.com; 39 Garnet Hill Road) is a great base for hiking in the Siamese Ponds Wilderness, fly-fishing on the Hudson, or paddling Thirteenth Lake. In winter, the resort offers a ski center—with rentals and a kids' program—and a network of almost 40 miles of cross-country-ski trails. The main log house has a massive stone fireplace and 16 rooms; the Birches and the Tea House can accommodate families and larger groups. There's also a restaurant and pub—don't miss Mary Jane's Famous Onion Pie. $$.

NORTHVILLE

Inn at the Bridge (518-863-3174; www .innatthebridge.com; 641 Bridge Street) is a restored turn-of-the-century Victorian mansion offering six guest rooms with private baths—four with a view of Great Sacandaga Lake (guests arriving by boat can tie right up to the inn's dock). A locally sourced breakfast is included with room, along with afternoon tea, and the bar serves craft beers on the weekends. The bistro is open for lunch and dinner seasonally. $$.

The **Orendaga on Northville Lake** (518-863-8013; www.orendaga.com; 732 South Main Street) is a collection of five

COTTAGE COUNTRY

Vacationing at these cute colonies is a trend stretching back to the 1920s, when visitors began to drive to the Adirondacks. Descendants of the very first cottagers are keeping the tradition alive.

Housekeeping cottages generally have kitchens, a beach on a nice lake, a dock, porches, and room to play horseshoes or volleyball or just sit under a huge pine in an Adirondack chair. Following are some of the lakeside highlights in this part of the park:

In Blue Mountain Lake, **Prospect Point** (518-352-7378; www.prospectpt.com) is a family favorite, with more than a dozen charming cabins—some that are winterized—lining the curving shore. Canoes, rowboats and paddleboats are available to guests, and the place's brunches are something special.

Binder's Cabins (518-648-5500) is open year-round in Indian Lake. Located right off Route 28, these have been a mainstay of local lodging for more than five decades, a popular base-camp for rafters, anglers, hikers, hunters, boaters, and cross-country skiers.

Long Lake has **Donnelly's Sunset Point** (518-624-6551), a handful of housekeeping cabins with screened porches and charcoal grills. It sits on a surprisingly private point of the lake, with a sandy beach and a fire ring—just waiting on s'mores—at the water's edge.

Waterfront seclusion is what you'll find at **Morningside Camps and Cottages** (518-251-2694; www.morningsidecamps.com), in Minerva. There are 19 camps—a combo of log cabins and chalets, all with complete kitchens, a stone fireplace or woodstove, and decks or screened porches—plus a two-story suite in the nineteenth-century farmhouse. There's also a tree house for the kids, as well as rowboats, canoes, volleyball court, and beach.

---

beautifully restored cabins and suites in a private setting that's also close to the village's historic downtown. The grounds include a private beach and dock; motorized boats are not allowed on Northville Lake. $$.

OLD FORGE/THENDARA

Great Pines (315-369-6777; www.greatpines.com; 4920 State Route 28, Old Forge), on Fourth Lake, takes classic Adirondack style and gives it a modern twist. Formerly the historic North Woods Inn, this impeccably remodeled resort offers a variety of accommodations: seven guest rooms and two suites in the main lodge, plus 20 motel-style rooms and three cabins. It's convenient to biking, hiking, fishing and more in summer, as well as snowmobile and cross-country ski trails in winter. There are two restaurant choices on-site, fine dining with a view at the Lodge, or comfort food and cocktails at the Lean-To (see page 99). $$.

Van Auken's Inne (315-369-3033; www.vanaukensinne.com; 108 Forge Street, Thendara) was a year old when the Adirondack branch of the New York Central made its first stop at Thendara station in 1892. Since then, the trains have come and gone (and are back again for scenic excursions from Thendara), while Van Auken's has remained a constant presence across the way. The second floor—where 20 bedrooms used to share two baths—now has 12 guest rooms, each with a private bath. Original details and antique furniture have been incorporated into these modern accommodations, and some rooms open onto the second-floor veranda. Van Auken's restaurant is open for lunch and dinner, plus there's a pub and a 1930s-themed speakeasy with a lineup of live music. $$.

SPECULATOR/PISECO

Bearhurst Lakeside Cottages (978-424-1931; www.bearhurst.com; 116 Bearhurst Drive, Speculator) was built in 1894 by Herman Meyrowitz (fashionable optical shops in Paris, Geneva, and Milan still carry his name), and it occupies a quarter-mile of shoreline on Lake Pleasant. Guests stay in five of the original outbuildings, including the icehouse, pump house, summer kitchen, and boathouse, all of which have been converted into modern accommodations while still maintaining historical charm. There's a private beach, dock space for guests' boats, and a pretty, rustic gazebo for watching the sunset over the lake. $$.

Irondequoit Inn (844-322-5500; www.irondequoitinn.com; 471 Old Piseco Road, Piseco) offers a traditional taste of the Adirondacks—a simple, off-the-beaten-path getaway that guests return to year after year. Established in 1892, this lakeside resort features a main lodge with seven guest rooms—most with private baths—cozy common areas and a wraparound porch. There are also five winterized cabins, as well as several beachside campsites available for do-it-yourselfers during the summer. $$.

STILLWATER

Stillwater Hotel (315-376-6470; www.stillwateradirondacks.com; 2591 Stillwater Road, Stillwater) is on Stillwater Reservoir, which is several miles back from the main highways via a winding gravel road. It's understandably popular with snowmobilers because the snow cover is excellent and several trail systems are accessible from the property. There are seven winterized motel rooms—the only accommodations that you can drive to on the reservoir. $$.

WEVERTOWN

Dillon Hill Inn (518-251-2912; www.dillonhill.com; 58 Dillon Hill Road) is a bed & breakfast with an Adirondack-country vibe. The centerpiece is a lovely nineteenth-century farmhouse offering five guestrooms with private baths, but there's also a pair of two-bedroom cabins on the pretty six-acre property. It's fine base for launching

LEWEY LAKE COURTESY OF TED COMSTOCK, SARANAC LAKE

AN AMERICAN TRAGEDY

I n July 1906, 20-year-old pregnant factory worker Grace Brown and her 22-year-old boyfriend, Chester Gillette, rented a boat from the Glenmore Hotel on Big Moose Lake.
Brown was later discovered beneath the water, allegedly killed by Gillette with a tennis racket. Gillette's sensational trial—and subsequent death by electric chair—put this Herkimer County hamlet on the map, as did Theodore Dreiser's acclaimed 1925 novel based on the case, *An American Tragedy*, and the 1951 movie starring Elizabeth Taylor, *A Place in the Sun*. The Glenmore burned to the ground in 1950.

BIG MOOSE'S GLENMORE HOTEL   COURTESY OF TED COMSTOCK, SARANAC LAKE

skiing or whitewater-rafting adventures at nearby North Creek. $$.

CAMPGROUNDS From Memorial Day through Labor Day, the **Department of Environmental Conservation** (518-402-9428; www.dec.ny.gov) operates public campgrounds. Facilities at state campgrounds include a picnic table and grill at each site, water spigots for every ten sites or so, and lavatories. DEC public campgrounds do not supply water, electric, or sewer hookups for recreational vehicles. If you require these amenities, there are privately owned campgrounds in many communities.

Reservations can be made for a site in the state campgrounds by contacting **Reserve America** (1-800-456-CAMP; www.reserveamerica). Its website includes details about every state campground, as does the DEC's campsite listings on its site, so you can see for yourself if Site #4 at Lake Durant is on the water (it is). Or contact the campground itself. DEC campgrounds will take you on a first-come, first-served basis if space is available.

Alger Island (315-369-3224; Petrie Road, Old Forge), on Fourth Lake. Access by boat, lean-tos, tents only.

Brown Tract Pond (315-354-4412; Uncas Road, Raquette Lake). Canoe to Raquette Lake or Fulton Chain. Swimming, canoe or rowboat rentals, no powerboats allowed.

Caroga Lake (518-835-4241; Route 29A, Caroga Lake). Swimming, showers, boat launch.

Eighth Lake (315-354-4120; Route 28, between Raquette Lake and Inlet). Swimming, showers, canoe or rowboat rentals, boat launch.

Forked Lake (518-624-6646; Forked Lake Campsite Lane, Long Lake). Primitive walk-in or canoe-in sites, launch for cart-top boats.

Golden Beach (315-354-4230; Route 28, Raquette Lake). On Raquette Lake. Swimming, showers, boat or canoe rentals, boat launch.

Indian Lake Islands (518-648-5300; Route 30, Sabael). Access by boat, tents only, boat launch.

Lake Durant (518-352-7797; Routes 28 and 30, Blue Mountain Lake). Swimming, showers, canoe rentals, boat launch; handicapped-accessible campsite. Access to Blue Ridge Wilderness and Northville–Lake Placid Trail.

Lake Eaton (518-624-2641; Route 30, Long Lake). Swimming, showers, canoe or rowboat rentals, boat launch.

Lewey Lake (518-648-5266; Route 30, Lake Pleasant). Swimming, showers, canoe or rowboat rentals, boat launch.

Limekiln Lake (315-357-4401; Limekiln Lake Road, Inlet). Swimming, showers, canoe or rowboat rentals, boat launch. Access to Moose River Recreation Area.

Little Sand Point (518-548-7585; Old Piseco Road, Piseco). On Piseco Lake. Swimming, canoe or rowboat rentals, boat launch.

Moffit Beach (518-548-7102; Page Street, Lake Pleasant). On Sacandaga Lake. Swimming, showers, canoe or rowboat rentals, boat launch.

Nicks Lake (315-369-3314; Bisby Road, Old Forge). Remote lakeside

location. Swimming, trout fishing, nearby hiking trails, no motorboats.

Northampton Beach (518-863-6000; Houseman Street, Mayfield). On Great Sacandaga Lake. Swimming, showers, canoe or rowboat rentals, boat launch.

Point Comfort (518-548-7586; Old Piseco Road, Piseco). On Piseco Lake. Swimming, showers, canoe or rowboat rentals, boat launch.

Sacandaga (518-924-4121; Route 30, Northville). On Sacandaga River. Swimming, showers, no powerboats.

Tioga Point (315-354-4101; Route 28, Raquette Lake). On Raquette Lake. Access by boat; some lean-tos, although it's best to bring a tent. Beautiful spot.

✳ Where to Eat

DINING OUT Calling ahead is a necessity in this region—imagine driving 50 minutes from Blue Mountain Lake to Big Moose to find the lights out. But if you plan ahead there are some sweet spots in these hamlets, and not just places that open in summer. The following are highlights.

BIG MOOSE

Big Moose Inn (315-357-2042; www .bigmooseinn.com; 1510 Big Moose Road), overlooking Big Moose Lake, is a favorite destination for visitors and year-round residents; some people even arrive by seaplane. The menu includes fine-dining choices as well as lighter fare—including the always-in-demand Blackened Prime Rib Sandwich—in the Tavern. Closed in April and November.

INLET

Seventh Lake House (315-357-6028; www .seventhlakehouse.com; 479 Route 28), which serves dinner only, changes up its extensive menu according to season. The place is elegantly simple, with an

THE MIDDLE OF NOWHERE

Beaver River on Stillwater Reservoir is one of the toughest settlements to reach in the Adirondacks—you can't drive there, though you can hike, cross-country ski, snowmobile, or paddle in.

In the late 1800s, the place was a stop along the Mohawk & Malone line, and hunters rushed here by rail, the hamlet's surrounding state-owned wilderness a big-game paradise. Boardinghouses and hotels sprang up. Then, in 1924, the hamlet's namesake river was dammed for hydropower. The resulting Stillwater Reservoir socked in the train-access-only community, giving it a last-frontier vibe. The train stopped chugging here in 1965, further disconnecting this remote community.

Today most of the outpost's year-round population of 20 or so, as well as its summer residents, embrace its remoteness, even its lack of electricity (power comes from generators). For visitors who want to explore this spit of land, particularly snowmobilers drawn by seemingly endless trails and plenty of white stuff, the **Norridgewock Lodge** (315-376-6200; www.beaverriver.com) is open year-round; the **Beaver River Hotel** (315-376-3010) closes in winter.

IN THE NINETEENTH CENTURY, BEAVER RIVER WAS BIG-GAME SHANGRI-LA COURTESY OF TED COMSTOCK, SARANAC LAKE

imposing fireplace and lots of picture windows. There's also a comfortable bar and a canopied deck stretching across the back.

LONG LAKE

Adirondack Growl & Grub (518-624-2816; www.growlandgrub.com; 8590 Newcomb Road), located behind Hoss's Country Corner, is a unique combination of deli and draft-beer filling station. Enjoy soups, sandwiches, and suds there, or take your grub and growlers to go.

ADK Trading Post (518-624-2357; www.adktradingpost.com; 1601 Route 30), stationed just outside of town, is a great pit stop for creative paninis, soups, and breakfast sandwiches. There's also a gift shop and liquor store.

THE HOLE STORY

By the time a line forms on summer mornings outside **Mary's White Pine Bakery** (315-357-5170; 152 Route 28), in Inlet, Doug Hugelmaier has been awake for hours. To make what he points out are "dough-nuts, not batter-nuts," Hugelmaier begins mixing at midnight so the dough has time to rise. The results—filled with jelly or real Bavarian cream; slathered with half-moons of chocolate and vanilla frosting in a riff on the black-and-white cookie; or dipped in maple glaze—plus an assortment of other baked goodies, draw steady crowds from Memorial Day through Columbus Day. "If we're not busy, we're closed," Hugelmaier says.

Misnomer though they may be, cake donuts have no shortage of fans in this corner of the Adirondacks, either. Just down the road from Mary's, in Eagle Bay, **The Donut Shop** (315-357-6421; 5474 Route 28; www.eaglebaydonuts.com) fries up as many as 1,200 plain or cinnamon-sugar donuts a day in peak season. Co-owner Dave Rowe is a former engineer who devised a compressed-air batter gun to ensure a consistent product. Humans aren't the only ones who find the aroma of **The Candy Cottage**'s mini-donut machine irresistible: the year owner Larry Starer installed the contraption, black bears attempted to break in two days in a row. (315-369-2310; 3031 Main Street, Old Forge; www .candycottage.net).

No matter your donut dream, there's somewhere in the Adirondack Park to fulfill it. Classic cider donuts can be found at **Gunnison Orchards**, in Crown Point (518-597-3363; Route 9N); they taste best warm from the fryer on a crisp

DONUT LOVERS WON'T BE DISAPPOINTED AT CAKE PLACID, IN LAKE PLACID COURTESY OF CAKE PLACID

autumn day, but there's no bad time to eat one of these traditional treats. **Donuts & More** (518-356-3210; 111 Elm Lake Road), in Speculator, doesn't stop at Technicolor frostings; its creative toppings might include caramel with pretzels, granola and fresh blueberries with a cinnamon-roll drizzle, or s'mores. The donuts at **Cake Placid** (518-523-9866; 2051 Saranac Avenue; www.cakeplacid.com) are as artistic as its fantastical cakes—filled with cannoli cream, topped with maple frosting and crunchy toffee, or frosted and sprinkled with fruity kids' cereal. At the **Washboard** (518-359-2339; 48 Park Street), it's no problem if you get a dollop of frosting—maybe maple, flecked with real bacon bits—on your shirt; this Tupper Lake institution doubles as a Laundromat.

Lakeside Knoshery (518-624-5253; 1240 Main Street) is a tiny walk-up-window joint that might be easy to miss—but you shouldn't. It transports classic New York City deli treats, like pastrami piled high on rye, plus latkes, knishes, and bagels and lox, to the Adirondack shore. Open July and August.

MAYFIELD

Lanzi's on the Lake (518-661-7711; www.lanzisonthelake.net; 1751 Route 30), on the western shore of Great Sacandaga Lake, is a popular destination. Ample docks and a long outdoor deck invite boaters in summer, and skiers dine by the stone fireplace in winter. It can become crowded on weekends, so reservations are recommended.

NORTH CREEK

BarVino (518-251-5533; www.barvino.net; 272 Main Street) is a chic, sweet spot on North Creek's Main Street. The decor is hip, the wine and beer lists lengthy, and the menus, which change constantly, are mostly imaginative small plates. Live music each week is another draw.

Basil & Wicks (518-251-3100; www.basilandwicks.com; 3195 Route 28) offers American fare in a comfortable atmosphere for hungry skiers, white-water rafters, and hikers. The bar has a nice fireplace and music many weekends, and families can head for a casual dining room.

Becks Tavern (855-846-7365; www.goremountainlodge.com/becks-tavern; 881 Peaceful Valley Road), located next to Gore Mountain Lodge, is the new kid in town, with German-inspired dishes and a full bar.

Café Sarah (518-251-5959; 260 Main Street) is an institution on North Creek's Main Street, serving up delicious baked goods, plus specialty coffees, breakfast burritos, soups and paninis. This is a local hot spot, so it bustles year-round.

NEW BREWERY ON THE BLOCK

The Fulton Chain Craft Brewery (315-369-1181;www.fccbrewery.com;127 North Street) brings farm-to-tap suds to Old Forge, crafting its stock with locally sourced ingredients. There's a rotating selection of ten beers on summer and fall weekends, as well as some weekdays during the fall. Favorites include its Adventure Canoe IPA, Go Fluff Yourself peanut butter ale, and Bear Road, a blueberry coffee stout.

Izzy's Market and Deli (518-251-3000; 282 Main Street) has set up shop in a restored turn-of-the-century general store, peddling unique foodstuffs and inventive sandwiches that keep visitors and locals lining up for more.

OLD FORGE

Five Corners Café (315-369-2255; www.fivecornerscafe.com; 3067 Route 28) is a funky little space on Old Forge's main drag. Owners Kathy and Paul Rivet—who used to run Van Auken's Inne in Thendara—have created a neighborhood restaurant vibe, serving tasty bistro fare with the freshest seasonal ingredients. A wine and beer bar and patio offer more seating options in this pocket-sized place.

The Lean-To at Great Pines (315-369-0181; www.greatpines.com; 4920 Route 28) offers casual dining in full-blown Adirondack style, with all the bark and rough-cut lumber you could ask for. This is comfort food with a North Country twist—including several variations of poutine, a regional delicacy (see page 159). The deck overlooks Fourth Lake, and docks allow for boat-up access. The Lean-To's sister restaurant, **The Lodge**, delivers a fine-dining experience with sweeping views of the lake.

Sisters Bistro (315-369-1053; www.sistersbistro.com; 3046 Main Street) has

SACANDAGA SAGA

Cities downstream of Adirondack rivers, fed up with destructive flooding, celebrated on March 27, 1930, when the gates of the new Conklingville Dam were shut, and 283 billion gallons of water swallowed the valley. But schools, farms, homes, stores, and businesses were also lost.

Today, the resulting Great Sacandaga Lake, a 29-mile-long reservoir with 125 miles of shoreline, is a summertime draw for swimmers, anglers, and boaters. Sometimes in October, when the reservoir's levels dip low, stumps, stone fences, foundations, and roads emerge.

THE SACANDAGA VALLEY WAS FLOODED TO CREATE GREAT SACANDAGA LAKE, A 29-MILE-LONG RESERVOIR THAT ENDED DESTRUCTIVE DOWNSTATE FLOODING COURTESY OF JOHNATHAN ESPER, WWW.WILDERNESSPHOTOGRAPHS.COM

a pretty Victorian mansion and eclectic decor as backdrop for its gourmet fare. Foodies all over the park are talking about Sisters' artful presentations and flavors—not to mention, where else in these parts can you order a Mango Martini? Open Memorial Day to Columbus Day.

OLMSTEDVILLE

The Owl at Twilight (518-251-4696; www .theowlattwilight.com; 1322 Route 29) is an unexpected treat: an upscale eatery hiding in this quiet pocket of the park that transports diners with its unique Latin American fare. The menu may be cosmopolitan, but the produce and herbs are hyper-local—fresh from the garden out back.

SPECULATOR

Logan's Bar & Grill (518-548-3287; www .logans921.com; Route 8) is former Anthony Bourdain–sous chef Steve Tempel's low-key restaurant in the heart of the park. Tempel, who has also been a contestant on various Food Network cook-offs, named the place after his son and, according to locals, has created an Adirondack family-style joint right down to the moose cutout on his restaurant's facade.

Melody Lodge (518-548-6562; www .melodylodge.com; 111 Old Indian Lake Road) feels almost like an Adirondack Great Camp, with its antiques, massive stone fireplaces, and view down Page Hill toward Lake Pleasant. The rambling inn was built in 1912 as a singing school for young girls, and became a restaurant and hotel in 1937. The lodge's menu has been updated recently to add fresh choices to old favorites. Closed Monday and Tuesday in winter.

CASUAL BITES Would you believe there's gelato in Inlet, and that the pistachio is divine? A trip to **Northern Lights Creamery** (315-357-6294; 162 Route 28) is a must. Also in Inlet, the **Red Dog Tavern**

(315-357-5502; www.reddogtavern.com; 2682 South Shore Road) has good ribs and other bar food. And after a night on the town, there's **Blue Line Coffee House** (315-357-5116; 157 Route 28) for all of your caffeine needs.

Long Lake's **Flavor** (518-624-2677; 1142 Main Street, behind Hoss's) is a can't-miss stop for dark roast coffee and Paris-worthy croissants, plus delicious scones, teacakes and more. Open June through August.

Breakfast, lunch or dinner, you can't go wrong with Northville's **Klippel's Kozy Korner Cafe & Deli** (518-863-8550; 221 Bridge Street), with its wide variety of downhome diner favorites. And find the freshest bites at the **Johnson's Family Farm** store (518-863-6104; www .johnsonsfamilyfarm.net; 132 North Main Street), offering local produce and meat, as well as farm-to-cup juices and smoothies, homemade soups, baked goods, and more. Open Thursday to Sunday May through November.

Ask the locals in Old Forge where they go for breakfast, and they'll point to **Walt's Diner** (315-369-2582; 3047 Main Street), a place famous for its hearty servings—including plate-size pancakes. For lighter fare, there are some great choices for coffee, baked goods, and other quick bites: **Lucy and Bob's Bakery Bistro** (315-369-4404; www.lucyandbobs .com; 2963 Route 28) and **Ozzie's Coffee Bar** (315-369-6246; 3019 Route 28). **Adirondack Dog House** provides the most playful fare, with every combination of hot-dog toppings imaginable, plus wraps, hamburgers, and deliciously wacky specials. Just outside of town there's **Daikers** (315-369-6954; www .daikers.com; 161 Daikers Circle), a hot spot—especially with snowmobilers—for bar food and live music on weekends. During the warm-weather months, eating on the spacious deck overlooking Fourth Lake is a treat.

Speculator's **Oxbow Inn** (518-548-7551), an all-season hangout with a long and colorful history, is enjoying a renaissance with a winning combination of new owners and old bar-food favorites.

✱ Selective Shopping

Want The Gap, J. Crew, or Eddie Bauer? Then head to Lake George or Lake Placid. In this, the heart of the park, it's all Adirondackana, antiques, artwork, books, and furniture.

ADIRONDACKANA/GENERAL STORES Adirondackana defines all kinds of material things that complement the countryside and evoke textures (bark, wood grain), smells (balsam, cedar), tastes (maple, apple), and forest colors (deep green, gold, sienna). In Blue Mountain Lake there's the **Adirondack Experience Store** (518-352-7311; www .theadkx.org; 9097 Route 30), open Memorial Day Weekend through Columbus Day; in Inlet, **Adirondack Reflections** (315-299-2471; www.adirondack reflections.net; 164 Route 28); in Northville, the **Adirondack Country Store** (518-863-6056; www.adirondack countrystore.com; 252 N. Main Street); in North Creek, **Hudson River Trading Co.** (518-251-4461; www.hudsonrivertrading co.com; 292 Main Street); and in Old Forge, **Moose River Trading Company** (315-369-6091; www.mooserivertrading .com; NY 28, Thendara).

Adirondack style often dominates our general stores, too—chances are you'll find glass percolator tops and camping gear an aisle over from the suspenders and boot socks, near a display of balsam pillows and birch-bark frames, which are around the corner from the chips and salsa. If you can't find it at one of these stores, you can probably live without it:

Pine's Country Store (518-648-5212; www.pinescs.com; 1 East Main Street), in Indian Lake; **Hoss's Country Corner** (518-624-2481; www.hossscountrycorner .com; 1142 Main Street), in Long Lake;

Old Forge Hardware (315-369-6100; www.oldforgehardware.com; 104 Fulton Street); **Lake Supply** (315-354-4301; Main Street), in Raquette Lake; the **Lake Store** (518-648-5222; 5450 Route 30), in Sabael; **Speculator Department Store** (518-548-6123; speculatordepartmentstore.com; 2901 Route 8); and the **Shop** (315-376-2110; www.stillwatershop.com; 2590 Stillwater Road at the boat launch), in Stillwater.

ANTIQUES The best fair is unquestionably September's **Adirondack Antiques Show & Sale**, at the Adirondack Experience, in Blue Mountain Lake (518-352-7311; www.theadkx.org), and the concurrent **Adirondack Mountains Antiques Show** (518-648-5112; www .indian-lake.com), in Indian Lake. The following shops are among the handful in this region: **Dragonfly Cottage** (315-327-9007; 2987 Main Street, Old Forge), the **Red Barn** (518-863-4828; 202 S. Main Street, Northville), and **Wide River Antiques** (518-624-4749; 1128 Main Street, Long Lake).

ART GALLERIES AND ARTISTS' STUDIOS The best nineteenth-century American painters came to the Adirondacks to interpret wild scenery on paper and canvas, and many artists still rely on the great outdoors for inspiration, no matter what the medium.

Indian Lake is where you'll find Kathy Larkin and Jane Zilka's **Abanakee Studios** (518-648-5013; www .abanakeestudios.com; Route 28), open late June through August. In Old Forge there's the fine-arts establishment **Gallery 3040** (315-369-1059; 3040 Route 28) and **Starving Artist Gallery** (765-720-2069; 3071 Route 28), a co-op of local artists. Sculptor John Van Alstine and his eight-acre **Adirondack River Sculpture Park** are in Wells (518-924-9204; www.johnvanalstine.com); Van Alstine's wife, **Caroline Ramsdorfer** (www.carolineramsdorfer.at), is also a renowned sculptor.

BOAT BUILDERS In Olmstedville, Peter Hornbeck builds popular, lightweight **Hornbeck Boats** (518-251-2764; www .hornbeckboats.com; 131 Trout Brook Road).

BOOKS You'll find independently owned bookstores in this region, most with extensive collections of Adirondack titles, including the **Adirondack Experience Shop** (518-352-7311; www.theadkx .org; 9097 Route 30), in Blue Mountain Lake, open daily late May through Columbus Day; the **Adirondack Reader** (315-357-2665; 156 Main Street), in Inlet, closed January through April; **Hoss's Country Corner** (518-624-2481; www .hossscountrycorner.com; 1142 Main Street), in Long Lake; **Hudson River Trading Co.** (518-251-4461; www .hudsonrivertradingco.com; 292 Main Street), in North Creek; **Old Forge Hardware** (315-369-6100; www.oldforge hardware.com; 104 Fulton Street); and **Charlie Johns Store** (518-548-7451; www .charliejohns.com; The Four Corners), in Speculator.

ARTIST BARNEY BELLINGER, OF SAMPSON BOG STUDIO, IN MAYFIELD, IS A MASTER CRAFTSMAN COURTESY OF SAMPSON BOG STUDIO

CLOTHING The following have classic woolens, practical sportswear, footwear, and high-tech outer gear:

French Louie ADK Sports (315-357-2441; www.frenchlouieadksports .com; 156 Main Street), in Inlet; **Mountainman Outdoor**

IN SEPTEMBER, THE ADIRONDACK EXPERIENCE'S ANNUAL RUSTIC SHOW IS A REGIONAL HIGHLIGHT COURTESY OF NANCIE BATTAGLIA

GARNET, EMBEDDED IN THE ADIRONDACK MOUNTAINS, IS THE REGIONAL STONE OF CHOICE COURTESY OF MELODY THOMAS, WWW.MELODYTHOMASPHOTO.COM

Supply Company (315-369-2300; www.mountainmanoutdoors.com; 2855 Route 28), in Old Forge; and **Speculator Department Store** (518-548-6123; speculatordepartmentstore.com; 2901 Route 8).

FURNITURE Regional woodworkers create furniture in a variety of styles, from Shaker-inspired designs to rugged sculptural pieces to the straightforward Adirondack chairs that now come in an infinite range of permutations. Get a good overview at the Adirondack Experience's (518-352-7311; www.theadkx.org;

9097 Route 30) **Rustic Furniture Fair**, held every September.

Charles Grover Woodworks (518-636-6772; charlesgroverwoodworks.com), in Long Lake, makes handcrafted Adirondack chairs and other outdoor furniture.

Mayfield's **Sampson Bog Studio** and **Art Funk and Junk** (347-582-1605; 171 Paradise Point Road) are home to Barney Bellinger's twig mosaic and birch-bark tables, desks, wall shelves, benches with fine hand-painted details and graceful lines, plus his new projects that incorporate vintage cars and tramp art.

In Northville, **William Coffey** (518-774-0531; 322 North Third Street) blends rustic and contemporary styles with stunning results.

Shelter: Adirondack Furniture and Gifts (315-369-5014; www.adkshelter.net; 3109 State Route 28), in Old Forge, showcases master craftsman Jim Kiefer's unique rustic pieces for camp and home.

Otter Lake Rustics (315-369-6530; www.otterlakerustics.com; 13977 NY 28) creates rustic furniture, carved doors, and other Adirondack-style decor in Otter Lake.

JEWELRY AND GEM SHOPS Garnet's the stone of choice in this region—it's embedded in these mountains and in beautiful bling that you can buy at the following:

In North River, there's the **Gore Mountain Mineral Shop** (518-251-2706; www.garnetminestours.com; Barton Mines Road) and **J and J Brown Garnet Studio** (518-251-3368; www.garnetstudio.net; 68 Casterline Road). In Old Forge, **Allen's** (315-369-6660; 3017 Main Street) offers fine jewelry, including Adirondack-themed pieces.

NORTHWEST LAKES

COURTESY OF MARK BOWIE, WWW.MARKBOWIE.COM

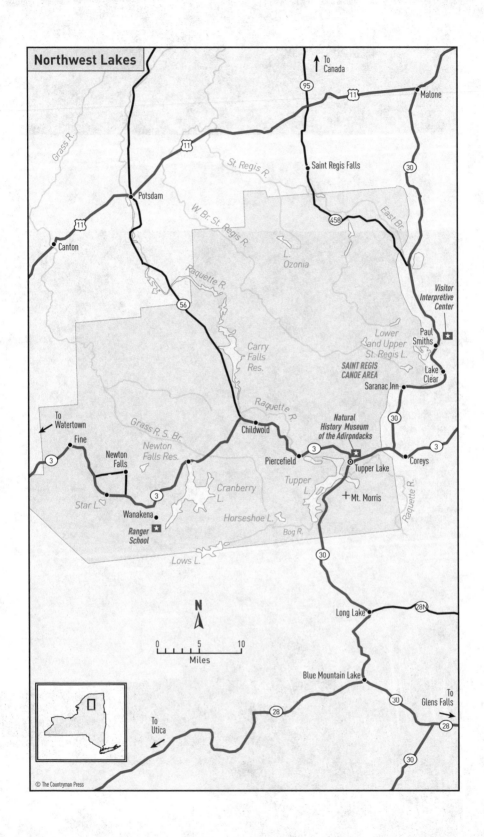

NORTHWEST LAKES

Want remote? The Adirondacks' Northwest Lakes region is wild, woodsy country, with teensy hamlets that emerge like rustic oases. It's paddler Shangri-La: the waters of the Saint Regis Canoe Area are seemingly endless—a pristine, motorless network of lakes and ponds. All this is a fitting backdrop for hidden hunting lodges, one of the most exclusive resorts in the Northeast, a ranger school, black bears, moose, and eagles, and a state-of-the-art natural history museum. But you can't explore this part of the park without acknowledging its woods-work heritage. Beginning in the mid-nineteenth century, logging was—and continues to be—the regional vocation. It shaped a culture that's celebrated in places like Tupper Lake, where a chain-saw-carved lumberjack serves as the town's mascot, and annual gatherings involve log-rolling, ax-flinging, and speed-chopping.

✳ To See

The Oswegatchie wilds, full of tall trees, huge bucks, and wily brook trout, drew native son and artist Frederic Remington to the region, where he painted fishermen, logging camps, and humble guides' cabins. Writers such as Irving Bacheller documented the dialect and tales of manly men; his *Eben Holden: A Tale of the North Country* was among the first American bestsellers. While the High Peaks and central Adirondacks attracted numerous Hudson River School painters, Marc Chagall spent time near Star Lake in the 1940s. Finding an Adirondack-influenced Chagall is difficult, perhaps because his wife, Bella, was very ill at the time. Sadly, she died in the hospital in Tupper Lake in 1944.

MUSEUMS AND NATURE CENTERS You can't come to the Adirondacks without visiting **The Wild Center** (518-359-7800; www.wildcenter.org; 45 Museum Drive, Tupper Lake), a slick, state-of-the-art natural history museum. Think adorable otters somersaulting in a glass tank, plus more than 900 other live critters, some that scurry, slither, and swim in and out of the museum via a reflective pond. Exhibits tell the story of this park's natural history—who doesn't love touching a glacier? (There's a freezy chunk that mimics the ice sheet that coated this place just ten thousand years ago.) A theater shows a variety of movies, among them *A Matter of Degrees*, narrated by Long Lake summer resident Sigourney Weaver. The museum's schedule is packed with lectures, workshops, and performances; museum

EXPLORING THE NATURAL WORLD ON A KID-SIZE WEB ALONG THE WILD CENTER'S WILD WALK, IN TUPPER LAKE COURTESY OF THE WILD CENTER

THE WILD CENTER, IN TUPPER LAKE, IS A MUST-SEE FOR ALL VISITORS TO THE ADIRONDACKS COURTESY OF THE WILD CENTER

staffers stroll about with porcupines, skunks, and raptors, and lead guided treks on the museum's network of trails. Kids love the natural playground, roots, twigs,

THE WILD WALK AT THE WILD CENTER BRINGS VISITORS HIGH ABOVE THE FOREST FOR A BIRD'S-EYE VIEW OF THE LANDSCAPE COURTESY OF THE WILD CENTER

and all. And the new Wild Walk is an extraordinary—and truly wild—trail in the treetops. Along the Walk is a four-story tree house, a giant spider web, and a massive bald eagle's nest in which you can perch yourself to take in the surrounding landscape. Also new are the canoe trips through the Raquette River's oxbow, plus the museum's iForest, where composer Pete M. Wyer's music is piped along a forest trail, providing an immersive experience. Admission in 2017: $20 adults, $13 ages 4–14, discounts available for seniors and groups. Open seven days in summer, Friday through Sunday in winter, plus Presidents' Week and Martin Luther King Jr. Day; closed in April.

Paul Smith's College Visitor Interpretive Center (518-327-3000; www.adirondackvic.org; Route 30, Paul Smiths), the former state-funded Paul Smiths Visitor

WOODSWORK: AN ADIRONDACK EDUCATION

Appropriately, **Paul Smith's College** (1-800-421-2605; www.paulsmiths.edu), in Paul Smiths, and the State University of New York–Environmental Science and Forestry Ranger School (315-470-6500; www.esf.edu/rangerschool), in Wanakena, are based in this region of the Adirondack Park. Paul Smith's, on the shores of Lower Saint Regis Lake, offers four-year programs in hospitality, culinary arts, forestry, recreation, fish and wildlife, or liberal arts. The Ranger School uses its wilderness digs to give students training for an associate's degree in environmental conservation, forest technology, or land surveying.

Paul Smith's hosts the intensive **Adirondack Woodsmen's School** (518-327-6990; www.adirondackwoodsmenschool.com), a three-session, summertime college-credit program that teaches proficiency in speed chopping, ax flinging, log rolling, sawing, and other woodsmen's skills.

You can see the finest lumber skills at the annual **Woodsmen's Days** (518-359-9444; www.woodsmendays.com) in Tupper Lake. This event underlines the importance of logging in the Adirondack economy today. There's a parade with sparkling log trucks hauling the year's biggest, best logs; contests for men and women (chainsaw carving, ax tossing), beasts (skidding logs with draft horses), and heavy equipment (precision drills for skidders and loaders); and games for kids. It's all on the second weekend in July, in the municipal park on the lakefront in Tupper Lake.

COURTESY OF TED COMSTOCK, SARANAC LAKE

Interpretive Center (VIC), is now operated by the college and the Adirondack Park Institute. The facility explains the region's natural history through exhibits, guided hikes, and workshops for kids and adults, and it has miles of interpretive and back-country trails, open year-round for hiking, snowshoeing, and cross-country skiing. Dogs are allowed on trails, but they must be leashed. In summer it has a wonderful butterfly house with flowers, plants, and indigenous insects.

✳ To Do

BICYCLING Mountain-biking at the **Peavine Swamp trail**, accessible from Route 3 in Cranberry Lake or from the northeast at the end of the Ranger School campus, in Wanakena, is incredible in late summer and early fall. This well-marked system in the

PAUL SMITH'S COLLEGE'S VIC HOSTS THE GREAT ADIRONDACK BIRDING CELEBRATION, WHICH INCLUDES TREKS TO WHITEFACE TO SEARCH FOR THE ELUSIVE BICKNELL'S THRUSH COURTESY OF JEFF NADLER, WWW.JNPHOTO.NET

Cranberry Lake Wild Forest has three loops of about 10 miles of intermediate-to-difficult riding. You'll roll through old-growth forest and encounter hills, roots, and rocks. But there are lots more routes for mountain bikes (and, in winter, trendy fat-tire bikes) and long stretches of woodsy highways for skinny ones.

CANOEING AND KAYAKING For flatwater fans, there are long trips linking lakes, such as the 44-mile route from Long Lake to Tupper Lake. In the Saint Regis Canoe Area, it's possible to paddle for weeks on end and visit a different pond or lake each day.

New York's land acquisitions—during the past two decades, vast tracts have been added to the Adirondack Park—mean even more opportunities for exploration, including beautiful, motorless Little Tupper Lake and Rock Pond, and the myriad white-water rivers that formerly belonged to Champion International Company. More

THE NORTHWEST LAKES' SAINT REGIS CANOE AREA IS PADDLERS' HEAVEN COURTESY OF MARK BOWIE, WWW.MARKBOWIE.COM

TEAR UP THE ADIRONDACKS

For a weekend each June, teardrop trailer enthusiasts from across the United States and Canada come to Fish Creek Pond campground for the **ADK Spring TearUp** (www .tearuptheadk.com). During the gathering, impromptu groups paddle the nearby waterways, hike the peaks, have potlucks, and kick back by fires—and most important, ramble campsite to campsite, checking out all the teardrops.

Popular after World War II, when the military's excess aluminum was used to build them, teardrop trailers—traditionally four by eight feet—with their funky stand-up rear-galley kitchens and overall cute-as-a-button appeal, have made a comeback. They can be pulled behind any vehicle, even a motorcycle.

The Fish Creek event lures teardrop lovers who tow fancy stainless-steel, air-conditioned, souped-up trailers with sound systems and satellite radio and television, but also hobbyists who restore vintage models or build trailers from scratch.

lakes opened to paddlers, such as Round Lake, adjacent to Little Tupper Lake. Four-mile-long Little Tupper Lake offers gorgeous paddling, swimming, and loon-watching, with several primitive campsites.

FISHING Lake trout in Star Lake, landlocked salmon in Lake Ozonia, bass in Lake Lila, walleye in Tupper Lake, and brook trout near Cranberry Lake and interior ponds—these are just a sampling of the fish native to waters in this corner of the Adirondack Park.

To get in the proper frame of mind for fishing, nothing beats a trip to a local fish hatchery. The **Adirondack Fish Hatchery** (518-891-3358; NY 30, Saranac Inn) specializes in raising landlocked salmon for stocking lakes.

GOLF Golf courses in this area include the **Clifton-Fine Golf Course** (315-848-3570; 4173 Main Street, Star Lake), a par-36, 2,800-yard course with nine holes; and **Tupper**

POSTCARD OF CRANBERRY LAKE   COURTESY OF TED COMSTOCK, SARANAC LAKE

SAINT REGIS CANOE AREA

State Route 30 is the main road to the **Saint Regis Canoe Area**, west of Saranac Lake and northeast of Tupper Lake. Off Route 30 the DEC's Fish Hatchery Road, near Lake Clear, has two put-ins, and Floodwood Road, near Saranac Inn, has three parking areas near canoe access points. Floodwood is also a launching place for ponds in the Saranac Lakes Wild Forest to the south.

Signature routes include the **Seven Carries**, originally a way to travel between Prospect House, on Upper Saranac Lake, and Paul Smith's Hotel, on Lower Saint Regis Lake. Today it's a popular day-trip or overnight. Pond and put-in options vary—there aren't always seven carries, but the name endures.

The **Nine Carries** can start on Little Clear Pond, Hoel Pond, or Upper Saint Regis Lake and follow a variety of pond-hop itineraries ranging from 13 to 18 miles (including 1.5 to 2.5 miles of carries). Consult maps and guidebooks to design your own route.

A hike up **Long Pond Mountain** (about 1.5 miles, 900-foot ascent) adds variety to outings in the Long Pond-to-Hoel Pond area. The trail is gorgeous. The take-out on a northern lobe of Long Pond is well marked and also leads to Mountain Pond.

Saint Regis Mountain's 3.4-mile trail is north of most of the ponds, but its unbroken views of the waters below attract nearly as much traffic as the rest of the canoe area combined. There's a preserved 1918 fire tower at the summit.

Nearby outfitters offer boats and gear for rental or purchase as well as guided trips: **Saint Regis Canoe Outfitters** (518-891-8040; www.canoeoutfitters.com), on Floodwood Road at the Long Pond portage, with its couch and woodstove, is as much woodland lounge as shop. **Mac's Canoe Livery** (518-891-1176; www.macscanoe.com), at the edge of the canoe area, 5859 State Route 30, in Lake Clear, is close to the Fish Hatchery Road put-ins. **Raquette River Outfitters** (518-359-3228; www.raquetteriveroutfitters.com), on Route 30, in Tupper Lake, is also a fine source of information.

Lake Golf & Country Club (518-359-3701; Country Club Road), a par-71 course with 18 holes and 6,200 yards.

HIKING AND BACKPACKING In some parts of the park, you can leave the trailhead and not see another person until you return to your car and look in the rearview mirror. The Five Ponds Wilderness Area, between Stillwater Reservoir and Cranberry Lake, is especially remote. You might go several days without seeing a soul.

The **Cranberry Lake 50**, a collection of trails that forms a 50-mile loop around the Adirondacks' third-largest body of water, offers hikers a variety of stretches, from easy logging road rambles to pond hopping. The trail goes beyond its namesake's shoreline, extending into the Five Ponds Wilderness and the Cranberry Lake Wild Forest. On this network you'll find lean-tos and lovely ponds, particularly Curis and Cowhorn Ponds, but most important is what you'll find at www.cranberrylake50.org, which covers everything you need to know about the 50.

Mount Arab, a 2,545-foot peak in Piercefield, allows a quick but satisfying hike or snowshoe that concludes with a recently restored fire tower. From the lookout's cab you can see Tupper Lake below and the High Peaks in the distance. In season, a steward hangs out at the observer's cabin on the summit to answer questions about the fire tower, erected in 1918, and the area's natural history.

CROSS-COUNTRY SKIING AND SNOWSHOEING Many towns maintain cross-country-ski trails, and the **Paul Smith's College Visitor Interpretive Center** (518-327-3000;

www.paulsmiths.edu/vic) has miles of paths. There's also the **Cranberry Lake Trail** (315-386-4000; NY 3, Cranberry Lake) and the 15-kilometer backcountry **Deer Pond Loop** (518-359-3328; NY 30, Tupper Lake). The **Saranac Inn Horse Trail System**, off NY 30 near Saranac Inn, has several short trails in the Saint Regis Canoe Area and an 11-mile round trip on the **Fish Pond Truck Trail**—excellent for cross-country skiing.

The **Jackrabbit Trail** is a superb resource, some 35 miles of groomed trails connecting Paul Smiths with Keene. The trail combines old logging roads and abandoned rail lines. Dogs aren't welcome on groomed portions of this trail.

DOWNHILL SKIING AND SNOWBOARDING **Big Tupper Ski Area** (518-359-3730; www.skibigtupper.org; Ski Tow Road, Tupper Lake) is a hometown hero, if ever a mountain can be. Big Tupper was shuttered for years until local volunteers, in an attempt to revive Tupper's sleepy economy, opened the locally popular ski area. There's no snowmaking here, just a no-frills, two-chair, 25-plus-trail mom-and-pop-type operation that's affordable and fine for skiing and snowboarding. In 2016 the mountain stayed closed due to little snow and financial issues, but insiders insist the mountain will open next season.

SNOWMOBILING Besides the Old Forge–Inlet area, there are more than 400 miles of snowmobile trails in the Tupper Lake–Saranac Lake–Lake Placid area, and near Cranberry Lake, there are miles and miles of trails. Many trail networks throughout the park cross private timberlands as well as the state forest preserve.

TRIATHLONS Tupper Lake's **Tinman Triathlon** (518-359-7571; www.tupper-lake .com), a USA Triathlon–sanctioned event that is half the length of Ironman, is a draw for amateur athletes looking to test their mettle, as well as professionals preparing for the real deal. Competitors converge in late June on Tupper Lake's Municipal Park and swim 1.2 miles in Raquette Pond, bike 56 miles past Cranberry Lake, then run 13.1 miles along Route 3; the footrace has earned a reputation as "mosquito alley."

WATERFALLS In this region is **Bog River Falls**, a two-tier falls at Big Tupper Lake, in Tupper Lake. It's visible from County Road 421. Also, **High Falls** is on a remote stretch of the Oswegatchie River, in Cranberry Lake. And **Raquette Falls** is on the Raquette River in Tupper Lake. See Russell Dunn's *Adirondack Waterfall Guide* to learn more about cascades across the park.

WILDERNESS AREAS These portions of the Forest Preserve are 10,000 acres or larger and contain little evidence of modern times. Wilderness areas are open to hiking, cross-country skiing, hunting, fishing, and other similar pursuits, but seaplanes may not land on wilderness ponds, nor are motorized vehicles welcome.

TUPPER RISING

The giant Adirondack Club and Resort project, in Tupper Lake, which combines the development of dozens of Great Camp–style homes with a marina on Tupper Lake, resuscitation of Big Tupper ski area, and, eventually, condominiums on and near its slopes, is giving locals plenty to celebrate. At press time the resort—tied down for more than a decade by environmental lawsuits, approval delays, and money troubles—has been lumbering to life. Locals say the project will boost the local economy and draw celebrities who might buy the massive homes (country star Tim McGraw's name has come up) as well as investors like golfer Greg Norman, who visited Tupper several years ago to survey the property.

GREAT ADIRONDACK BIRDING FESTIVAL

Birders can participate in the Great Adirondack Birding Festival, at Paul Smith's College's Visitor Interpretive Center (518-327-3000), in Paul Smiths, in June. It's a birding extravaganza with workshops, lectures from top ornithologists, and expeditions with an emphasis on boreal species.

IN JUNE, THE GREAT ADIRONDACK BIRDING FESTIVAL ATTRACTS BIRDERS FROM AFAR COURTESY OF JEFF NADLER, WWW. JNPHOTO.NET

In the Northwest Lakes region is the **Saint Regis Canoe Area**, with 20,000 acres, west of Paul Smiths. Its 58 lakes and ponds are the ultimate for paddling; the views are postcard-perfect from Saint Regis and other mountains, and there's a trail network for hiking and cross-country skiing.

WILD FOREST AREAS More than a million acres of public land in the park are designated as wild forest, and are open to snowmobile travel, mountain biking, and other recreation.

In this region is **Cranberry Lake Wild Forest**, between Cranberry Lake and Piercefield, with snowmobile and hiking trails and trout ponds. Also, 9,837-acre **White Hill Wild Forest**, near Parishville. Its 35-acre Clear Pond is the tract's centerpiece, though other pretty ponds and wetlands draw adventurers and bald eagles.

✳ Lodging

In the nineteenth century, Paul Smith built his wilderness resort for sportsmen, hosting guests such as Theodore Roosevelt, Charles Dickens, and P. T. Barnum. His famous hospitality skills launched today's Paul Smith's College, in Paul Smiths, but also a trend of backwoods lodging in these parts—you won't find cookie-cutter hotels or franchises around here. Following are the region's highlights.

LAKE CLEAR

Lake Clear Lodge & Retreat (518-891-1489; www.lodgeonlakeclear.com; 6319 NY 30) is acclaimed for home-style German cuisine, and overnight guests have enjoyed the family's gracious hospitality for half a century. On 25 secluded lakeshore acres, accommodations here combine modern conveniences with Old World charm. Four guest rooms in the 1886 lodge each have a private bath, three winterized chalets with fireplaces provide woodsy privacy, and three lakeside cottages cater to larger groups—perfect for weddings or retreats. Guests may use canoes, rowboats, a picnic area, and beach. Sleigh rides are popular in winter, and mountain-bike rentals, guide service, or overnight canoe trips for visitors can be arranged. The lodge allows pets in the chalets and vacation rentals and offers packages ranging from wellness weekends to romantic getaways. $$.

PAUL SMITHS

White Pine Camp (518-327-3030; www.whitepinecamp.com; White Pine Road), a real Great Camp, was once the summer White House of President Coolidge. Four of the cabins along Osgood Pond are available to guests by the week in July and August and for shorter visits in spring and fall; a couple of units are available for winter rentals as well. All 13 cabins—furnished with an eclectic assortment of rustic and Mission-style antiques—have porches, kitchens, separate bedrooms that accommodate two to eight people, and some either fieldstone fireplaces or woodstoves. Guests can use the beach, boathouse, Japanese teahouse, croquet lawn, bowling alley, canoes, rowboats, and kayaks. $$.

The Point (518-891-5674 or 1-800-255-3530; www.thepointresort.com; P.O. Box 1327). See box on page 116.

THE DARKEST SKIES

The Adirondack Public Observatory (www.apobservatory.org), in Tupper Lake, has a roll-off roof observatory to house its telescopes. But the nonprofit organization is more than a place for stargazing: it's a club of amateur and expert astronomers who present lectures and activities to, and raise public awareness within, the Adirondack community.

Its Tupper Lake base is a fitting place for an astronomy group. Minus brightly lit correctional facilities in some nearby towns, Tupper and most of the Adirondack Park are free of the light pollution that blots out the night sky and disrupts the reproduction and migration cycles of many species. Across the region, on the shore of Lake Champlain, David Levy, who discovered 22 comets—including Shoemaker-Levy 9—runs an annual Adirondack Astronomy Retreat at Twin Valleys Outdoor Education Center for that very reason.

SARANAC INN

Sunday Pond Bed & Breakfast (518-891-1531; www.sundaypond.com; 5544 NY 30) is perfect for paddlers or hikers

THE POINT LUXURY RESORT COURTESY OF THE POINT

AN ADIRONDACK FANTASY

The Point's twiggy gate swings open. You're told, "This is *your* camp. *You're* the Rockefellers." And it feels that way: the champagne placed in your hand as you tour the Upper Saranac Lake property, your handsome room with stone fireplace, the staff who seem to emerge from the trees with trays of cocktails and gourmet fare. The point offers an Adirondack fantasy that conjures William Avery Rockefeller II, who commissioned this Great Camp as his getaway, Wonundra (an Australian Aboriginal word for "Big Rock," the story goes). It was built post–Gilded Age, during the Depression. By the 1930s the Adirondack house party was still stylish and, in many ways, more exclusive. The Rockefellers were among those who continued their lavish life in the midst of the country's financial collapse. All the structures at Wonundra, including a main lodge, boathouse, guest cabin, and sap house, were constructed with native cut stone and Canadian logs, a sturdy approach compared to other trophy camps' delicate tangled-twig and peely birch-bark exteriors.

Today the resort offers guest rooms in the main house and the guest house; the garage has been renovated into a pub with billiards and jukebox, with guest rooms above and behind; and the boathouse, perched over parking spaces for an Elco lunch and a 1929-replica Hacker-craft, is one of the resort's most sought-after quarters. The decor is Adirondack-style, what The Point calls "rustic elegance." All guest rooms were recently renovated.

The property's 75 acres include tennis courts, a croquet court, and hiking trails. Name the watercraft—electric launches, guideboats, a Ski Nautique—and it's here, available for guests. Each night there's a campfire beside a tricked-out lean-to with built-in bar. And as a Relais & Chateaux Property, fine cuisine is a prerequisite. Dinner—black tie on Wednesdays and Saturdays—is served communally in the Great Hall.

Though staffers won't divulge names, word's trickled out that Robert De Niro, U2's Bono, Sigourney Weaver, British lords, Saudi princes, investment bankers, and politicians have stayed here. One rumor has Bill Gates being turned away because he brought his kids; children under 18 aren't permitted, though dogs are welcome.

All this elegance and hedonism comes at a price, with one night for a couple at The Point costing more than a week for two at most other resorts. $$$$.

THE POINT, ON UPPER SARANAC LAKE, IS THE MOST EXCLUSIVE RESORT IN THE ADIRONDACKS COURTESY OF THE POINT

who want to explore the Saint Regis Canoe Area, but prefer not to camp out. Adventures can begin from Sunday Pond's front door. In the Lyons' home—one of a very few in this corner of the park—guests can choose from three rooms or, for families, a spacious sleeping loft, all with private baths. There's also a new lean-to with outdoor shower on the property for those who prefer more rustic-style lodging. Breakfasts are ample and healthy; hearty trail lunches and dinners are available by request. $.

TUPPER LAKE

Shaheen's Adirondack Inn (518-359-3384; www.shaheensadirondackinn.com; 314 Park Street) is the place in town where locals send their visitor overflow. The motel looks like a 1950s throwback—there are plenty of cabin colonies and motor inns around Tupper that hark from that age—but Shaheen's simple rooms are clean, updated (though the wood paneling endures), and a

FAR OUT IN CRANBERRY LAKE

The psychedelic revolution came to Cranberry Lake in 1965, when Arthur Kleps opened his Morning Glory Lodge on the water's east shore. The camp became headquarters for the former North Country school psychologist's Neo-American Church, founded on the principle that "psychedelic substances such as LSD are sacraments in that they encourage enlightenment, which is the realization that life is a dream." Among Morning Glory Lodge visitors were LSD guru Timothy Leary, plus guests—"and a few hippies"—from around the country, including undercover federal agents, as Kleps documented in his 1975 book *Millbrook*. Morning Glory Lodge is long gone, but Kleps's church still exists at okneoac.com.

welcome respite for those who want to stay in town, close to restaurants, The Wild Center, and whatever northwestern Adirondack adventures await. $.

THE ROCKEFELLERS' UPPER SARANAC LAKE GREAT CAMP IS NOW A LUXURY RESORT COURTESY OF THE POINT

THE GREAT WINDFALL

On September 20, 1845, almost half a century before the Adirondack Park was formed, what's been described as a tornado leveled everything in its 275-mile-or-so path, from Watertown, across Lake Champlain—even sucking up the steamer *Burlington*'s deck planks—into Vermont. Thousands upon thousands of acres of timber were toppled.

An excerpt from the 1892 *Annual Report of the Forest Commission of the State of New York* describes the "most marked destruction" by the Great Windfall "occurring about 6 miles north of Lake Massawepie. . . . The path of the cyclone is still to be seen here, extending for 25 miles in length and varying from a half to over a mile in width.

"Not a single tree was left standing," wrote Frederick J. Seaver in *Historical Sketches of Franklin County and Its Several Towns*. "All were snapped off or uprooted, with a result a tangle of trunks and limbs and tops that was impenetrable."

Old maps depict the scarred swath as a stripe that runs from Newton Falls to present-day Windfall Pond, north of Tupper Lake. Writer Paul Jamieson commented in his guidebook *Adirondack Canoe Waters: North Flow* that the storm's course can be traced by names such as the "Windfall Road . . . three Windfall Brooks, and two Windfall Ponds." Post–Civil War pioneers, drawn to the windfall's clearing, settled in Franklin County. Today there's barely evidence of the destruction, though it's believed that Route 3 from Cranberry Lake to Tupper Lake follows the storm's path.

WANAKENA

Packbasket Adventures Lodge (315-848-3488; www.packbasketadventures .com; 12 South Shore Road) is Wanakena Ranger School graduate and Adirondack guide Rick Kovacs's dream come true. Rick spent time in Vermont as a back-to-the-lander, but the Green State's surge in development was a turnoff for him and his wife, Angie Oliver. Remote Wanakena had everything they hoped for, so they established Packbasket Adventures Lodge and Guide Service so other folks could enjoy it, too. Expect comfortable Adirondack rustic-style accommodations—log furniture, wrought-iron decor—in their four-bedroom, four-bath lodge and adjacent cozy log cabin. Guests are loyal repeat customers, often sportsmen hunting or angling in the region, many who also hire Rick for fly-fishing instruction. Meals are provided, and Rick will even set up picnic lunches in nearby lean-tos.

CAMPGROUNDS From Memorial Day through Labor Day the **Department of**

Environmental Conservation (518-402-9428; www.dec.ny.gov) operates the following public campgrounds in the Northwest Lakes region:

Cranberry Lake (315-848-2315; 243 Lone Pine Road, Cranberry Lake). Beach for swimming, showers, rowboat or canoe rentals, the trailhead to easy but pretty Bear Mountain.

Fish Creek Pond (518-891-4560; 4523 NY 30, Saranac Lake). A quintessential Adirondack campground with swimming beaches, showers, canoe or rowboat rentals, boat launch, and nature programs.

Rollins Pond (518-891-3239; NY 30, near Fish Creek Pond campsite), offers showers, canoe or rowboat rentals, and boat launch.

✳ Where to Eat

In these parts, lumberjack flapjacks and camp-stove meals come to mind, though there are a handful of indoor spots where you can find a fine meal. As with most Adirondack ventures, be sure to call ahead since hours of operation can change like the weather.

LAKE CLEAR

Lake Clear Lodge & Retreat (518-891-1489; www.lodgeonlakeclear.com; 6319 NY 30), a charming Adirondack inn, was the town's first post office and an early stagecoach stop; the decor today is European-Adirondack fusion. And the food today is traditional—heirloom recipes like schnitzels, wursts, beef stroganoff, and spaetzle—but also focuses on wellness and local bounty and products. Chef Cathy Hohmeyer, whose family built the lodge in 1886, follows the 100-mile philosophy: all food is sourced from within a 100-mile radius. Hohmeyer's is "culinary naturopathy" cuisine, which focuses on mind, body, and soul, and the way they relate to the food we eat. Ask about the Adirondack Three-Course Great Camp Dinners, the cooking demos, the history of beer workshops and tastings, and, after dinner, head down to the Bierkeller, where there are some 125 kinds of beer from around the world.

PAUL SMITHS

Paul Smith's Saint Regis Café (518-327-6355; www.paulsmiths.edu; Routes 86 and 30) may be a training restaurant for the culinary students at Paul Smith's College, but don't assume anything less than fine food. Wannabe chefs work beside faculty in a nice dining room with views of Lower Saint Regis Lake in the Joan Weill Student Center. Lunches (the restaurant is open 11:30–2) include a gourmet prix-fixe meal. Also on campus is Paul Smith's **Adirondack Waterside Palm** (open 5 to 9 PM), serving delicious dinners prepared by the school's culinary students and inspired by the legendary Palm steakhouses (Palm co-owner Wally Ganzi is a Paul Smith's grad).

TUPPER LAKE

Amado Bakery & Bistro (518-359-5356; www.amadony.com; 10 Cliff Avenue) is a bright spot—and part of an exciting revival in Tupper Lake. The new, colorful, cozy cafe in a 1940s-era bakery offers macaroons, cakes, éclairs, and

FISH CREEK IS A CLASSIC ADIRONDACK CAMPGROUND COURTESY OF TED COMSTOCK, SARANAC LAKE

GILDED-AGE REVIVAL

The Vanderbilts, Rockefellers, Astors, Guggenheims, and other families of fabulous wealth came to the Adirondacks to escape the grind and pollution of industrialized urban centers. They punched through howling wilderness on buckboard or, later, privately-owned locomotives to their sprawling estates, Pine Knot, Santanoni, Uncas, Topridge, and Nehasane among them. These Great Camps—often compounds of dozens of structures—were made from native materials, resulting in stunning feats of architecture. These were places to entertain and impress their guests: presidents, actors, industrial moguls, scholars, royalty—accessories themselves. At these estates no expense was spared, no detail overlooked, from the twigified to the taxidermied. Gilded-Age society knew that, in these parts, "rustic" didn't necessarily mean . . . rustic.

In 2015 Jack Ma, the founder of Alibaba—China's version of Amazon.com—and one of the richest people in China, purchased a 28,100-acre parcel in the town of Santa Clara that includes trout ponds, a fish hatchery, a mountain, miles of the Saint Regis River, and numerous camps and cabins. It's a Great Camp and grand spread, complete with elite owner and entourage. But in a twist on what would seem a Gilded Age–revival, Ma, a member of the global board of directors of The Nature Conservancy and co-founder of the environmental conservation organization Paradise International Foundation, bought the property for $23 million, according to the *Wall Street Journal*, "as an occasional personal retreat," but "principally for conservation purposes."

other baked goods, but its eclectic dinners reflect the owner's Brazilian roots. Brazilian *moqueca*—coconut curry with red palm oil—and *feijoada* (pork, sausage, and black bean stew) spice up an already interesting and extensive menu that includes steak, seafood, paninis, and homemade sausage. Amado also offers homemade "pot pie floaters"—your choice of filling topped with mashed potatoes and mashed green peas, with gravy on the bottom of the plate—perhaps a nod to hearty old-time lumberjack meals.

Well Dressed Food: Fine Foods & Provisions (518-359-5280; welldressedfood.com; 87 Park Street), in an airy, tin-ceilinged space in downtown Tupper, has an espresso bar and exceptional food. Whether you take your meal to go or to stay (or from the heat-and-eat freezer), the breakfasts, deli options, lunches (salads, paninis, flatbread pizzas), and dinners (the fixed-price menu might include bacon-wrapped scallops or chili-lime chicken) are delicious and inventive, prepared and served by a large, accommodating, and efficient staff.

WANAKENA

Pine Cone Grill, Inc. (315-848-2121; www.wanakenapinecone.com; 68 Ranger School Road), a classic North Woods tavern, is known for its burgers. Ask students at the nearby ranger school—or anyone who happens to pass through—and they'll rave about the Lumberjack Burger (a *really* big burger), the Stuffed Smoky Bleu 'n' Bacon Burger, the Jack 'n' Coke Burger (exactly what it says)—the list goes on. There's more to the menu, of course, and plenty of reasons to be grateful for such deliciousness—even a dedicated "Bacon Day" on April 22—in the backcountry.

CASUAL BITES Microbreweries **Big Tupper Brewing** (518-359-9440; www.bigtupperbrewing.com; 12 Cliff Avenue) and **Raquette River Brewing** (518-0420-8461; www.raquetteriverbrewing.com; 11 Balsam Street #2) bring an exciting variety of beers to the area, serve as gathering places (there's cornhole at Raquette River Brewing's beer garden), and, in the case of Big Tupper Brewing, offer pub fare in a brand-new brewery, the fresh-sawed lumber still aromatic.

P-2's Irish Pub (518-359-9980; www.p2s irishpub.com; 31 Main Street) is a bustling little joint that draws locals, plus Wild Center employees thirsty for a post-work Guinness. There's often live music here, and someone just might share the location of a nearby fishing honey hole.

For a quick meal or snack, **Sky-line Ice Cream** (518-359-7288; sky lineicrecream.com; 1976 Route 30) is worth a visit. Hits are soft serve, poutine, Michigan hot dogs, malts, and broaster (pressure-fried) chicken.

The Marketplace Pub & Deli (518-359-9500; www.themarketplacepub.com; 2594 NY 30) has such a non-descript exterior, you could cruise by without noticing it. But this local favorite, with its worn wood paneling and mounted deer, has a deli, a bar, and a pocket-sized deck. Meals are consistent and no-nonsense.

The Washboard Donut Shoppe & Laundromat (518-359-2339; 48 Park Street) is one of many hybrid businesses in the Adirondacks, and it means you can eat some seriously delicious homemade old-fashioned donuts—flavors range from bacon, maple, and peanut butter to chocolate, cinnamon, and raspberry—during the spin cycle.

✳ Selective Shopping

Obviously, this isn't the area to shop for a cocktail dress. But you can find Adirondack art, handmade boats, adventure supplies, or funky antiques (**The Old Stuff Store**, at 337 Park Street, in Tupper Lake, is a local favorite).

ARTISTS **Diane Leifheit** (518-327-3473; www.dianeleifheit.com), of Gabriels, works *en plein air* in a variety of media.

Snow Line Design (315-262-3150; www.snowlinedesign.com) is Suzanne Langelier Lebeda's South Colton studio,

THE SWEET STUFF

You can find maple syrup, candies, liquor, or just about any other configuration of the sweet treat—and plenty of sugar-bush tours and pancake breakfasts—across the Adirondacks and beyond (check out www.nysmaple.com for details on the early-spring maple circuit). But if it's the science of the sticky stuff that interests you, **Paul Smith's College Visitor Interpretive Center** (518-327-6241; paulsmiths.edu; 8023 Route 30) offers maple-sugaring education at its demonstration sugaring operation. The **Wild Center**, in Tupper Lake (518-359-7800; www.wildcenter.org; 45 Museum Dr.), also focuses on maple in spring, with demonstrations and, to the delight of visitors (be warned, it goes fast), maple cotton candy.

where she paints, draws, and creates graphic design work.

In Tupper Lake, **Casagrain Gallery** (518-359-2595; 68 Park Street) is where artist Gary Casagrain exhibits his paintings. Also in Tupper is photographer Burdette Parks's **Round Lake Studios** (518-359-9324; www.roundlakestudios.com).

BOAT BUILDERS In Lake Clear, James Cameron, of **Boathouse Woodworks** (www.adkguideboat.com; 518-327-3470; P.O. Box 317), crafts traditional wooden Adirondack guideboats built to order. In Tupper Lake, Rob Frenette, of **Spruce Knee Boatbuilding** (518-359-3228; NY 30 near Moody Bridge), makes Rushton-design wooden canoes and rowboats, guideboats, and sailboats, all built to order. He also does wooden boat repairs and seat caning.

GENERAL STORES The old-school general store is pretty much it in the way of shopping in the backcountry. Stores really take the word general to heart, so you can pick out a nice gift as well as the fixings for an afternoon picnic, including sunglasses, bug dope, and sustenance.

Cranberry Lake's **Emporium** (315-848-2140; NY 3) is a tiny place crammed with souvenirs, maps, fishing tackle, and canned goods, but there's even more—it's a marina with gas pumps, water taxi, and a big, long, weathered wooden dock. **Lakeside General Store** (315-848-2501; 7140 NY 3), also in Cranberry Lake, is open May through October. It's a liquor store and laundromat, and it has a campground and gas pumps, plus just about any supplies you need, but it is only open May through October.

HIGH PEAKS
AND NORTHERN
ADIRONDACKS

COURTESY OF MARK KURTZ, WWW.MARKKURTZPHOTOGRAPHY.COM

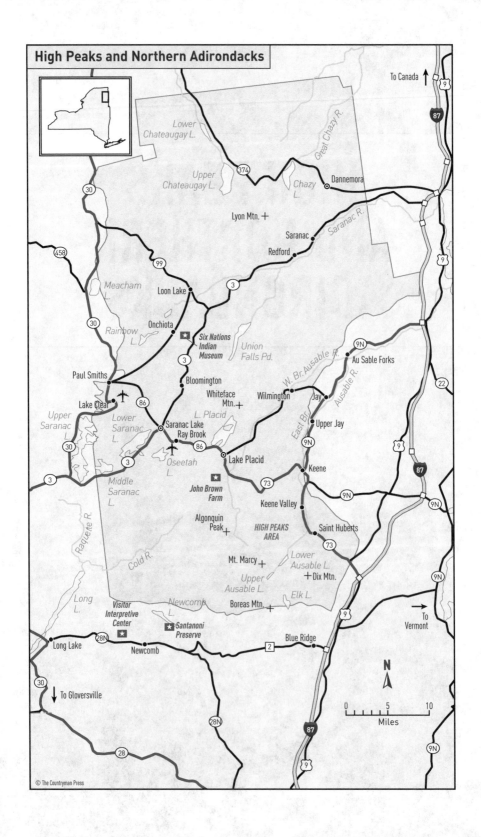

High Peaks and Northern Adirondacks

To Canada

Lower Chateaugay L.

Upper Chateaugay L.

Chazy L.

Dannemora

Lyon Mtn.

Saranac

Redford

Saranac R.

Great Chazy R.

Meacham L.

Loon Lake

Rainbow L.

Onchiota

Six Nations Indian Museum

Union Falls Pd.

Au Sable Forks

Paul Smiths

Bloomington

Whiteface Mtn.

Wilmington

Jay

W. Br. Ausable R.

Ausable R.

Lake Clear

Upper Saranac

Lower Saranac L.

Saranac Lake
Ray Brook

L. Placid

Upper Jay

East Br.

Oseetah L.

Lake Placid

Keene

Middle Saranac L.

John Brown Farm

Keene Valley

Raquette R.

Algonquin Peak

HIGH PEAKS AREA

Saint Huberts

Cold R.

Mt. Marcy

Lower Ausable L.

Dix Mtn.

Long L.

Upper Ausable L.

Elk L.

Newcomb

Boreas Mtn.

Visitor Interpretive Center

Santanoni Preserve

Blue Ridge

To Vermont

Long Lake

Newcomb

To Gloversville

N

0   5   10
Miles

© The Countryman Press

HIGH PEAKS AND NORTHERN ADIRONDACKS

The High Peaks region is all about drama, whether it's the lofty mountains, pristine lakes, Olympic glory, or arts centers. This part of the Adirondack Park attracts the masses, which means a variety of lodging and meals, interesting galleries, and cool events. Sure, Lake Placid's Main Street is a draw, but there's way more to this region if you know where to look.

✳ To See

Winslow Homer painted woodsmen in Keene Valley. Harold Weston, who lived most of his life in Keene Valley, made bold, burly oils of the High Peaks that were exhibited widely from the 1920s to the 1970s, and now reside in major collections throughout the world. Rockwell Kent spent his last decades at his farm in Au Sable Forks, painting the Ausable River Valley and designing houses for friends. Composers Charles Ives and Béla Bartók both spent extended periods working in the Adirondacks. Ives created the "Concord" Sonata while visiting Elk Lake, and began the "Universe" Symphony, one of his last major works, while at the summer home of his wife's family, in Keene Valley. Bartók wrote the Concerto for Orchestra at a modest cottage in Saranac Lake, where he was taking the cure for tuberculosis. And Robert Louis Stevenson worked on his *The Master of Ballantrae*, among other pieces, while taking the cure at a Saranac Lake cottage. These hills are still alive with artists—musicians, dancers, writers, painters, actors—and cultural centers that support their work and encourage others to appreciate it.

ARCHITECTURE The Ausable River Valley holds many historic buildings that are visible along roadways. South of Keene Valley, it's worth a quick detour off NY 73 at Saint Hubert's to see the massive Victorian inn, the **Ausable Club**. It is "members only" inside the building, but you can get a rare glimpse of the kind of hostelry that visitors once enjoyed throughout the Adirondacks. North on US 9, between Upper Jay, Jay, and Au Sable Forks, there are fine Federal-style stone and brick houses and churches; in Jay, a **covered bridge** that spans the Ausable River, built in 1857, was dismantled in 1997 and rebuilt with an adjacent park.

The **Olympic Village**—Lake Placid, that is—has only a few buildings left from its earliest days, when the settlement of North Elba, near the ski jumps, was an iron mining center; one that's easy to spot on Old Military Road is the **Stagecoach Inn**. Another, off Old Military, is **John Brown's Farm** (518-523-3900; 115 John Brown Road). In 1849, abolitionist John Brown came to North Elba to help Gerrit Smith foster a self-sufficient enclave for free black citizens. Smith owned more than 100,000 acres across northern New York, and his plan was to give 40 acres to each would-be African American homesteader. The idea may have been doomed from the start since the families—many of them from northern cities—were not prepared to farm in the harsh climate or work

MANHUNT

In June of 2015, the eyes of the world turned to the Adirondacks' tangled wilderness after killers Richard Matt and David Sweat implausibly broke out of high-security Clinton Correctional Facility, in Dannemora, dubbed "Little Siberia." And it certainly was implausible—a breakout scheme that involved forbidden romance, a tool frozen in hamburger, hacking out of cells and into tunnels, and emerging from a manhole at midnight on a street lined with homes. It was a plot worthy of a made-for-TV movie—in fact, it did become a Lifetime movie, *NY Prison Break: The Seduction of Joyce Mitchell*. (A Showtime miniseries directed by Ben Stiller and starring Patricia Arquette was also in the works at press time.) But it was an intense reality show for those who were caught in the area as it turned into a militarized zone. Wanted signs appeared at quiet trailheads, SWAT teams swept into backyards, law enforcement lined wooded lanes, helicopters circled, recess was cancelled for local kids—in some cases, whole school days were scrapped. More than 1,200 officers combed acre upon acre of dense forest. The two convicts haunted the area for 23 days, but their sojourn in the Adirondacks was no vacation—blackflies, endless rain, scraps of scavenged food—and the ending could have been scripted, too: Matt was shot and killed near Malone; Sweat was shot and captured on his final sprint for the Canadian border.

the rugged, unprepared ground. Most of the residents of "Timbuctoo," as it became known, left within a few years of their arrival. Brown lived only a few years at the farm, leaving his family for months at a time to pursue a failing wool business and work on antislavery concerns. After his final adventure in Harpers Ferry, Virginia (modern-day West Virginia), Brown was executed on December 2, 1859. In 1870, the property was acquired by a group of the abolitionist's admirers. Today the farmhouse and outbuildings, managed by New York as a state historic site, contain exhibits related to John Brown's life, and his "body lies a-mouldering in the grave" nearby. Brown's birthday, May 1, brings a major gathering of people to the site sponsored by the Westport-based group **John Brown Lives!** (www.johnbrownlives.org).

In Saranac Lake, which was incorporated in 1892, the tuberculosis industry inspired its own architecture, manifested in "cure porches" and "cure cottages." The group **Historic Saranac Lake** (518-891-4606; www.historicsaranaclake.org) sponsors lectures, concerts, and tours from time to time, highlighting buildings of note; ongoing restoration projects include the cure cottage used by composer Béla Bartók and the 1894 laboratory of tuberculosis treatment pioneer Dr. E. L. Trudeau.

Saranac Lake is also where you can see the **Robert Louis Stevenson Memorial Cottage and Museum** (518-891-1462; www.robertlouisstevensonmemorialcottage.org; 44 Stevenson Lane). Robert Louis Stevenson took the cure for TB here from 1887 to 1888. He slept in an unheated porch all winter and took in plenty of fresh air while hiking and skating. During his Adirondack stint, Stevenson wrote a dozen essays for *Scribner's Monthly*, started *The Master of Ballantrae*, and worked on *The Wrong Box*, a collaborative effort with Lloyd Osbourne. In a letter to Henry James, the Scotsman described his tiny cottage: "Our house . . . is on a hill, and has sight of a stream turning a corner in the valley—bless the face of running water!—and sees some hills too, and the paganly prosaic roofs of Saranac itself; the Lake it does not see, nor do I regret that; I like water (fresh water, I mean) either running swiftly among stones, or else largely qualified with whiskey." The Stevenson Society was founded in 1916 to commemorate the writer's life and works; one of the group's original projects was to interest Gutzon Borglum, the sculptor best known for creating Mount Rushmore, in designing a bronze bas-relief depicting Stevenson—now displayed next to the cottage's front door. The society still manages the property and museum, which has displays of Stevenson letters, photographs, memorabilia, and first editions, and sponsors readings and lectures.

ARTS CENTERS AND ARTS COUNCILS **Bluseed Studios** (518-891-3799; www.bluseed studios.org; 24 Cedar Street, Saranac Lake) is home to a bustling arts scene. This seven-thousand-square-foot 1930s train warehouse is an oasis for artists and the community. It has exhibitions, studio space, weekend and one-day workshops—everything from printmaking and letterpress to ceramics and photography—and an eclectic music series that features regional and national performers.

Lake Placid Center for the Arts (518-523-2512; www.lakeplacidarts.org; 17 Algonquin Drive, Lake Placid) is a multi-arts center with a community focus, and the facility is top-notch. It boasts a theater that seats about 300, well-equipped studios, and a bright, airy gallery. Exhibitions are slated throughout the year, including juried shows for regional artists and craftspeople. Presentations include visiting theater groups; contemporary American and foreign films; folk, blues, and Zydeco music; dance-company residencies; gala programs by soloists of the New York City Ballet;

ABOLITIONIST JOHN BROWN'S FARM IN NORTH ELBA   COURTESY OF JOHN DIGIACOMO, WWW.PLACIDTIMES PHOTOGRAPHY.COM

LADY IN THE LAKE

In 1963, a group of divers, exploring caves more than 100 feet below the surface of Lake Placid, discovered the body of 56-year-old Mabel Smith Douglass, founder and former dean of the New Jersey College for Women at New Brunswick. Douglass, who had disappeared from her Camp Onondoga on the west shore of the lake 30 years earlier for reasons that are still a mystery—though most sources allege she committed suicide—was found remarkably intact, probably because of the depth and extreme coldness of her resting place. The novel *Dancehall*, by Bernard F. Conners, is loosely inspired by the lady in the lake.

and excellent classical and chamber performances. The Lake Placid Sinfonietta plays here on Sunday evenings in July and August. The LPCA also is home to the Community Theatre Players, who offer three or four shows annually. For kids, in July and August, there's the free "Young and Fun" performance series on weekday mornings.

Upper Jay Art Center (518-946-8315; www.upperjayartcenter.com; Recovery Lounge, Upper Jay Upholstery, NY 9N, Upper Jay) was, at first, an underground scene—locals gathering at brothers Scott and Byron Renderer's Upper Jay Upholstery to hear the Renderers' band Monsterbuck and their friends play music. But nowadays, the shop's 1920s former Model-T assembly plant, just across the Ausable River from what was the Land of Makebelieve theme park, is a thriving nonprofit arts organization drawing culture seekers. The Renderers turned their funky, cavernous space, called the Recovery Lounge, into an arts center. There are impromptu performances by regional and national acts as well as Arts Nights, drawing hundreds of people to see paintings, sculpture, exceptional theater performances, and films, often by local artists, some of whom are nationally recognized, such as photographer Nathan Farb and painters Harold Weston and Paul Matthews. On Sunday afternoons in January locals bring their fiddles, guitars, or whatever and jam the winter blues away.

DANCE The sensual and athletic **Elisa Monte Dance** (www.elisamontedance.org) spends three weeks in residence at the Lake Placid Center for the Arts. The arts center also presents modern dance concerts, including stars of the New York City Ballet.

Contemporary dance ensemble **Rebecca Kelly Ballet** (www.rebeccakellyballet.com) makes Au Sable Forks its summer base—NYC's Soho is its home the rest of the year—in Tahawus Lodge, a former Masonic Temple, for classes and workshops. The lodge, with its first-floor gallery space, is a cultural light in an old mill town.

MUSEUMS **Six Nations Indian Museum** (518-891-2299; www.sixnationsindianmuseum .com; 1462 County Route 60, Onchiota) reflects this region's indigenous roots. Native peoples traveled to the Adirondacks for spring fishing, summer gathering, and fall hunting; the mountains, forests, and lakes offered abundant resources. At many local institutions, this information is overshadowed by all the other stories those museums have to tell, but at Six Nations, the kaleidoscopic collection of baskets, beadwork, quill work, tools, weapons, paintings, drums, cradle boards, hats, pottery, and clothing all celebrate the lives and times of the Haudenosaunee (Iroquois) who first inhabited the surrounding uplands 13,000 years ago. Artifacts fill cases, line the walls, and hang from the ceilings.

In Lake Placid, the train depot is home to the **Lake Placid–North Elba Historical Society Museum** (518-523-1608; www.lakeplacidhistory.com; 242 Station Street). There's a nostalgic country store display, sporting gear and memorabilia from the 1932

Olympics, and a music room honoring famous former residents Victor Herbert and Kate Smith.

In the Olympic Center is the **Lake Placid Winter Olympic Museum** (518-302-5326; www.lpom.org), open daily, year-round. Photographs, vintage films, equipment, trophies, clothing, and memorabilia illustrate the 1932 and 1980 Olympic Games that came to town. This place is a must-see for Lake Placid visitors, and every year the exhibitions and collection expand.

Just outside of the Adirondack Park, near Malone, is the **Wilder Homestead** (518-483-1207; www.almanzowilderfarm.com; 177 Stacy Road), the setting for the novel *Farmer Boy* by Laura Ingalls Wilder. The farmstead was the home of the author's husband, Almanzo Wilder, in the mid-1800s.

✳ To Do

In this part of the park you can find backcountry solitude, extreme adventure, and everything in between when it comes to muscle-powered activity. Deep snow draws alpine and cross-country skiers; fast water appeals to fly-fishers and paddlers. Trails go up steep peaks, skirt tranquil ponds and even link communities. Bicyclists can head for singletrack routes or cruise country roads. In all five seasons (the extra one is "mud season"), there's somewhere to go and something to do if sitting isn't your idea of fun.

BIKING The **Whiteface Regional Visitors Bureau** (518-946-2255; www.whitefaceregion.com), in Wilmington, has a new brochure with area mountain-bike trails. In fact, Wilmington's the hot new mountain-biking spot in the North Country, with an expanding trail system on state land around town, plus more and more offerings around **Whiteface Mountain** (518-946-2233; www.whiteface.com; NY 86, Wilmington). **Barkeater Trails Alliance** (www.barkeatertrails.org), a volunteer crew of trail-builders and maintainers, has everything to do with booming mountain-biking scene at **Hardy Road** and the flume, in Wilmington, plus **Henry's Woods**, in Lake Placid. Also, **Mount Van Hoevenberg**, in Lake Placid, has great bike trails (and a mountain-bike center, with rentals, run by High Peaks Cyclery), but unlike riding on state trails, it requires paying a use fee.

A reminder: all-terrain bicycles are barred from wilderness and primitive areas in the Adirondack Park. In the state land areas designated as wild forest, you'll find old logging roads that make excellent bike routes, and in most of these places, you'll find far fewer people.

MOUNTAIN BIKING AT WHITEFACE MOUNTAIN COURTESY OF DREW HAAS, WWW.ADKBCSKI.COM

As far as skinny wheels: in much of the northern Adirondacks, road cyclists appear in spring, training for the Lake Placid Ironman, so locals, whether they like it or not, are used to cyclists zooming along roadways. Wear a helmet! For bike repairs, rentals, and sales, visit **Human Power Planet Earth** (518-524-6177; www.humanpowerplanetearth .com; 52 Dorsey Street, Saranac Lake), **High Peaks Cyclery** (518-523-3764; www .highpeakscyclery.com; 2733 Main Street, Lake Placid), **LeepOff Cycles** (518-576-9581; 23 Market Street, Keene Valley), **Maui North** (518-523-7245; www.mauinorth.net; 134 Main Street, Lake Placid), or **Placid Planet** (518-523-4128; www.placidplanetbicycles .com; 2242 Saranac Avenue, Lake Placid).

BOAT TOURS Sadly, **Lake Placid Marina & Boat Tours** (518-523-9704; www .lakeplacidmarina .com; 24 George and Bliss Road) retired its classic wooden boat *Doris II*, but it still offers scenic narrated (don't believe everything they tell you) trips on Lake Placid. These days, an enclosed pontoon boat will chug you around.

CANOEING AND KAYAKING **Adirondack Paddler's Map**, a waterproof and tear-proof guide for multiday trips with enough details for navigating, includes trailheads, portages, and whitewater ratings across the region. It's available at **Saint Regis Canoe Outfitters**, in Saranac Lake (1-888-775-2925), or at www.canoeoutfitters.com.

If you're overwhelmed by making a decision about where to go, or need a primer on paddling technique, consult one of the following outfitters: **Adirondack Lakes and Trails Outfitters** (518-891-7450; www.adirondackoutfitters.com; 541 Lake Flower Avenue, Saranac Lake), **Adirondack Rock and River Guide Service** (518-576-2041; www.rockandriver.com; Alstead Hill Lane, Keene), **Cloud-Splitter Outfitters** (518-582-2583; NY 28, Newcomb), **High Peaks Mountain Adventures** (518-523-3764; www .highpeaksma.com; High Peaks Cyclery, 331 Main Street, Lake Placid), **Jones Outfitters Ltd.** (518-523-3468; www.jonesoutfitters.com; 331 Main Street, Lake Placid), **Saint Regis Canoe Outfitters** (518-891-1838; www.canoeoutfitters.com; 73 Dorsey Street, Saranac Lake), or **Tahawus Guide Service** (518-891-4334; Lake Placid).

FAMILY FUN **Santa's Workshop** (518-946-2212; www.northpoleny.com; NY 431, Wilmington), near Whiteface Mountain, claims to be one of the oldest theme parks in the world, dating back to 1946, and it's the place to mail your Christmas cards, as the postmark reads, "North Pole, NY." Don't expect something slick like Disney World—this place suits the nostalgic set with small children. You'll find Santa and his lap, reindeer (arrive early enough so your kids can feed them before the animals' bellies are too full), gentle rides for children, and singing and dancing. Tickets could be pricey, depending on the season; the theme park is open most of summer and select weekends leading up to Christmas.

On the other end of the spectrum, the **Olympic Regional Development Authority** (518-523-1655; www.orda.org) offers an Olympic Sites Passport, which provides VIP entry to all Lake Placid region Olympic venues: the gondola up Whiteface; the Whiteface Veterans Memorial Highway that you can drive to the summit; the Lake Placid Olympic Museum; the Olympic Speed Skating Oval; the Olympic Sports Complex with its bobsled, luge and skeleton track; and the 120-meter jump tower's elevator at the Olympic Jumping Complex. Also popular are bobsled rides, with a professional driver and brakeman, though in 2017 these cost $75 a pop for adults, $70 ages 13–19, and $65 ages 12 and under.

If sliding down a frozen chute is something your family wants to try but the bobsled price tag is a bit much, Lake Placid's **toboggan run**, near the Mirror Lake beach, is a

TROUBLE BRUIN

As humans have become comfortable sleeping out in the wilds, some wild animals have learned to recognize coolers, packs, tents, and even car trunks as potential food sources. Hungry black bears or pesky raccoons may not be in evidence when you set up camp, but it's best to take all precautions. If your site has a metal locker for food storage, use it. Otherwise, stash your supplies and cooking gear well away from your tent: put them in a pack or strong plastic bags and suspend it between two trees with a sturdy rope at least 20 feet off the ground. Tie it off by wrapping several times around one tree and tying a complicated knot; bears have been known to swat down food stashes within their reach, climb saplings, and even bite through ropes. Don't try to outsmart bruins by putting your food in an anchored boat away from shore; bears swim well. In some places, the campsite caretaker can give you an update on the bear situation. Also, special poles for bear bags can be found in some High Peaks Wilderness campsites. Bear-proof canisters for food can be rented at places such as EMS in Lake Placid; however, there are reports that some bears have learned how to rip tops off these sturdy tubes. As soon as humans think they have outsmarted the bears, the wild ones come up with creative solutions.

If a bear does visit your camp, loud noises (yelling, banging on pots, loud whistles) usually discourage it. Attacks are extremely rare in the Adirondacks. Keep your dog under control in the event of a close encounter of the ursine kind.

AVOID UNINVITED GUESTS TO YOUR CAMPSITE BY USING BEAR CANISTERS AND STASHING SUPPLIES AND COOKING GEAR WELL AWAY FROM YOUR TENT COURTESY OF ERIC DRESSER, WWW.ECDPHOTO.ADDR.COM

HIKERS SHOULD AVOID FRAGILE PLANTS ATOP THE REGION'S HIGH PEAKS COURTESY OF BRENDAN WILTSE

cheap thrill. It's open winter weekends, weather permitting; check with the North Elba Parks Department (518-523-2591).

Saranac Lake's **Adirondack Carousel** (www.adirondackcarousel.org; 6 Depot Street in the William Morris Park) is made of 18 hand-carved critters indigenous to the Adirondack Park: blackfly, moose, brook trout, and toad among them.

High Falls Gorge (518-946-2278; www.highfallsgorge.com; NY 86, Wilmington) has waterfalls and trails (check them out on snowshoes!) on the Ausable River.

Tucker Farm's Autumn Corn Maze (518-327-5054; www.tuckertater.com; 112 Hobart Road, Gabriels), with its varying themes, is open August through early November.

Whiteface Mountain Cloudsplitter Gondola Ride (518-946-2223; www.whiteface.com; NY 86, Wilmington) is recommended for fall foliage. Open late June through Columbus Day.

FISHING A 5-mile-long section of the **West Branch of the Ausable River** between Lake Placid and Wilmington is designated for catch-and-release fishing only. With the no-kill rules in effect for more than a decade, the action on the river has been transformed; the fly-fishing here can be the stuff dreams are made of.

GOLF Adirondack golf courses range from informal, inexpensive, converted cow pastures to challenging, busy, championship links. This region's courses include:

Ausable Club (518-576-4411; www.ausableclub.org; 137 Ausable Road, St. Huberts). Nine holes; Scottish-links–type course. Open to nonmembers in September only, Monday through Thursday.

Craig Wood Golf Course (518-523-9811; www.craigwoodgolfclub.com; Cascade Road, Lake Placid). Eighteen holes, par-72, 6,500 yards. Named after Lake Placid native Craig Wood, who won both the US Open and Masters in 1941.

Crowne Plaza Resort & Golf Club (518-523-2556; www.lakeplacidcp.com; Mirror Lake Drive, Lake Placid). Two 18-hole courses: the Mountain course and the Links course.

High Peaks Golf Course (518-582-2300; Santanoni Drive, Newcomb). Nine holes, par-33, 2,600 yards, magnificent High Peaks views.

Saranac Inn Golf & Country Club (518-891-1402; www.saranacinn.com; 125 County Route 46, Saranac Inn). Eighteen holes, par-2; 6,600 yards, beautifully maintained course.

Saranac Lake Golf Club (518-891-2675; NY 86, Ray Brook). Nine holes, par-36, 3,000 yards.

Whiteface Club Golf Course (518-523-2551; 373 Whiteface Inn Lane, Lake Placid). Eighteen holes, par-72, 6,500 yards, challenging course with beautiful views.

HIKING AND BACKPACKING There are trails leading to pristine ponds, roaring waterfalls, spectacular peaks, and hidden gorges; perhaps the toughest choice for an Adirondack visitor is selecting where to go.

In some parts of the park, you can leave the trailhead and not see another person until you return to your car and look in the rearview mirror. Parts of the **Northville–Lake Placid Trail** are many miles from the nearest road; going end-to-end on this long trail requires a minimum of 10 days and a solid amount of backcountry knowledge, but you can pick shorter sections for 3-day junkets. Parts of the High Peaks—especially from southern access points—offer similar overnights. It's possible to find solitude even in the middle of the busy summer season if you select the right destination. There are also plenty of easy hikes of 2 to 5 miles that traverse beautiful terrain throughout the park.

The **Adirondack Mountain Club** (518-523-3441; www.adk.org), based in the High Peaks at the **Heart Lake Program Center** at Adirondak Loj, in Lake Placid, leads trips and gives map-and-compass, woodcraft, and low-impact-camping workshops.

HORSEBACK RIDING AND WAGON TRIPS New York's North Country may not have the wide, open spaces of the Wild West, but there are hundreds of miles of wilderness horse trails to explore. Public horse trails in this region are:

FLY-FISHING ALONG THE AUSABLE RIVER COURTESY OF DREW HAAS, WWW.ADKBCSKI.COM

BEAVER MEADOW FALLS IN THE HIGH PEAKS COURTESY OF JOHN DIGIACOMO, PLACIDTIMESPHOTOGRAPHY.COM

LAKE PLACID HORSE SHOWS

If you enjoy just watching horses, there are two excellent annual horse shows in Lake Placid, located a canter away from the Olympic ski jumps: the **Lake Placid Horse Show** in late June and, in July, the **I Love NY Horse Show** (518-523-9625; www.lakeplacidhorseshow .com; 514 Cascade Road, Lake Placid). The shows attract about 800 horses, their riders and trainers, plus grooms, farriers, veterinarians, vendors, and sponsors. Competitions begin at 8 AM each day and happen in four different rings, so spectators can watch a variety of action. In "model" classes, nearly naked animals are paraded before judges to show off their conformation and scrutinized for their perfect looks. Equitation is all about the rider's posture, hands, and way of handling his or her well-matched mount. The hunter division is for horses that approach the ideal in a foxhunting creature, one that moves with exceptional fluidity and intelligence, with beautiful proportions from head to hock.

Jumping events feature 15 to 20 obstacles arranged in the ring, with low, simple rails for juniors and double or triple jumps as high as five feet for the Grand Prix. Horses in this championship turn are covering the ground at about 12 miles per hour, but excess speed can result in knocking down an obstacle, a fall, or a balk—all of which are faults that affect the overall score. Riders get the chance to walk the course, which coils around the ring in different patterns, and the order for competing can give later contestants the advantage of seeing how others handle the route.

THE LAKE PLACID HORSE SHOWS ATTRACT ABOUT 800 HORSES, THEIR RIDERS AND TRAINERS, PLUS GROOMS, FARRIERS, VETERINARIANS, VENDORS, AND SPONSORS COURTESY OF JOHN DIGIACOMO, WWW. PLACIDTIMESPHOTOGRAPHY.COM

Although horse shows have the aura of a closed society, Lake Placid's events are family-friendly and welcoming to the novice. Leashed dogs are also welcome. You can bring a picnic, grab a burger, ask for an autograph on your program, and zero in on the contests that catch your interest.

Cold River Horse Trails. Six miles east of Tupper Lake off NY 3, very difficult 13- and 32-mile-loop dirt trails; lean-tos and corral. Connects with easier Moose Pond and Santanoni trails.

Meacham Lake. Three and a half miles north of Paul Smiths, off NY 30; 10 miles of trails, although they include two separate dead-end routes; lean-tos and barn.

Moose Pond Trail. Starts at Santanoni trailhead just north of Newcomb off NY 28N; 10 miles.

Raquette Falls Horse Trail. Branches off Cold River Trail; 1.6 miles.

Santanoni Trail. North of Newcomb off NY 28N; 10-mile round-trip. Hitching trails and two-wagon teams that transport people.

ICE SKATING The modern sport of speed skating was launched in Saranac Lake and Lake Placid. In the early 1900s, more world records were set—and broken—by local bladesmen than at any other wintry place. Nowadays, there's backcountry skating on remote lakes and ponds or skating on plowed rinks in the towns, and even indoor figure skating or hockey on Zamboni-maintained ice sheets.

If you'd like to try wilderness skating, wait until January. Cold, clear, still weather produces the most consistent surface. Ice that's 2 inches thick will support one person on skates, but it's better to wait for at least 3 inches to form, as currents and springs can create weak spots. Ice is thinner near shore, and be sure to steer clear of inlets, outlets, and other tributaries. Ponds in the High Peaks are often good for skating by New Year's Day, especially if there's been little snow. You can scout **Chapel Pond**, off NY 73 south of Keene Valley, or the **Cascade Lakes**, on the same road, north of Keene, or **Heart Lake**, at the end of the Adirondak Loj Road.

In Lake Placid, you can enjoy terrific ice outdoors most evenings at the **Olympic Speed Skating Oval** (the James B. Sheffield Olympic Skating Rink), on Main Street, or you can skate in the **Olympic Arena** (518-523-1655; www.whiteface.com; 2634 Main Street) at scheduled times for a small charge. If you want to try speed skating, you can get rental skates, a lesson, and ice time in Lake Placid. Lake Placid's Olympic ice gets lots of attention in annual **Can-Am Hockey** tournaments, camps, and clinics. Hockey

LUGE AT THE OLYMPIC SPORTS COMPLEX AT MOUNT VAN HOEVENBERG COURTESY OF ORDA

HIGH PEAKS OLYMPIC VENUES COURTESY OF ORDA/DAVE SCHMIDT

fans can check out www.whiteface.com, for schedules. **Tupper Lake** (518-359-2531; McLaughlin Street) maintains rinks for hockey and skating; Saranac Lake's **Civic Center** (518-891-3800) has good ice indoors and an active youth hockey program. You can also try curling with the Lake Placid Curling Club (518-524-3314). Some seasons there are even little volunteer-made rinks behind Keene's community center and Wilmington's too, though you'll have to ask around town about their hours and availability.

OLYMPIC SPORTS Lake Placid is the only place in North America that has hosted two Winter Olympic Games, in 1932 and 1980. During the '32 Games, the American team won the bobsledding events, took silver and bronze medals in speed skating, hockey, figure skating, and bobsledding, and was therefore regarded as the unofficial Olympic champion. In 1980, Eric Heiden garnered five gold medals in speed skating, and the US hockey team won the tournament following a stunning upset over the Russians in the semifinal round. The legacy of Olympic glory lives on here at the **Olympic Training Center on Old Military Road**, where hundreds of athletes eat, sleep, and work out in a high-tech setting, and in several specialized sports facilities in and around Lake Placid. Every season, competitors come to town for coaching and practice.

There's just one place in the Northeast where you, too, can ride a real bobsled on an Olympic run: the **Olympic Sports Complex at Mount Van Hoevenberg**, a few miles from downtown Lake Placid. This thrill does not come cheap: in 2017 it was $75 for an adult, depending on the season, for the longest minute you'll ever spend (note that the sleds are piloted by professional drivers). Rides are available starting around Christmas through early March, depending on the track conditions. There's also a bobsled with wheels that shoots down the track when there's no ice on it. Call for details (518-523-1655; www.whiteface.com; Olympic Center, Lake Placid).

Watching international luge, skeleton, and bobsled competitions is almost as exciting as trying it yourself, and perhaps easier on the cardiovascular system. Races are held nearly every winter weekend. Dress warmly for spectating; you'll want to walk up and down the mile-long track to see and hear the sleds zoom through. At some vantage

AERIAL SKI-JUMPING IN LAKE PLACID COURTESY OF ORDA

points, sliders fly by nearly upside down, and the racket of the runners is a lesson in the Doppler effect. You'll definitely want to see several push starts, where track stars have a decided advantage.

In the **Olympic Arena**, at the center of Lake Placid, you can watch youth and collegiate ice hockey tournaments, exhibition NHL games, indoor short-track speed skating, figure skating competitions, and skating exhibitions such as "Stars on Ice," year-round.

Ski jumping on the **90- and 120-meter jumps** is thrilling; seeing people fly through the air is far more impressive in person than the sport appears on television. If watching from the bleachers, dress warmly. The 120-meter jump tower has a sky deck accessible by elevator and a chairlift that provides the perfect spot to watch jumpers and surrounding mountains from above. Annual favorite competitions are the **Fourth of July Ski Jump** and October's **Flaming Leaves Festival** (with blues, brews, and BBQ); these are Lake Placid spectator events where you will avoid hypothermia. Also, at the jumping complex, you can watch the US freestyle skiers training in warm weather. The skiers go off jumps, tumble through the air, and land in a huge aerated pool of 750,000 gallons of water with their skis still attached.

At **Whiteface Mountain** you can see occasional international freestyle, downhill, and slalom races, as well as snowboard cross and parallel giant slalom races. Or you can try riding the slopes yourself.

RACES AND SEASONAL SPORTING EVENTS Events are listed in chronological order.

Adirondack International Mountainfest (518-576-2281; www.mountaineer.com; the Mountaineer, Keene Valley) includes clinics, slide shows, and lectures by renowned ice and rock climbers, in mid-January.

Lake Placid Loppet (518-523-1655; www.orda.org; Olympic Regional Development Authority, Lake Placid), popular 25- and 50-kilometer citizens' races at Mount Van Hoevenberg, is supposed to happen in late January, though in past years there wasn't enough snow.

Empire State Winter Games (518-523-1655; ORDA, Lake Placid) brings competitors in figure skating, luge, bobsled, speed skating, ski jumping, cross-country skiing, and other events, in Lake Placid, in early March.

Pond Skimming (518-946-2223; www.whiteface.com; Whiteface Mountain, Wilmington), a goofy display at Whiteface, challenges skiers and snowboarders to jump across a pool of freezing water, in April.

THE LONGEST DAY

Lake Placid Ironman (www.ironmanlakeplacid.com) is the real deal: a grueling 2-plus-mile swim in Mirror Lake, 112-mile bike race from Lake Placid to Keene and back (twice), followed by a marathon. During this annual July event, international competitors give it their all in the High Peaks for a spot at Kona. In September an Ironman 70.3 follows the same route as the original triathlon, but is half the distance.

In much of the northern Adirondacks, road cyclists appear in spring, training for both Lake Placid Ironmans, so locals are used to cyclists zooming along roadways.

'Round the Mountain Canoe Race (518-891-1990; Saranac Lake Chamber of Commerce, Saranac Lake), a 10-mile canoe race on Lower Saranac Lake and the Saranac River, happens in early May.

Whiteface Mountain Uphill Bike Race (518-946-2255; www.whiteface race.com; Wilmington) is a race up the Whiteface Mountain Veterans Memorial Highway, in June.

Willard Hanmer Guideboat and Canoe Races (518-891-1990; Saranac Lake Chamber of Commerce, Saranac Lake) take over Lake Flower with guideboats, canoes, rowing shells, war canoes, and kayaks, in early July.

Lake Placid Ironman (www.ironmanlakeplacid.com; Lake Placid) is an epic competition that includes a 2-plus-mile swim in Mirror Lake; 112-mile bike race from Lake Placid to Keene and back (twice), followed by a marathon, in late July.

Can-Am Rugby Tournament (518-891-1990; www.canamrugby.com; Saranac Lake Chamber of Commerce, Saranac Lake), North America's largest rugby meet, attracts more than 100 teams competing in fields throughout Lake Placid and Saranac Lake, in early August.

Olga Memorial Footrace (518-891-0375; www.saranaclake.com; Saranac Lake), 5- and 10-kilometer runs in Riverside Park, happen in August.

Summit Lacrosse Tournament (518-441-8228; www.lakeplacidlax.com) includes teams of kids, old-timers, men, and women competing at the North Elba Horseshow Grounds, in mid-August.

Whiteface Mountain Uphill Footrace (518-946-2255; www.whitefacerace.com; Wilmington) is a race up the Whiteface Mountain Veterans Memorial Highway, in September.

CLIMBING Plenty of steep, arduous rock walls can be found in the High Peaks. Possibilities for rock and ice climbers abound, from nontechnical scrambles up broad, smooth slides to gnarly 700-foot pitches in the 5.11+ difficulty range. Adirondack climbers—from wannabes to folks with permanently chalky palms—all depend on a thick green guidebook, *Climbing in the Adirondacks: A Guide to Rock and Ice Routes*, by Don Mellor. This book is indispensable, as the approaches to many of the best climbs

THE ADIRONDACKS IS A HOT DESTINATION FOR ICE CLIMBERS COURTESY OF DREW HAAS, WWW.ADKBCSKI.COM

involve a hike or bushwhack to the base. It also outlines hundreds of climbs and explains the local ethic on clean wilderness climbing: leave as little trace as possible and place a minimum of bolts. Also helpful is Jim Lawyer and Jeremy Haas's *Adirondack Rock*, a guide to new climbing routes and a remapping of old ones.

Climbers can get tips in a few places. **The Mountaineer** (518-576-2281; www.mountaineer.com; NY 73, Keene Valley) sells climbing gear, topo maps, and guidebooks; advice is free. Many climbers' questions can be answered at the **Adirondack International Mountaineering Festival** each January, sponsored by the Mountaineer. Climbing gear can also be found in Lake Placid at **Eastern Mountain Sports** (518-523-2505; www.ems.com; 2453 Main Street) and **High Peaks Cyclery** (518-523-3764; www.highpeakscyclery.com; 2733 Main Street), which has an indoor-climbing wall.

SCENIC FLIGHTS A 15- to 20-minute flight covering about 50 miles of territory costs less than the average evening out. You can make arrangements for longer flights, but in 2017 a typical short trip cost about $55 per person. **Adirondack Flying Service** (518-523-2473; www.flyanywhere.com; 73 Cascade Road, Lake Placid) will bring you over the High Peaks, the Olympic venues, or the lakes of this region.

SCENIC HIGHWAYS Most Adirondack byways are pretty darn scenic: even **Interstate 87**—the Northway—won an award as "America's Most Beautiful Highway" the year it was completed. Not too far from Lake Placid, **Whiteface Mountain Veterans Memorial Highway** (518-946-2223; www.whiteface.com; off NY 431, Wilmington) has a great view, too, looking down on other summits and silvery lakes. It's a state-operated toll road open daily from late May through the fall.

CROSS-COUNTRY SKIING AND SNOWSHOEING The Adirondack Park is paradise for cross-country skiers. Most winters there's plenty of snow, upward of 100 inches, especially in the higher elevations. A wide range of destinations entices skiers, from rugged expeditions in the High Peaks to gentle groomed paths suitable for novices, plus hundreds of miles of intermediate trails. Many of the marked hiking trails on state land are not only suitable for cross-country skiing or snowshoeing, they're actually better for winter recreation, as swampy areas are frozen, and ice-bound ponds and lakes can be easily crossed.

THE HIGH PEAKS

D ozens of mountaintops rise 4,000 feet or more above sea level in the Adirondack Park. You don't need to be a technical climber to enjoy the views, but you should be an experienced, well-prepared hiker capable of putting in at least a 12-mile round trip. For trail descriptions and access points, consult the *Adirondack Mountain Club's High Peaks Region* guidebook. The following "Forty-Six" are in the area bounded by Newcomb on the south, Elizabethtown on the east, Wilmington on the north, and the Franklin County line on the west.

Peak	Elevation (in feet)	Peak	Elevation (in feet)
1. Mount Marcy	5,344	24. Mount Marshall	4,380
2. Algonquin Peak	5,115	25. Seward Mountain	4,347
3. Mount Haystack	4,961	26. Allen Mountain	4,347
4. Mount Skylight	4,924	27. Big Slide Mountain	4,249
5. Whiteface Mountain	4,866	28. Esther Mountain	4,239
6. Dix Mountain	4,839	29. Upper Wolf Jaw	4,185
7. Gray Peak	4,830	30. Lower Wolf Jaw	4,173
8. Iroquois Peak	4,830	31. Phelps Mountain	4,161
9. Basin Mountain	4,826	32. Street Mountain	4,150
10. Gothics Mountain	4,734	33. Sawteeth Mountain	4,150
11. Mount Colden	4,734	34. Mount Donaldson	4,140
12. Giant Mountain	4,626	35. Cascade Mountain	4,098
13. Nippletop Mountain	4,610	36. Seymour Mountain	4,091
14. Santanoni Peak	4,606	37. Porter Mountain	4,085
15. Mount Redfield	4,606	38. Mount Colvin	4,085
16. Wright Peak	4,580	39. South Dix Mountain	4,060
17. Saddleback Mountain	4,528	40. Mount Emmons	4,040
18. Panther Peak	4,442	41. Dial Mountain	4,020
19. Table Top Mountain	4,413	42. East Dix Mountain	4,006
20. Rocky Peak Ridge	4,410	43. Blake Peak	3,986
21. Hough Peak	4,409	44. Cliff Mountain	3,944
22. Macomb Mountain	4,390	45. Nye Mountain	3,944
23. Armstrong Mountain	4,390	46. Cousachraga Peak	3,820

The **Adirondack Forty-Sixers** is an organization dedicated to these High Peaks. To earn its member's patch, you must have climbed all of the mountains listed above. The group performs trail work and education projects; for information, visit www.adk46r.org.

Designated wilderness and wild forest areas offer great ski touring on marked but ungroomed trails. Another option for exploring the wild wintry woods is to hire a licensed guide.

SKIING THE HIGH PEAKS BACKCOUNTRY COURTESY OF DREW HAAS, WWW.ADKBCSKI.COM

CROSS-COUNTRY-SKI CENTERS, TRAIL NETWORKS, AND OUTFITTERS **Adirondak Loj** (518-523-3441; www.adk.org; Adirondack Loj Road, Lake Placid) has 12 kilometers of backcountry trails that connect with numerous challenging wilderness trails, guided tours, lessons, food, and lodging.

Cascade Ski Touring Center (518-523-9605; www.cascadeski.com; NY 73, Lake Placid) grooms 20 kilometers of trails and connects with the Jackrabbit Trail, offers night skiing (ask about its full-moon parties), rentals, lessons, and a ski shop. (Ask about the local food nights, when area farmers dish their bounty to live music and dancing.)

Dewey Mountain Recreation Center (518-891-2697; www.deweyskicenter.com; NY 30, Saranac Lake) maintains 20 kilometers of groomed trails, has night skiing, lessons, and guided tours, and is great for snowshoeing, too.

Olympic Sports Complex at Mount Van Hoevenberg (518-523-2811; www.whiteface .com; NY 73, Lake Placid) is a 50-kilometer groomed Olympic trail system that connects with the Jackrabbit Trail. It also has rentals, lessons, and a ski shop. Cross-country sales, rentals, maps, and other gear can be found at **Blue Line Sports, LLC** (518-891-4680; 81 Main Street, Saranac Lake), **Eastern Mountain Sports** (518-523-2505; www .ems.com; 2453 Main Street, Lake Placid), **High Peaks Cyclery** (518-523-3764; www .highpeakscyclery.com; 2733 Main Street, Lake Placid), **Maui North** (518-523-7245; www.mauinorth.net; 134 Main Street, Lake Placid), and **The Mountaineer** (518-576-2281; www.mountaineer.com; NY 73, Keene Valley).

DOWNHILL SKIING AND SNOWBOARDING Naturally, downhill season in the Adirondacks depends on the weather (this is not a region known for its powder). Often, snowmaking begins in early November, and some trails may open by Thanksgiving, but, increasingly, it can be January before the snow is reliable throughout an entire ski area. Whatever the weather, it's not a bad idea to call ahead for the ski conditions before you go.

Compared to ski areas in Vermont or the Rockies, those in the Adirondacks seem undeveloped. The emphasis at the hills is on skiing and snowboarding, not on hot-tub lounging, nightlife, or après-ski ambience. At the base of a mountain, you won't find condos or designer restaurants for fancy meals and lodging—you have to go to town. Following are some downhill ski areas within the Adirondack Park:

Mount Pisgah (518-891-0970; www .mtpisgahadk.com; Mount Pisgah Road, off Trudeau Road, Saranac Lake) was mentioned in *The Bell Jar*. Sylvia Plath skied there in the 1950s and chronicled her spectacular tumble in the book. The mountain today, with its T-bar and slopes geared to beginner and intermediate skiers, is still very much a family ski area

WHITEFACE MOUNTAIN'S GONDOLA DELIVERS SKIERS INTO THE CLOUDS COURTESY OF ORDA

CATCHING AIR ON WHITEFACE'S SLOPES COURTESY OF ORDA

BIRD LAND

Many interior lakes and ponds are home to kingfishers, ducks, herons, and loons. Listen and watch for that great northern diver in the early morning and at dusk. Peregrine falcons and bald eagles, absent from the park for much of the twentieth century, have been reintroduced. Cliffs in the High Peaks are now peregrine falcon aeries, and you should be able to spot a bald eagle or two near Meacham Lake or Franklin Falls Pond. In the evening, listen for owls: the barred owl, known by its call, "Who cooks for you, who cooks for you," is quite common. In the fall, look up to see thousands of migrating Canada and snow geese.

Learn more about loons at Saranac Lake's new Adirondack Center for Loon Conservation (518-354-8636; www.adkloon.org; 15 Broadway). Whether it's loon research, conservation and management, or education and outreach—or a cool loon postcard or print—this is the epicenter for the Adirondacks' beloved *Gavia immer*.

IT'S NOT UNUSUAL TO HEAR A LOON'S MOODY YODEL ON ADIRONDACK LAKES COURTESY OF JOHN DIGIACOMO

with a friendly atmosphere. Tubing is also a big deal here. There's snowmaking for most of the hill, plus a ski school, patrol, and a cozy base lodge with a snack bar. Pisgah is one of the few places left in the Adirondacks where you can enjoy night skiing; local residents often hit the slopes after work.

Whiteface Mountain (518-946-2233; www.whiteface.com; 5021 NY 86, Wilmington), at 3,430 feet, has the longest vertical drop in the East. New York governor Averill Harriman dedicated Whiteface Mountain, a state-owned facility, in 1958; the event was marred slightly when the chairlift he was riding came to a dead halt and Harriman had to be rescued by ladder from his lofty perch. On its 86 trails, there's lots of intense, expert skiing. Tackling the mountain's double-black-diamond slides when they're open is a real adventure. The mountain is big enough—though not a place you can get lost in—to accommodate scads of skiers without building up long lift lines. Eight chairlifts, plus a high-speed gondola, propel skiers up the slopes. There's an excellent Kids Kampus—play-and-ski program for tots—and a first-rate ski school. Whiteface is constantly expanding offerings for snowboarders, including a quality half-pipe and terrain parks. World Cup snowboard athletes compete here. Other races, on boards and skis, happen during the season—check www.whiteface.com for a calendar of events. Three lodges supply food, drink, and a place to discuss the slopes, plus a full ski shop with rentals. In 2017 a weekend adult ticket was about $95, though there are sizable midweek discounts and special promotions.

SNOWMOBILING More than 400 miles of snowmobile trails weave through the Tupper Lake–Saranac Lake–Lake Placid area. Many trail networks throughout the park cross private timberlands as well as the state forest preserve. Public lands designated as wild forest areas are open to snowmobiling; wilderness areas are not.

SPAS In Lake Placid, there are spas at the **Mirror Lake Inn Resort & Spa** (518-523-2544; www.mirrorlakeinn.com) and the **Whiteface Lodge** (518-523-0560; www.thewhitefacelodge.com). In Wilmington, you can get a massage at **River Stone Wellness Center** (802-309-5447; www.riverstonewellness.com; 1181 Haselton Road).

WATERFALLS Among the cascades in this region are **Beaver Meadow Falls** in the High Peaks Wilderness Area; **Blue Ridge Falls** on the Branch in North Hudson; the **Flume** on the West Branch of the Ausable River in Wilmington; **Hanging Spear Falls** on the Opalescent River in the High Peaks Wilderness; and **Wanika Falls** on the Chubb River in Lake Placid. See Russell Dunn's *Adirondack Waterfall Guide*.

WILDERNESS AREAS Wilderness areas are open to hiking, cross-country skiing, hunting, fishing, and other similar pursuits, but seaplanes may not land on wilderness ponds, nor are motorized vehicles welcome.

    Dix Mountain. 45,000 acres, southwest of Keene Valley. Adjacent to High Peaks wilderness; rock climbing at Chapel Pond; views from Noonmark, Dix, and many other mountains.

    Giant Mountain. 23,000 acres, between Elizabethtown and Keene. Roaring Brook Falls; extensive hiking trails; views from Rocky Peak Ridge, Giant, and other mountains.

    High Peaks. 226,000 acres, between Lake Placid and Newcomb. Excellent trail network; rock climbing at Wallface and other peaks; small lakes and ponds; views from

JAY MOUNTAIN COURTESY OF JOHNATHAN ESPER

Mount Marcy, Algonquin, and numerous other summits. Some interior destinations (Lake Colden and Marcy Dam) and peaks are very popular, to the point of being over-used—more than 12,000 people climb Mount Marcy every year.

Jay Mountain. 7,100 acres, east of Jay. Lengthy ridge trails.

McKenzie Mountain. 38,000 acres, north of Ray Brook. Trails for hiking and cross-country skiing; bordered by the Saranac River, Lake Placid, and McKenzie, Moose, and Franklin Falls Ponds; views from McKenzie and Moose Mountains.

Sentinel Range. 23,000 acres, between Lake Placid and Wilmington. Small ponds for fishing, few hiking trails, views from Pitchoff Mountain. This area is remote and receives little use.

WILD FOREST AREAS More than a million acres of public land in the park are desig-nated as wild forest, which is open to snowmobile travel, mountain biking, and other recreation.

Debar Mountain. Between Loon Lake and Meacham Lake. Horse trails, hiking, fish-ing in the Osgood River.

Saranac Lakes. West of Saranac Lake village. Excellent canoeing, island camping.

✳ Lodging

Of all the regions in this book, this is where you'll find year-round lodging and places suited to conferences and other gatherings. Not to mention all sorts of choices—motels, hotels, hostels, bed & breakfasts, backwoods cabins, luxury lodges, lean-tos, and Airbnbs galore. The following have character that can only enhance your Adirondack getaway.

ELK LAKE

Elk Lake Lodge (518-532-7616; www .elklakelodge.com; 1106 Elk Lake Road) is the quintessential Adirondack lodge. (Staying here and exploring the property should be on every Adirondacker's bucket list.) Set on a private lake ringed by the High Peaks, in the midst of a 12,000-acre preserve, the place offers everything an outdoorsperson could ask for: great fishing, unlimited wilderness hiking, and canoeing on an island-studded lake that's off limits to motorboats. Of course, if just hanging out, listening to the loons, and admiring the view are your kinds of rec-reation, there's that, too. There are a half-dozen rooms in the turn-of-the-century lodge, all with private baths. Around the lakeshore are seven cottages, some that

can accommodate 12. Several of the cab-ins are equipped with kitchens and fire-places or have decks overlooking the lake, and several have recently been renovated. The price of a stay at Elk Lake includes all meals, which are served in the dining room, where huge picture windows reveal the mountains and lake. Canoes and rowboats are available for guests. Open seasonally. $$$.

JAY

The **Book and Blanket** (518-946-8323; www.bookandblanket.com; 12914 NY 9N), in a restored Greek Revival home, has rooms named for authors: the Jack London chamber has a north-woods ambience, queen-size bed, and private bath with a whirlpool tub; the Jane Austen room has a queen-size bed and a quiet nook for reading; the F. Scott Fitzgerald room has a double bed and shares a bath. All of them—upstairs and down—have lots of books, and guests are encouraged to browse and borrow at will. Or they can kick back in front of the liv-ing room fireplace. $.

KEENE

The **Bark Eater Inn** (518-576-7100; www.barkeater.com; 124 Alstead Hill

ADIRONDACK LIFE

Published since 1969, *Adirondack Life* (www.adirondacklife.com) has earned numerous national awards for the quality of its photography and design and the depth of its editorial content. The magazine covers New York's 6-million-acre Adirondack Park, which has more wild country than Yellowstone, Yosemite, and Glacier National Parks combined. The bimonthly magazine, based in Jay, explores the region's people, places, wildlife, history, and public issues, and gives readers insider tips on outdoor recreation, from hiking and canoeing to ice climbing and backcountry skiing. In late spring, *Adirondack Life* publishes its "Annual Guide to the Great Outdoors," devoted entirely to outdoor pursuits; in fall, its "At Home in the Adirondacks" features architecture, interior design, gardening, and home products reflecting the region's signature style.

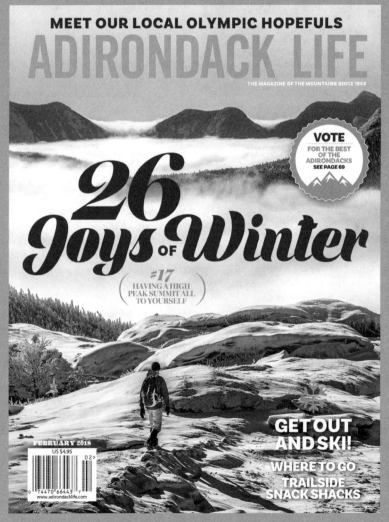

ADIRONDACK LIFE MAGAZINE HAS BEEN THE TRUSTED VOICE OF THE PARK SINCE 1969

DARTBROOK RUSTIC GOODS, IN KEENE, IS ONE OF THE MOST STYLISH SHOWROOMS AROUND, WITH ADIRONDACK RUSTIC FURNITURE AND GREAT CAMP ACCOUTREMENTS COURTESY OF NANCIE BATTAGLIA

page 164), where you can purchase pieces like the ones you'll covet in Dartbrook's cabins. $$.

KEENE VALLEY

Keene Valley Lodge (518-576-2003; www .keenevalleylodge.com; 1834 NY 73), from 1929 to 1949, was known as Beede Cottage; now it's a cozy inn with all the modern comforts in nine guest rooms. On the first floor of this big Italianate home, there's a suite with queen-size bed, full bath, and its own entrance. Most of the second-floor rooms have private baths and king-size beds, and all are furnished with antiques and hand-stitched quilts. A breakfast buffet is included in the rate. $$.

RoosterComb Inn (315-657-4839; www.roostercombinn.com; 3 Market Street) is a lovely, colorful place. The nineteenth-century home was one of the earliest boardinghouses around, taking in travelers when this area—called Keene Flats in the late 1800s—started attracting visitors. The inn, named after the peak just up the road, has a half-dozen rooms and is dog-friendly. Steve Bowers's Bald Mountain Rustics (www .baldmountainrustics.com) Adirondack-style furniture is located on the premises. $.

Trail's End Inn (518-576-9860 or 1-800-281-9860; www.trailsendinn.com; 62 Trail's End Way), a gambrel-roofed house with eyebrow windows on a quiet road, calls itself a hikers' lodge, implying that the accommodations aren't so fancy that you need to worry about blow-drying your hair before you come to breakfast. Some guest rooms upstairs have fireplaces, private porches, and whirlpool tubs. There are four double rooms that share baths, plus a two-bedroom cottage—with kitchen and washer/dryer—that accommodates up to six guests and even a pet. Hiking clubs or family groups can take over the entire place, which holds about 40 comfortably. The bus stops every day at the Noon Mark Diner (see page 157), a five-minute walk away,

Lane) is a former stagecoach stop on one of the most picturesque plots in the High Peaks. Guests can choose from five bedrooms in the recently renovated nineteenth-century farmhouse, with stunning views of the Sentinel Mountains. Hiking trails meander through the Bark Eater's 200–acre property; on-site gardens and a greenhouse supply fresh greens and vegetables, berries, and melons for hearty, gourmet breakfasts in the inn's dining room. $$.

Dartbrook Lodge (518-576-9080; www.dartbrooklodge.com; 2835 Route 73, at the intersection with 9N), a rehabbed compound of seven well-appointed Great Camp–style cabins, most with kitchenettes—plus a three-cabin complex with private entrance and a dreamy mountaintop retreat—is a welcome addition to drowsy Keene. Dartbrook offers travelers rustic luxury—think chic twiggy and bark decor, details such as balsam soap, and proximity to High Peaks adventures. On-site there's Dartbrook Rustic Goods (see

JAY COVERED BRIDGE

Since 1846, a structure—in a handful of incarnations thanks to floods, ice jams, logging rigs, and a runaway soda delivery truck—has connected the banks of the Ausable River in Jay. Today's pedestrian-only 175-foot-long stretch still has timbers from one of its nineteenth-century predecessors, drawing covered-bridge buffs. Beneath this centerpiece of the historic hamlet is a popular swimming hole, and folks come here to picnic, bike, or stroll around the surrounding park.

THE JAY COVERED BRIDGE, SHOWN HERE BEFORE ITS FACELIFT, HAS ANCHORED THIS QUAINT HAMLET SINCE 1857 COURTESY OF TED COMSTOCK, SARANAC LAKE

and from the inn, there's easy access to Roostercomb and other peaks. $$.

LAKE PLACID

Crowne Plaza Resort & Golf Club (518-523-2556; www.lakeplacidcp.com; 101 Olympic Drive) overlooks the Olympic Arena and Mirror Lake; has a heated pool, sauna, and whirlpool; access to Jackrabbit cross-country-ski trails; two championship golf courses; a health club; a lake view; and a restaurant and lounge. $$.

The **Haüs** (518-523-3005; www .thehauslakeplacid.com; 2439 Main Street), an "eco-chic boutique lodging" hidden along Lake Placid's Main Street, is more apartment rental than hotel. There's no elevator, no parking, no beach, no bar, spa, or restaurant, but no worries: the place is smack in the middle of the action, with Mirror Lake out back and eateries, shopping, and everything you could possibly need just out the door. Those who appreciate aesthetics, particularly a fresh take on Adirondack style, will dig this place. Nine elegantly designed suites offer various views, stainless-steel kitchens, hardwood floors, and can sleep from two to four people. $$.

The **Interlaken Inn** (518-523-3180; www.theinterlakeninn.com; 15 Interlaken Avenue, around the corner from Mirror Lake Inn) has walnut-paneled walls, tin ceilings, a polished garnet fireplace, a winding staircase, and antiques that make it a true oasis. Built in 1912 by one of the founders of the Bank of Lake Placid, the secluded, high-end spot has been operated as an inn for most of its existence. There are seven lovely guest rooms, two suites, and a carriage house, most with queen-size beds, all with private baths—some with Jacuzzis or a claw-foot tub. Downstairs, the dining room is elegant yet casual. Off the living room is the cozy bar, where there's a pub menu and an extensive wine list. The inn makes an elegant backdrop for small weddings and other gatherings. Closed in April. $$.

Lake House at High Peaks Resort (518-523-4422; www.highpeaksresort.com/lake-house; 1 Mirror Lake Drive) is the result of an old motor inn that got an update well beyond a fresh coat of paint. A full renovation and rebranding transformed the midcentury motel into a chic lodge with a retro vibe. The decor combines elements of 1960s design with rustic Adirondack touches—think vintage tourism posters and maps, Pendleton blankets, modernist furniture, and wood paneling. Each of the 44 pet-friendly guest rooms has a patio or balcony with a view of Mirror Lake, plus guests can borrow paddling gear—or in winter, ice skates and Norwegian kicksleds—to enjoy the lake up close. Anyone can have a cocktail or a pint of local craft beer by the fireplace in the cozy lounge, stocked with old-school board games. $$.

Lake Placid Lodge (518-523-2700; www.lakeplacidlodge.com; 144 Lodge Way) was originally built as a summer home at the turn of the last century. The place opened as a hotel in 1946, and more than six decades—and a devastating fire—later, it's one of the most stylish, exclusive places in the region. The luxurious lodge's rooms, suites, cottages, and cabins are decked out in Adirondack Great Camp style, with handcrafted rustic furniture,

handsome oil paintings, crackling stone fireplaces, rich fabrics, and tasteful taxidermy; its pub and restaurant are among the best in the park. And then there's the lakeside pinch-me view. Guests can lounge on the property's sandy beach, help themselves to canoes, sailboards, pedal boats, and bicycles, or stroll to the 18-hole Whiteface Inn golf course. $$$$.

Mirror Lake Inn Resort & Spa (518-523-2544; www.mirrorlakeinn.com; 77 Mirror Lake Drive), on a hillside overlooking Mirror Lake, is a lovely hotel in the heart of town. The resort has five lodging buildings—three across the street from Mirror Lake and the other two by a small private beach. All rooms are upscale, with mountain or lakeside views and fireplaces; suites are also available to accommodate families. The Colonial House Ultimate Suites on Mirror Lake are sensational, with fine furniture, Oriental rugs, cathedral ceilings, enormous living quarters, and marble tubs. On site is a nice restaurant, a cozy pub, and various nooks and crannies for guests to kick back in. And there's a spa: if your interest is relaxing, improving your skin, or launching a healthier lifestyle, the staff can help. The resort now hosts wedding receptions and is an

RUSTIC ELEGANCE AT LAKE PLACID LODGE COURTESY OF LAKE PLACID LODGE

STYLISH LAKE PLACID LODGE IS AN EXCEPTIONAL WATERFRONT RESORT   COURTESY OF LAKE PLACID LODGE

exceptional facility for conferences, with plenty of attractive meeting rooms for large or small groups. $$$.

Paradox Lodge (518-523-9078; www .paradoxlodge.com; 2169 Saranac Avenue) reopened as a cozy inn a century after it was originally built, in 1899. Although the place has been scrubbed, rewired, replumbed, painted, and decorated with an eclectic jumble of antiques and art, the house's underlying character is handsomely intact. Four rooms, all with private baths, are upstairs. The Cedar Lodge has four elegantly rustic upscale rooms, each with king-size bed, Jacuzzi tub, deck, gas fireplace, robes, and refrigerator. All rooms have air-conditioning, and guests have access to Paradox Bay and the inn's watercraft. Downstairs are two cozy dining rooms. If you stay at Paradox, do not miss the opportunity to eat here—some would argue Chef Moses "Red" LaFountain makes the most fabulous food in the North Country. $$.

The **Lake Placid Stagecoach Inn** (518-523-9698; www.lakeplacidstagecoachinn .com; 3 Stagecoach Way), built in 1833, is probably the oldest but loveliest spot in all of Lake Placid. This was a stop along what was a well-traveled stagecoach route that brought abolitionists to John Brown's nearby North Elba farm. Today, the place is gorgeous with its polished dark woodwork and eclectic decor, and charming with its fireplaces, narrow hallways, and stairwells. Four suites sleep anywhere from two to four people; a fine, complimentary breakfast is offered; and the inn's proximity to the Lake Placid Horse Show Grounds make this a sought-after—and recommended—getaway. $$.

Van Hoevenberg Lodge and Cabins (518-523-9572; www.vanhoevenbergcabins .com; 4529 Cascade Road) are owned and operated by Wayne Failing, a respected New York State–licensed guide, who, if you hire him, will take you on the rafting trip, hiking trek, or fishing or hunting adventure of your life. Eight cabins and three guest rooms in the lodge would make accommodations appealing in any Adirondack setting, but the attraction at Failing's spread is its proximity to excellent cross-country skiing, hiking, and mountain biking—and pets are welcome. The cabins and lodge are next to

A GEOGRAPHY LESSON

The village of Lake Placid is on tiny Mirror Lake. The lake named Placid is slightly west of downtown, and it's a big body of water with a trio of islands and gorgeous views.

the more than 50 kilometers of groomed tracks at the Olympic cross-country complex, which connects with the Cascade Ski-Touring Center and Jackrabbit Trails. You can head into the High Peaks Wilderness Area without parking your car at a trailhead and afterward enjoy an invigorating wood-fired sauna. $$.

The **Whiteface Lodge** (1-800-903-4045; www.thewhitefacelodge.com; 7 Whiteface Inn Lane) is a luxury resort that's appeared in all sorts of travel magazines, and has been included in *Condé Nast Traveler*'s Gold List, under "The World's Best Places to Stay." Although it isn't on waterfront or at the base of a mountain, there are nice views and the lodge itself is over-the-top in Adirondack-style detail and decor. The lodge has the feel of an elegant nine-teenth-century Adirondack Great Camp, but with all the comforts of the modern world. It's also an extraordinary place for families with kids, with many amenities and activities "on campus." Evening s'mores gatherings are a hit. The White-face Lodge operates as a resort hotel and private residence club—folks can buy full and partial ownership. Rooms are spacious and beautifully decorated—nothing has been overlooked here—and the resort includes a state-of-the-art spa, an outdoor boating club on Lake Placid,

MIRROR LAKE INN RESORT & SPA, IN LAKE PLACID, IS CLASSY COLONIAL   COURTESY OF MIRROR LAKE INN RESORT & SPA

TROPICAL STORM IRENE

In summer 2011, Tropical Storm Irene pushed Adirondack rivers, including the Ausable and Boquet and their tributaries, to record levels, flooding much of the northern and eastern Adirondacks: water surged through living rooms, ripped apart businesses, disintegrated roads, devastated farms, killed livestock, and carried away part of a fire station. After the flood, Au Sable Forks, Jay, Upper Jay, St. Huberts, Keene, Keene Valley, and Elizabethtown, among others, looked as though they'd been bombed by an unrelenting army. Post-storm, dozens of houses, particularly in the towns of Jay and Keene, had to be torn down because of structural damage, altering the riverside landscape. Irene also altered the mountainscape when torrential downpours caused landslides on some of the High Peaks. Today those slides appear as scars, a reminder of the power of nature.

IN AUGUST 2011, TROPICAL STORM IRENE DEVASTATED PARTS OF THE ADIRONDACKS, INCLUDING ROADS, HOMES, AND BUSINESSES IN UPPER JAY COURTESY OF DEB MACKENZIE, WWW.MACKENZIEFAMILY.COM

indoor and outdoor swimming pools, an outdoor skating rink, movie theater, bowling alley, bocce and tennis courts, and a separate facility with a massive porch and banquet hall that makes a perfect backdrop for wedding receptions or other gatherings. The on-site bar and its fireplaces and couches are perfect for cocktails and conversation; the lodge's KANU restaurant is recommended for a romantic meal or special occasion. $$$.

SARANAC LAKE

Fogarty's Bed and Breakfast (518-891-3755 or 1-800-525-3755; www .adirondacks.com/fogarty; 74 Kiwassa Road) was built in 1910 as a cure cottage for tuberculosis patients. This attractive home overlooking Lake Flower has handsome woodwork, leaded-glass windows, wonderful porches, and five bedrooms. Although Fogarty's is a quick walk from

OLD MOUNTAIN PHELPS

Legendary guide Orson Schofield Phelps, a.k.a. Old Mountain Phelps, named Skylight, Basin, Saddleback, Haystack, and Dial mountains. He slashed the first trail up Mount Marcy 150 years ago, made plenty of first ascents and paths over Great Range peaks, and led an esteemed crew of nineteenth-century intellectuals above the forests, into the clouds. Winslow Homer captured Phelps and another guide in his 1875 oil *Two Guides*, now hanging at the Sterling and Francine Clark Art Institute in Williamstown, Massachusetts, and the eccentric elfin guide was immortalized by writer Charles Dudley Warner in his 1878 *Atlantic Monthly* essay "The Primitive Man."

COURTESY OF KEENE VALLEY LIBRARY

Saranac Lake's business district and restaurants, it's in a peaceful neighborhood and has a dock on the lake for swimmers and boaters. Winter guests note that cross-country skiing at Dewey Mountain is about a mile away, and in early February, when the winter carnival is in full swing, you can look over to the fabulous ice palace on the opposite shore of the lake. An important Fogarty's feature: Because the house is set on a steep hillside, you've got to climb a lot of steps—73 to be exact—to get to the entrance. $.

The **Porcupine Inn** (518-891-5160; www.porcupineinn.com; 350 Park Avenue), designed by architect William Coulter, was built for Thomas Bailey Aldrich, *Atlantic Monthly* editor, author of *The Story of a Bad Boy*, and friend of Mark Twain. The name "Porcupine" isn't some cute modern affectation: this massive, six-gabled, gambrel-roofed house acquired that title in the early 1900s because "it had so many good points and because it was occupied by a quill driver"—the quill driver being author Aldrich. He brought his wife and sons to Saranac Lake not on some vacation whim but because one of his twin sons had tuberculosis, and the family hoped that the fresh mountain air and good

LAKE PLACID'S STAGECOACH INN HAS OLD-SCHOOL CHARM COURTESY OF NANCIE BATTAGLIA

doctors at nearby Trudeau Sanatorium could cure him. Sadly, the young man died. Nowadays, a happier chapter has unfolded for this grand home. With plenty of elbow grease and lots of enthusiasm, the place opened as a bed & breakfast. Downstairs is a comfortable living room with a fireplace, as well as a billiards room and wine bar. Five spacious guest rooms are on the second floor, up the beautiful Jacobean-style staircase. All have private baths; most have glassed-in "cure porches," an architectural element dating back to the days when TB patients were made to sleep in unheated rooms, swaddled in blankets. Breakfast is served in a big, bright dining area. An outdoor hot tub allows for soaking and relaxing in all weather. $$.

Saranac Lake Inn, a.k.a. **Gauthier's** (518-891-1950; www.saranaclakeinn.com; 488 Lake Flower Avenue) is eco-conscious lodging. Among their practices: only nontoxic, biodegradable cleaners are used in rooms, guests are offered organic Fair Trade coffee and tea purchased from local vendors, low-flow showerheads and compact fluorescent light bulbs have been installed, the pool is solar heated, and no pesticides or chemicals are used on the grounds, which are landscaped with native plants. Gauthier's is right on Lake Flower, which

means guests can take its canoes or paddleboats for a spin. $.

WILMINGTON

The Hungry Trout Resort (518-946-2217; www.hungrytrout.com; 5239 NY 86) is a motel with great views and close proximity to Whiteface Mountain, a nice restaurant, and R. F. McDougall's Tavern. There's an on-site guide service that offers fly-fishing lessons, as well as a tackle shop, plus the resort owns a super stretch of the Ausable River. $$.

Willkommen Hof Bed & Breakfast (518-946-SNOW or 1-800-541-9119; www .willkommenhof.com; 5367 NY 86) is a European-style guesthouse within a one-minute walk of the Ausable River's spectacular flume. The B&B has three rooms with private baths, a three-room suite, and three rooms that share baths, to house a maximum of 24 guests. Full breakfasts and after-ski treats are included in the room rate; hearty dinners may be arranged. World-famous trout waters are nearby, as are numerous state-marked trails for cross-country skiing, mountain biking, and hiking. (The innkeepers Heike and Bert Yost can suggest trips off the beaten path on foot or by

A WELL-APPOINTED ROOM AT THE WHITEFACE LODGE IN LAKE PLACID COURTESY OF THE WHITEFACE LODGE

HIGH PEAKS HOSTELS

In addition to tents and lean-tos, there are other affordable places to sleep in this region: **Adirondak Loj** (518-523-3441; www.adk.org; 1002 Adirondak Loj Road), in Lake Placid, has a sweeping panorama of Mount Marcy and Indian Pass, and the drive in sets you up for a visit to the Adirondack Mountain Club's (ADK) wilderness retreat. On Heart Lake in the midst of the High Peaks, the 1920s-era lodge is a rustic, comfortable place. In the living room, you can rock in an Old Hickory chair in front of the vast stone fireplace and choose from the shelves practically any book that's ever been written on the Adirondacks. Breakfast—the wake-up bell rings bright and early—is served buffet style, as is dinner, at picnic tables in an adjoining room. Bag lunches are available, and plain, home-cooked dinners are served when the lodge is busy. There are four private rooms, four bunk rooms, and a huge coed loft. The bunkrooms, which have four built-in log beds, are snug and cozy, like cabins on a ship; the loft can be a hard place to get a good night's sleep if there are any snorers in the crowd. You don't need to be a member of ADK to stay at the Loj, but you must make advance reservations. On Heart Lake are two cabins that accommodate four to 16 people during the fall, winter, and spring. For the intrepid traveler, ADK has three excellent backcountry cabins that are accessible by foot—all are a 3.5-mile hike in from Keene Valley: **Johns Brook Lodge**, which is open Memorial Day through Columbus Day (in July and August you can get two hot meals and bag lunches here); and **Grace Camp** and **Camp Peggy O'Brien**, which are open year-round and have tiers of bunks, gas lights, and propane heat. They're excellent bases for hiking, snowshoe, or ski weekends.

Again in Lake Placid, though away from the village on Route 73, is **TMax-n-Topo's Hostel** (518-523-0123; www.tmax-n-topo.com; 5046 Cascade Road), en route to Keene, where you can get a bunk for about $30, plus tax, per night. Four bunkrooms can accommodate up to 33 people, and upstairs are private rooms. The owners know just about everything about recreation in these parts.

Keene Valley Hostel (518-576-2030; www.keenevalleyhostel.com; 1755 Route 73) is in the middle of the High Peaks action. It's $30 for a night in the bunkhouse, linens and towels provided—there's lawn camping too—and you can book a shuttle that'll deliver you to Adirondak Loj, the Garden parking lot, Newcomb, or beyond.

MOUNT MARCY COURTESY OF TED COMSTOCK, SARANAC LAKE

bike, or guests can book Bert, a licensed guide, for an outdoor excursion.) Willkommen Hof is popular with Whiteface Mountain downhill skiers because it's just minutes away from the slopes. After all that exertion, guests can wind down in either the outdoor hot tub or indoor sauna. $.

CAMPGROUNDS The **Department of Environmental Conservation** (518-402-9428; www.dec.ny.gov) operates public campgrounds across the park, open from Memorial Day through Labor Day, though some can vary.

Camping is allowed year-round on state land, but you need a permit to stay more than three days in one backcountry spot or if you are camping with a group of more than six people. Special regulations apply in the High Peaks Wilderness Area. These permits are available from forest rangers. You may camp in the backcountry provided you pitch your tent at least 150 feet from any trail, stream, lake, or other water body. Along the Northville–Lake Placid Trail and on popular canoe routes you'll find lean-tos—three-sided Adirondack icons—for camping.

Reservations can be made for a site in the state campgrounds by contacting **Reserve America** (1-800-456-CAMP; www.reserveamerica). Some campgrounds will take you on a first-come, first-served basis if space is available. The following are public campgrounds in this region:

Buck Pond (518-891-3449; 1339 County Route 60, Onchiota). Swimming, showers, canoe or rowboat rental, boat launch.

Lake Harris (518-582-2503; 291 Campsite Road, Newcomb). Swimming, showers, boat launch. Near Adirondack Visitor Interpretive Center nature trails.

Meacham Lake (518-483-5116; 119 State Campsite Road, Duane). Swimming, showers, horse trails and barn, some primitive sites accessible by foot only, boat launch. Good place to see bald eagles in summer.

Meadowbrook (518-891-4351; 1174 NY 86, Ray Brook). Showers, no swimming. Closest campground to downtown Lake Placid.

Saranac Lake Islands (518-891-3170; 58 Bayside Drive, Saranac Lake). Access by boat, tents only. Beautiful sites.

Taylor Pond (518-647-5250; 1865 Silver Lake Road, Au Sable Forks). Boat launch.

Wilmington Notch (518-946-7172; 4953 NY 86, Wilmington). On the West Branch of the Ausable River. Great area for fly-fishing; fairly close to Lake Placid.

❋ Where to Eat

DINING OUT If you like your meal seasoned with a stunning view, you're in the right place. This part of the park doesn't lack for options, but it helps to know which ones don't reach for the Sysco cans or freezer bags when it comes time to prep your feast. The following are picked for quality of eats as well as ambience.

KEENE

Cedar Run Bakery and Market (518-576-9929; www.cedarrunbakery.com; 2 Gristmill Lane), a local hot spot open 7 AM to 7 PM every day, is a delicious and convenient option in this little mountain town. Although there are a couple of cafe tables inside and outside, most folks grab their muffins, scones, bagels, soup, and sandwiches to go. Everything here is fresh and tasty. This is where you can buy gourmet chips or chocolate, local artisan cheeses, or a fine cup of coffee; the market's coolers are stocked with scrumptious take-and-bake meals and desserts. And the attached wine and spirits shop has a good selection.

KEENE VALLEY

Noon Mark Diner (518-576-4499; www.noonmarkdiner.com; NY 73/Main Street) accommodates everyone from

High Peaks backpackers to investment bankers to kids on bikes who come to stoke up on the extensive diner menu. You can order breakfast anytime, if you're not up for the chili or a cheeseburger. Always order (or take out) some homemade pie (worth a visit for the coconut cream alone, though Noon Mark does have a mail-order pie business). An ice cream stand is off to one side of the huge front porch (open seasonally), if you want some walk-around dessert. This diner can be jammed on summer weekends, with a half-hour wait for a table and another half hour before your meal is served.

LAKE PLACID

Caffé Rustica (518-523-7511; www .cafferustica.com; 1936 Saranac Avenue, in the Price Chopper Plaza) is where to get delicious rustic Mediterranean meals, prepared by the capable hands of Kevin Gregg. You can't go wrong here. This isn't the place to go if you're hoping for a private dinner—tables in the front room are close together, like at crammed-in city restaurants. But this is where you go for a fine lunch or dinner. Gregg and his team are also popular local caterers. Or you can arrange to have a private shindig in the cafe's back room.

The Good Bite Kitchen (518-637-2860; www.thegoodbitekitchen.com; 2501 Main Street), in a pocket-sized Main Street space (a former storage hallway), has the best vegetarian food around. Sandwiches, salads, soups, bowls—it's all fresh, inventive, and prepared by Kayte Billerman, a graduate of Colorado's School of Natural Cookery. Most people take their food to go, but there are stools for eight should you choose to stay.

Interlaken Inn (1-800-428-4369; www .theinterlakeninn.com; 39 Interlaken Avenue) is a grand old small hotel tucked into a peaceful downtown neighborhood. This place has fantastic food in both its classy dining room and informal pub. (In

the latter there's a stamped-tin ceiling and an elegant bas relief of trees—not many restaurants or inns would do this kind of detail in a public space, nor do many put this kind of detail into the food itself.) There's an excellent wine and beer list, too. In the dining room, entrées vary with the seasons (in deep winter, ask about the fondue). Desserts, such as the crème brûlée, are scrumptious.

Lake Placid Lodge (518-523-2700; www.lakeplacidlodge.com; Whiteface Inn Road) is one of finest, most elegant restaurants in the Adirondacks. The decor is Great Camp posh, the view stunning, and dining here means the chance to be at a Relais & Châteaux property without busting the bank. In Maggie's Pub, try the cheese board and charcuterie plate. Entrées in the lodge's Artisans restaurant might include sumac-dusted beef strip loin or foie gras. If ever there's an over-the-top spot to celebrate, this is it.

Liquids and Solids at the Handlebar (518-837-5012; www.liquidsandsolids .com; 6115 Sentinel Road) is a farm-to-fork gastropub that attracts foodies from afar. The vibe is hip and happening and the place is pretty small, so you might have to wait a while for a table or a spot at the bar, where mixologist Keegan Konkowski concocts funky cocktails like her

MAGGIE'S PUB AT LAKE PLACID LODGE COURTESY OF LAKE PLACID LODGE

FRENCH (-CANADIAN) CUISINE

Not many people outside the maple syrup belt have heard of the Quebecois delicacy poutine, a plate of gravy-drowned cheese curds melting into a heaping pile of home-made fries. But here in the northern Adirondacks—thanks in part to a considerable influx of French-Canadian loggers a few generations back—it's a favorite treat.

North of the border, the gravy that graces poutine is peppery, with hints of vinegar, and the cheese is traditionally cheddar curds. The version you get at diners throughout the park is more apt to be smothered in the same brown gravy that tops your mashed potatoes, and—since squeaking-fresh curds can be harder to come by in these parts—mozzarella is a popular substitution. Even so, the result is the same: a gut- and spirit-warming marvel. Sample some for yourself at **The Swiss Kitchen** (518-359-3513; 92 Park Street), in Tupper Lake, or for a more creative version, **Liquids and Solids at the Handlebar** (518-837-5012; www.liquidsandsolids .com; 6115 Sentinel Road), in Lake Placid.

cilantro daiquiri, Balsamic Fizz, or guava margarita. The fried brussels sprouts are amazing, and there's always a poutine special. Fresh, seasonal food such as smoked pig belly in a blanket or saffron cavatelli is featured on the Smalls and Bigs menus. Most kids won't appreciate what's served here; don't come if you're looking for quick, traditional fare. Check out **Kreature Butcher Shop** (518-837-5200; on Facebook) next door if you're looking for local meats and sandwiches.

Lisa G's (518-523-2093; www.lisags .com; 6125 Sentinel Road) advertises "casual dining with a twist." That's not the only reason diners love this place: there's its proprietor's friendliness (Lisa G. is usually greeting, chatting, serving), its off–Main Street former opera-house digs, and its roomy deck out back along the Chubb River. There's something for everyone here, and meals can be creative pizzas or four kinds of chicken wings that include Greek-style or atomic hot, and there's a daily burger special. The dining room will accommodate an entire outing club, while the bar has smaller tables and comfy couches.

Salt of the Earth Bistro (518-523-5956; www.saltoftheearthbistro.com; 5956 Sentinel Road) opened in spring 2017 in a renovated house and quickly became a local favorite for its imaginative, reasonably priced dinners and chic yet relaxed atmosphere. The decor has

some whimsical touches, like a chandelier made from cheese graters and a vintage-TV-turned-diorama. The menu, which changes seasonally, is described as New American but with influences that bounce around the planet—a starter of house-made paneer cheese with a ginger and serrano pepper creamed spinach, fish tacos on handmade tortillas, seared duck breast in a coconut Thai red curry sauce.

SARANAC LAKE

Blue Moon Cafe (518-891-1310; blue moonadk.com; 46 Main Street) at breakfast means homemade bread and English muffins accompanying Greek omelets (with feta and spinach) and home fries. Regulars dig into bowls of steel-cut oats with a side of blueberries. At lunch, soups, burgers, and sandwiches are all made fresh; dinners, including Asian-influenced rice or noodle bowls with fresh vegetables, are reasonably priced and delicious. There's a small bar in the back dining room, and a friendly neighborhood vibe.

Fiddlehead Bistro (518-891-2002; see Facebook; 33 Broadway Street) is an exceptional new offering in Saranac Lake. The chef-owners do everything 100 percent, from the tiles to the tables to the wall decor—everything was made locally and they know by whom, in some cases even the tree or barn where the wood came from. The same attitude applies to the food. They are committed to sourcing locally as much as possible: think wild ramps and, yes, fiddleheads too. Menus change daily and with the seasons. Again, there's a personal relationship with those who raise the beef, chicken, and pork. Cocktails are made by a pro who likes to try new things, from local herbs and infusions, even chaga. Locals will tell you it's a treat to go to Fiddlehead.

Left Bank Café (518-354-8166; www .leftbankcafe36.com; 34 Broadway) brings a delicious French vibe back to Saranac Lake. (A half-century ago, this was a bakery of the same name, run by the father of Kenneth Weissberg, who now operates this place. The Weissbergs also own the Maison des Adirondacks bed & breakfast in Entrains-Sur-Nohain, France.) Breakfasts are croissants and crepes; lunches are panini and soups and salads; dinner may be tapas with wine; and there's always fine coffee to be sipped and savored in this rich, earthy space with dark polished wood—or on the skinny deck overlooking the Saranac River. The cuisine may be international, but the vibe is all community; the work of local painters, jewelry makers, and musicians is often featured here.

Little Italy Pizzeria (518-891-9000; www.littleitalypizzeriainc.com; 23 Main Street) appears to be a simple pizza joint, but is much more. Venture beyond the front counter and booths in this Saranac institution—this is, after all, the town's number one takeout/delivery pizza place—and you'll find yourself in a spacious dining room with Old Country decor and tables that accommodate parties from two to twenty. What you'll get here is straight-up Italian fare—no pretension, no nonsense. Just ziti, manicotti, lasagna, chicken parmesan, spaghetti with meatballs, gnocchi, ravioli, fettuccine Alfredo—all the standards.

WILMINGTON

The Hungry Trout (518-946-2217; www .hungrytrout.com; 5239 NY 86) is perched along a mile-long section of the legendary West Branch of the Ausable River. This motel/restaurant/fly shop complex has fine views of Whiteface Mountain, and a foaming waterfall can be seen from the dining room—the view upstages the food. The menu is extensive, with numerous trout (farm-raised) dishes, plus lamb, steaks, pasta, chicken, and salmon. If you'd like to sample this spot but prefer not to spend a bundle, try the tavern on the ground floor, **R. F. McDougall's** (as in Rat Face McDougall, a trout fly). It's casual, with a lighter menu and a variety of beers to choose from.

CASUAL BITES **Asgaard Farm & Dairy** (www.asgaardfarm.com; 74 Asgaard Way), in Au Sable Forks, makes absolutely delectable goat's-milk caramels and award-winning farmstead cheeses.

Keene Valley's **Ausable Inn** (518-576-9584; 1809 Route 73) is a popular hangout with a great post-adventure porch. At **Subalpine Coffee** (518-930-4645; www .subalpinecoffee.com; 1767 Route 73), you'll find specialty coffee and homemade baked goods.

In Lake Placid, the **Taste Bistro** at Mirror Lake Inn Resort & Spa (518-302-3000; www.mirrorlakeinn.com; 77 Mirror Lake Drive) is comfy and classy—you can order a fine glass of wine or microbrew with pommes frites or a Black Angus burger. (The resort's **Cottage**, across the road, is a lively spot with a nice outdoor deck, for cocktails.) **Base Camp Café and Camp Cocktail** (518-523-3888; Facebook; 2488 Main Street), in an Adirondack-style closet-size space, serves cappuccino and lattes, smoothies, and interesting bagels; in the evening it transitions to exotic small plates and specialty cocktails. **The Breakfast Club, Etc**. (518-523-0007; www.thebreakfastclubetc .com; 2431 Main Street) has delicious breakfasts—and all sorts of Bloody Marys and mimosas—all day long. **Downtown Diner** (518-523-3709; 2728 Main Street) has good breakfasts, and Bruce Springsteen has been known to

LAKE PLACID BREWERIES

Lake Placid Pub & Brewery (518-523-3813; www.ubuale.com; 813 Mirror Lake Drive) is a wildly popular destination on Mirror Lake—so much so, the owners recently added a floor and expanded their outdoor seating to accommodate the crowds. It's home to good fare, from ribs to quesadillas to specialty burgers. (Parents love the kids' glass-walled playroom on the second floor.) But the draw here is the brews—a half-dozen award-winning ales and beers on tap at all times, some brewed in the back of the restaurant, including the award-winning Ubu Ale and Lake Placid IPA.

Big Slide Brewery & Public House (518-523-7844; www.bigslidebrewery.com; 5685 Cascade Road), opened in 2016 by the owners of Lake Placid Pub & Brewery, adds delicious food and drink to the other side of Lake Placid, near the ski jumps and horse show grounds. (In summer visitors appreciate the dog-friendly patio.) Big Slide's already earned a reputation for delicious food: Caribbean Night is a hit, Sunday brunch is an insiders' favorite, and local food is always at front and center of the imaginative menu. And the beer? The brewers here like to push the envelope. A flight at Big Slide might include Big Slide IPA, of course, plus a sour beer, and then, depending on the season, maybe Chili Pepper Pale Ale, Coriander Berliner Weiss, or Red Rye Delbrueckii.

BIG SLIDE BREWERY & PUBLIC HOUSE   COURTESY OF BIG SLIDE BREWERY & PUBLIC HOUSE

LAKE PLACID PUB & BREWERY, ON MIRROR LAKE, IS A BEER-LOVER'S DESTINATION   COURTESY OF LAKE PLACID PUB & BREWERY

WHERE THE WILD THINGS ARE

Adirondack Wildlife Refuge (855-965-3626; www.adirondackwildlife.org; 977 Springfield Road, Wilmington) is a safe haven and rehab center for creatures that have been hit by cars, shot by hunters, tumbled from nests, or orphaned. But it's also an educational center where humans can learn about Adirondack habitats and the animals—hawks, owls, raccoons, hybrid wolves, eagles, bears—that call this place home.

pop in. **Green Goddess Natural Market** (518-523-4676; www.greengoddessfoods.com; 2051 Saranac Avenue) is the place to go for exceptional vegetarian or vegan fare in the on-site café, local produce in the market, and supplements and natural personal care items lining the aisles. **Lake Placid Club Boathouse** (518-523-4822), on Mirror Lake, has good meals and gorgeous scenery. **Lobster Reef** (518-523-9919; www.lobsterreeflp.com) is the brand-new spot on Main Street for tapas and substantial lobster rolls. **Saranac Sourdough** (518-523-4897; 2126 Saranac Avenue) has delicious deli-style sandwiches and subs, soups and salads, and baked goods. **'Dack Shack** (518-523-3111; www.simplygourmetlakeplacid.com; 2099 Avenue), in the former Howard Johnson's, has tasty lunches and dinner specials. Its on-site deli, **Simply Gourmet**, has endless sandwiches (actually, 46) to choose from, as does its sister site, **Big Mountain Deli & Creperie** (518-523-3222; 2475 Main), by the library on Main Street. **Smoke Signals** (518-523-2271; www.smokesignalsq.com; 2489 Main Street) is a barbecue hot spot and, upstairs, where you can hear live music. **Top of the Park** (518-523-3632; www.topofthepark.bar.com; 2407 Main Street) has cocktails, tapas, and nice views of Mirror Lake. **Villa Vespa** (518-523-9789; www.villavespa.net; 2250 Saranac Avenue) carries homemade Italian sauces,

frozen and dried pastas, and ready-to-heat entrées. The ravioli—about three inches in diameter—are wonderful.

Saranac's **Saranac Pantry** (Route 3) is a bakery, café, and farm store that features local bounty.

In Saranac Lake, **Donnelly's**, open Memorial Day through Labor Day, is, without a doubt, the place for soft-serve ice cream (518-891-1404; intersection of NY 86 and 186). See Donnelly's "flavor schedule" on its Facebook page. **Lakeview Deli** (518-891-2101; www.lakeviewdeli.com; 137 River Street) is where to go for a quick lunch in the Adirondacks' All-America City. **Nori's Village Market** (518-891-6079; www.norisvillagemarket.com; 138 Church Street) has a natural-foods deli with daily lunch specials and excellent salads, plus all you'd expect from a good health food store. **Origin Coffee** (518-354-8102; www.origincoffeeadk.com; 77 Main Street) is a slick new cafe with the best gourmet drinks in town. Breakfasts and lunches are delicious, too.

On the former theme park, Land of Makebelieve, in Upper Jay, **Adirondack Mountain Coffee Café** (518-496-6080; www.adkmountaincoffee.com; 8 Arto's Way) is the brand new place to find hearty breakfasts and lunches. **Sugar House Creamery** (518-300-0626; www.sugarhousecreamery.com; 18 Sugar House Way) is where you'll find exceptional farmstead cheese, including Alpine-style Dutch Knuckle or soft-ripened Little Dickens, made from the milk of the Brown Swiss cows grazing about the property. In winter the creamery hosts Snowy Grocery, on Sundays, 11 AM–2 PM, when local growers bring their goods for an off-season mini-farmers market. In May, hundreds of people attend Sugar House's Green Grass Getdown to watch the cows prance to pasture at the start of grazing season.

In Wilmington, **Pourman's Tap House** (518-946-6160; www.pourmanstaphouse.com; 8 Whiteface Memorial Highway), a new establishment in an old motel at the base of Whiteface Memorial Highway, has an après-ski following for the fried food and beer selection. The bartender at the **Wilderness Inn II** (518-946-2391; www.wildernessinnadk.com; 5481 NY 86)—the place bedecked year-round in holiday lights—knows how to make a fine mixed drink; you can order light fare in the bar.

Several area **farmers' markets** are exceptional places to find local produce, as well as crafts and other items. In Keene, it's Sundays from June through October on Marcy Field, between Keene and Keene Valley. Lake Placid's market is Wednesdays, June through October, at St. Agnes School's parking lot. Saranac Lake's is Saturdays, from June through October, at Riverside Park. Learn more about these farmers' markets as well as other ones in the Adirondacks at www.adirondackharvest.com.

✳ Entertainment

Nearly every town with a summer tourist draw presents outdoor or indoor musical programs. A few examples: if you're traveling to the High Peaks, in Jay, the **Jay Entertainment and Music Society** (518-946-7362; www.jemsgroup.com) presents music and other programs, on Saturday evenings in July and August at the village green. (It also puts on a winter coffeehouse series and other events as its Amos & Julia Ward Theater on the green, a 130-plus-seat structure that hosts concerts, art exhibitions, workshops, and other community events.) Saranac Lake has music on Friday nights at **Riverside Park**, on Lake Flower (518-891-1990; www.saranaclake.com). Lake Placid's summertime **Songs at Mirror Lake Series** (www.songsatmirrorlake.com) features local bands as well as regional ones, and happens at Mids Park on Main Street at 7 PM on Tuesdays.

Hill and Hollow Music (518-293-7613; www.hillandhollowmusic.com; 550 Number 37 Road, Saranac) hosts fine, mostly classical, music in an off-the-beaten-path corner of the Adirondacks. The organization also sponsors retreats and community dance programs, and it coordinates special events that weave dance with food and historical reenactment.

Lake Placid Sinfonietta (518-523-2051; www.lakeplacidsinfonietta.org; various locations, Lake Placid) was established almost a century ago as the house orchestra at the Lake Placid Club (the exclusive resort of Melvil Dewey, of the Dewey decimal system), where it played for the guests. Now the summertime chamber orchestra is a valued community resource, presenting free Wednesday night Pops in the Park concerts in the Paul White Memorial Shell in Mid's Park, overlooking Mirror Lake in the center of town (7 PM; bring a lawn chair) and concerts on stages across the Adirondack Park. On Sunday nights, the Sinfonietta performs its Symphony Series at the Lake Placid Center for the Arts.

Loon Lake Live (518-891-0757; www.loonlakelive.org) presents small classical ensembles in cozy spaces such as Loon Lake's Jewish Center, the Saranac Lake Free Library, and Harrietstown Hall, in Saranac Lake. Each concert, played in summer by fine professional musicians, is preceded by a master class with the performers.

Pendragon Theatre (518-891-1854; www.pendragontheatre.com; 15 Brandybrook Avenue, Saranac Lake), a highly successful local troupe, was awarded the prestigious Governor's Art Award, and has received acclaim for performances at the Edinburgh International Arts Festival, the Dublin Theatre Festival, and in Stockholm at the English-Speaking Theater. During the summer and fall, Pendragon puts on three or four shows in repertory format. During the school year and in winter, actors tour local classrooms and perform in regional venues.

There's exceptional theater at **Upper Jay Arts Center** (518-946-8315; www.upperjayartcenter.com; Recovery

THE ADIRONDACKS' BLUEGRASS BROTHERS

The Gibson Brothers, from Ellenburg, in the most northern reaches of the Adirondacks, are chart-topping bluegrass stars. Siblings Eric and Leigh Gibson, who grew up on their family farm, have repeatedly won top honors International Bluegrass Music Association awards, held in Nashville. They often play big-time shows and festivals, such as Mountain Stage and Grey Fox, but it's not unusual to see them perform in the North Country, usually to support regional causes. Check www.gibsonbrothers.com for tour information.

AWARD-WINNING BLUEGRASS STARS LEIGH AND ERIC GIBSON   COURTESY OF THE GIBSON BROTHERS

Lounge, Upper Jay Upholstery, NY 9N). Productions, directed by UJAC co-founder Scott Renderer (a former actor with the Wooster Group, in New York City), have included Michael Hollinger's *Opus*, Martin McDonagh's *The Pillowman*, Patrick Meyers's *K2*, and Sam Shepard's *True West*.

✳ Selective Shopping

Shopping here ranges from quirky to funky to woodsy, though you can find a Gap outlet on Lake Placid's main drag. But the real finds aren't skinny jeans or some other trend: look for a piece of Adirondackana, adventurewear or gear for your next excursion, a classic Adirondack chair or some other rustic furniture, or Adirondack art—painted or sculpted or written in these parts. Or, perhaps, it means picking up "Adirondack-scented"

lotions and candles at **Pure Placid** (518-637-3596; www.pureplacid.com) on Main Street, in Lake Placid.

In Keene, **Dartbrook Rustic Goods** (518-576-4360; www.dartbrookrustic.com; Routes 73 and 9N) is the place to go for authentic Adirondack rustic furniture and Great Camp–style accessories. You can't come to the High Peaks without a stop at this gorgeous showroom and its extension (**Dartbrook South**) just up the road.

The **Birch Store** (518-576-4561; www.birchstore.com; 1778 Main Street), in Keene Valley, sells hip shoes and apparel, cards, lotions, and interesting jewelry, combined with traditional Adirondack camp furnishings: blankets, birch-bark baskets and frames, chairs, balsam pillows, and wicker ware in a classy vintage storefront.

In Lake Placid, **Adirondack Decorative Arts & Crafts** (518-523-4545; 2512

Main Street) is a delightful four-story shop with a huge inventory—everything from birch bark–patterned table linens to one-of-a-kind twig furniture, oiled canvas jackets, bark lampshades, jewelry, Lightfoot's soap, and the best selection of woodsy cabinet hardware. **Adirondack Store and Gallery** (518-523-2646; www .theadirondackstore.com; 109 Saranac Avenue) is the place that launched the Adirondackana trend decades ago. If you're looking for anything—pottery, wrapping paper, doormats, sweaters, stationery, cutting boards—emblazoned with loon, trout, pinecone, or moose motifs, search no further. There's also an excellent selection of Adirondack prints, woodsy dinnerware and rustic furniture, and camp rugs and blankets.

Adirondack Trading Company (518-891-6278; 48 Broadway), in Saranac Lake, is a gift shop with plenty to choose from, especially cards, picture frames, and tchotchkes with bear and moose themes.

ANTIQUES In these parts, antiquing isn't what it was even a decade ago, but if you know where to look you can still find something special, even artifacts from logging and farming days and good-quality mass-produced nineteenth-century furniture. Redford glass, made in the Saranac River Valley during the early 1800s, is highly prized and hard to find. Vintage rustic furniture, which was discarded willy-nilly in the 1950s as camp owners modernized, is scarce, but Old Hickory pieces have the right look and feel and are widely available. If you're hunting for a pair of snowshoes or antlers to hang at home, you shouldn't have any trouble finding them here. Some shops stock wood engravings and hand-tinted etchings of Adirondack scenes. These prints—many of them by Winslow Homer or Frederic Remington—originally appearing in *Harper's Weekly*, *Every Saturday*, and other magazines—are affordable. Stereoviews of the grand hotels, postcards from 1910 to 1930, and photographs by George Baldwin, H. M. Beach, "Adirondack" Fred Hodges, and others are charming and not too dear. For photographs of the lakes, mountains, and resorts by Seneca Ray Stoddard, a contemporary of William Henry Jackson and Mathew Brady (all three Adirondack-born), you can expect to pay more, but the images are exceptional. Another name on the list for ephemera fans is Verplanck Colvin: mountain panoramas, diagrams, and maps from his 1870–90 surveys are meticulous curiosities.

In Bloomingdale, **Red Canoe Antiques** (518-897-8228; on Facebook; 1495 Route 3) sells antiques and vintage pieces for the home, camp, or porch.

Lake Placid has **Alan Pereske Antiques** (518-570-6933; 2158 Saranac Avenue), where you shouldn't be deceived by the small roadside storefront; there are rooms and rooms to see with quality oak, pine, and rustic furniture, paintings and prints of local interest, glass, toys, and ephemera. **Antediluvian Antiques & Curiosities** (518-523-3990; www .antediluvian.biz; 2022 Saranac Avenue) has fine art, tramp art, Victorian taxidermy, and lots of other funky stuff.

Bear Stump Antiques (51 Bloomingdale Avenue), in Saranac Lake, has Depression glass and other collectibles, used furniture, and funky pieces.

GALLERIES In Lake Placid, **Cornerstone Gallery** (518-569-7992; 2439 Main Street) sells Adirondack art and furnishings. **A Point of View Gallery** (518-578-5490; 6047 Sentinel Road) features photographer Rolf Schulte's work, but also that of other area artists.

In a former Methodist church in Keene, **Keene Arts** (914-309-7095; 10881 Route 73) hosts exhibitions, films, concerts, and workshops.

In Saranac Lake, there's **Adirondack Artists Guild** (518-891-2615; www .adirondackartistsguild.com; 52 Main Street), a gallery that features local artists of note, with changing exhibitions. **Small Fortune Studio** (518-891-1139; www

ADIRONDACK CAMERA OBSCURA

The seafoam-green shingled hut on Mark Ellis's Saranac Lake lawn, across from Lake Flower, is one of 50 or so freestanding camera obscuras in the world. First, a little background on how camera obscuras (Latin for "dark chambers") work: when light, which travels in a straight line, passes through a single point, or pinhole, into a dark, enclosed space, it projects an inverted image on the opposite side of the interior surface—exactly how the human eye operates. This optical effect has been used for art and entertainment through the ages. Some scholars think it played a part in Paleolithic drawings, and there's evidence the Old Masters used camera obscuras. Lenses were eventually incorporated to further focus the light, as well as mirrors added to better direct it. Ellis welcomes artists and photography buffs who want to visit by appointment; see www.adirondackcameraobscura.com or call (518) 891-2266.

.fortunestudio.com; 76 Main Street) is the base for venerable and internationally regarded painter Tim Fortune, who creates realistic Adirondack landscapes.

BOAT BUILDERS **Placid Boatworks** (518-524-2949; www.placidboats.com; 263 Station Street), in Lake Placid, is a top-quality carbon/Kevlar canoe-building outfit.

In Saranac Lake, a long line of boat builders has occupied the **Woodward Boat Shop** (518-891-3961; www.guideboats.com; 9 Algonquin Avenue) on the edge of town, including Willard Hanmer, whose boats are displayed at the Adirondack Experience. Chris Woodward learned the trade from Carl Hathaway, who was taught by Willard himself. He offers traditional wooden Adirondack guideboats with oars and yoke, plus boat repairs. **Spencer Boatworks** (518-891-5828; www.spencerboatworks.com; 956 NY 3, Bloomingdale Road) makes inboard wooden boats built along classic runabout lines, and does inboard-motor repairs.

BOOKS Along Lake Placid's Main Street, the **Bookstore Plus** (518-523-2950; www.thebookstoreplus.com; 2491 Main Street) is the place to go for Adirondack titles, not to mention any other book you're looking for. In Saranac Lake, you can find new titles and trading cards at the new **Book Nook** (518-354-8439; 74 Broadway).

CRAFT SHOPS AND WOODWORKERS In Jay, the **Alpaca Shoppe** (518-946-7886; www.alpacashoppe.com; 13036 NY 9N), which sells apparel, accessories, blankets, and yarns made from alpaca fiber.

Regional woodworkers create furniture in a variety of styles, from Shaker-inspired designs, to rugged sculptural pieces, to the straightforward Adirondack chairs that now come in an infinite range of permutations. Many studios are in private homes, so don't expect a large ready-made inventory. **L. Post Rustics** (518-647-5114; www.lpostrustics.com; 2056 Route 9N), in Au Sable Forks, is gorgeous, high-end stuff.

CREATIONS BY CERAMICIST BROOKE NOBLE, OF BLOOMINGDALE COURTESY OF BROOKE NOBLE

Swallowtail Studio (518-946-7439; www.swallowtailstudio.com; 55 Trumbulls Corners Road) is Wayne Ignatuk's award-winning sculptural furniture, with fine dovetailing and mortise and tenon construction. Spencer Reynolds's **Twisted Tree Rustics** (518-647-5378) has end tables, coffee tables, lamps, and wall art.

Dartbrook Rustic Goods, in Keene, is where you can find traditional Great Camp–style furniture (518-576-4360; www.dartbrookrustic.com; Routes 73 and 9N).

Bald Mountain Rustics (www .baldmountainrustics.com), at the Rooster Comb Inn, in Keene Valley, is base for Steve Bowers's funky rustic chairs, benches, beds, cabinets, tables, frames, and other items for the home.

JEWELRY Lake Placid's **Arthur Volmrich** (518-523-2970; 2413 Main Street) carries amusing earrings and necklaces mixing antique charms, buttons, and stones with modern components, turquoise bracelets and watchbands, and custom rings. **Darrah Cooper Jewelers** (518-523-2774; www.darrahcooperjewelers .com; 2416 Main Street) has fine jewelry, including sterling silver and gold charms and earrings representing miniature North Country objects like pack baskets, canoe paddles, and pinecones. **Spruce Mountain Designs** (518-523-9212; www.spruce-mountain.com) does Adirondack nature in sterling silver and gold.

Tupper Lake native Rachel King makes her **Earth Girl Designs** earrings in the Adirondacks (they're available on Etsy.com and at local shops such as Green Goddess, in Lake Placid, and the Community Store, in Saranac Lake).

CERAMICS AND SCULPTURE Architectural-design elements, folk-art figures, realistic wildlife, and modern concrete sculpture are just a few of the things shaped by Adirondack hands. **Brooke Noble**, of Bloomingdale, is a ceramicist who sculpts funky, interesting vessels.

INSTALLMENT AT THE JAY INVITATIONAL OF CLAY COURTESY OF BEN STECHSCHULTE

Jay Crafts Center (518-946-7824; www.jaycraftcenter.com; NY 9N) is Cheri Cross's showroom, with pottery lamps, bowls, vases, and dinnerware. **Youngs' Studio and Gallery** (518-946-7301; www.adirondackpottery.com; 6588 NY 86) features Sue Young's creative pottery (Raku and stoneware) and limited-edition etchings of Adirondack landscapes by her husband, Terry, plus a full range of other local crafts.

Matt Horner, of **Matt Horner Stone Work** (518-524-0879; www.matthorner stonework.com), in Keene, creates cool stone vessels and other pieces.

✳ Special Events

The following events (in chronological order) emphasize history, music, storytelling, crafts, and skills, or a combination of the arts.

SARANAC LAKE'S HOBOFEST IS A POPULAR NEW MUSIC EVENT COURTESY OF SHAUN ONDAK, WWW.SHAUNONDAK.COM

Saranac Lake Winter Carnival (518-891-1990; www.saranaclake wintercarnival.com), in February, is reputedly the oldest winter carnival in the country. On the shore of Lake Flower, there's an awesome ice palace, dramatically lit by colored spotlights each evening. Events include ski races, a parade, concerts, theater, and kids' activities.

Lake Placid Film Forum (518-523-3456; www.lakeplacidfilmforum .com), early in June, brings directors, screenwriters, and indie film producers together to meet and greet the public each year. Venues throughout Lake Placid, including the Palace Theater, show films from morning to midnight.

I Love Barbecue Festival (www.ilbbqf .com) is a barbecue competition sanctioned by the Kansas City Barbecue Society, with vendors and two full days of music by local bands at Lake Placid's speed skating oval at the beginning of July.

Jay Invitation of Clay & Ausable Valley Studio Tour (www.nortemaar.org; Randys Lane), in July, is an exhibition of regional and visiting ceramicists (with demos and workshops), plus a tour of artists' studios in the Ausable Valley.

Hobofest (www.hobofest.com), organized by local arts organizations, is a hip, daylong September event that brings talented musicians and the community together.

Oktoberfest (518-946-2223; www .whiteface.com), at the end of September, draws Bavarian culture lovers to Whiteface Mountain, in Wilmington, for oom-pah-pah and *gemütlichkeit*. There's live music and German-style dancing, a crafts fair, ethnic food and beer booths, children's activities, and rides on the ski area's chairlift to view the fall foliage.

CHAMPLAIN VALLEY

COURTESY OF JOHN DIGIACOMO,
WWW.PLACIDTIMESPHOTOGRAPHY.COM

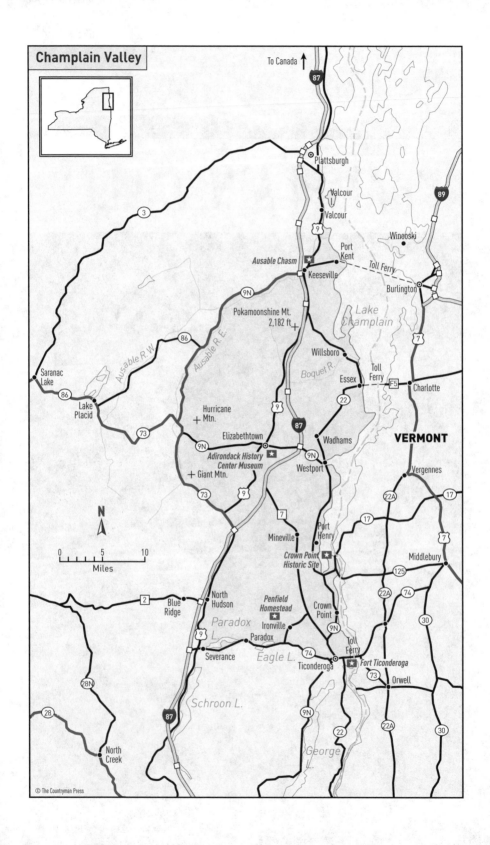

CHAMPLAIN VALLEY

his classic corridor is the right parts pretty, drowsy, and historical. Lake Champlain is a recreational playground in itself, but along its coast is an extensive trail network, meticulously preserved neighborhoods—including Essex, an entire village that's listed on the National Register of Historic Places—agricultural fairs, fascinating forts, and what remains of a once thriving iron-ore industry. This terrain may look a world away from the Adirondacks' interior, but it's a special place with a charm all its own, a pastoral setting with a lively farm-to-fork culture that's just a day trip away from the peaks and paddles in the heart of the park.

✳ To See

From carefully preserved nineteenth-century neighborhoods to first-rate professional theater, and from high-stakes fishing derbies to the "Grand Canyon of the Adirondacks," there's plenty to appreciate in this historic region.

ARCHITECTURE/ HISTORICAL DISTRICTS The Champlain Valley is rich in architectural sights. Beginning in the south, the town of Ticonderoga is a major destination for history lovers. **Fort Ticonderoga** is about 2.5 miles north of the village on NY 22, but you can find the crumbling walls and rusting cannons of **Fort Mount Hope** by exploring near the old cemetery on Burgoyne Street, not far from the village waterworks. At the head of the main drag, Montcalm Street, is a replica of **John Hancock's Boston home**, built by Horace Moses in 1926. Moses made his fortune with the Strathmore Paper Company and funded many town beautification projects, including the **Liberty Monument**, a bronze statue by Charles Keck that's in the center of the traffic circle across from Hancock House. **Pride of Ticonderoga** (518-585-6366; www.prideofticonderoga .org; 111 Montcalm Street), a nonprofit revitalization organization, offers a walking tour brochure that highlights Ticonderoga's bustling nineteenth-century industrial history.

Near today's bridge to Vermont, off NY 22, is Fort Crown Point; there were several fortifications along the lake harkening back to the French occupation of the Champlain Valley in the 1730s. **Crown Point State Historic Site** (518-597-4666; 21 Grandview Drive, Crown Point) sits on a thumb-shaped point that parts the waters, with Bulwagga Bay to the west and the long reach of the lake on the east. The sweeping view to the north once provided an ideal spot for guarding the territory. The French built a gargantuan stone octagon here in 1734, Fort St. Frederic, which was attacked repeatedly by the British from 1755 to 1758 and finally captured by them in 1759. Colonial forces launched their assault on the British ships in Lake Champlain from Crown Point in 1775. In 1910, the ruins of the French, British, and colonial forts were given to New York State. There's an excellent visitor center that explains the archaeology and political history of this haunting promontory through exhibits and audiovisual programs, and several miles of interpretive trails winding around stone walls and redoubts. The site is open May through October. Admission: $4 adults, $3 seniors, free for kids 12 and under.

West of Crown Point is **Ironville**, a well-preserved early-nineteenth-century community, with several white clapboard homes, a lovely church, numerous farm buildings,

EVERY ADIRONDACK VISITOR SHOULD GO TO FORT TICONDEROGA, A STRUCTURE AND CHUNK OF LAND THAT CHANGED THE COURSE OF AMERICAN HISTORY PHOTOGRAPH BY RICHARD TIMBERLAKE, COURTESY OF FORT TICONDEROGA

and peaceful, tree-shaded roads. On the way to Ironville, in Factoryville, you'll see the only octagonal house in the Adirondacks.

Historic markers erected by New York State abound along NY 22 as you approach **Port Henry**. The original settlement here supplied lumber for the forts at Crown Point and for Benedict Arnold's naval fleet. Later, the discovery of abundant iron ore shaped the town. Evidence of this prosperity appears in an ornate downtown block, elaborate churches, and the exuberant high Victorian **Moriah Town Office** building, formerly the headquarters of the Witherbee, Sherman & Co. Iron Company.

The Essex County seat is **Elizabethtown**, founded in the 1790s. The county courthouse complex is impressive, and about half a mile away are brick buildings built by the illustrious Hand family, which produced a dynasty of civic leaders and attorneys, including Supreme Court Justice Learned Hand. The well-preserved Greek Revival **Hand House** and the Hands' freestanding law office are on US 9, near the flashing light. About 8 miles east of Elizabethtown, along Champlain's shore, is **Westport**, which was first settled in 1770. Buildings from that era have all disappeared, but a few homes near the lake on Washington Street, off NY 9N and 22, were built in the 1820s. Westport was a vital port, shipping iron, lumber, wool, and other farm products before the Civil War, and a thriving summer community afterward. Download the *Walking Tour of Westport, New York* at www.westportheritagehouse.com.

The Adirondack community richest in architectural treasures is undoubtedly **Essex**. During the brief peaceful period between the French and Indian War and the American Revolution, William Gilliland, an Irish immigrant, bought up huge tracts of land along Lake Champlain. He envisioned a string of prosperous communities and by 1770 had established Essex. Unfortunately, the town lay smack in the path of General Burgoyne as British troops marched from Canada to Saratoga, and just a decade after the settlers arrived, their town was destroyed. By 1800, Essex was again thriving thanks to iron mining, stone quarrying, a tannery, shipbuilding, and other commerce. By 1850, the population of the town was 2,351, but when railroads came to eastern New York in the 1870s, fortunes changed for Essex and other lakeside towns. The 1850s marked the peak of the town's prosperity. Thereafter the population dwindled steadily to its current level of about 1,000 residents. Because of this decline and the lack of economic opportunities, there was little need for new housing; old buildings were preserved out of necessity. Today, Essex contains one of the most intact collections of **pre–Civil War buildings** in the Northeast. *Essex, New York Architecture: A Doodler's Field Guide* is sold at several local businesses. See www.essexonlakechamplain.com/architecture for details.

Continuing on NY 22, **Willsboro** and **Keeseville** contain many historic buildings. Keeseville has several homes made of buff-pink native sandstone that date back to the 1830s, and buildings in the full range of nineteenth-century styles from Dutch Colonial to Federal and Greek Revival to Gothic Revival and Romanesque. The **Stone Arch Bridge** over the Ausable River, built in 1842, is the largest single-span arch bridge in the country. From the bridge you can see the huge factory buildings that made horseshoe nails, an indispensable product of the nineteenth century. The former AuSable Horse Nail Factory Company offices is now home to Adirondack Architectural Heritage.

Maps with interpretive signs along the route are available through the **Champlain Valley National Heritage Partnership** (802-372-3213; www.champlainvalleynhp.org) and highlight historic sites, farmsteads, local industries, and vistas from Keeseville to Ticonderoga.

Adirondack Architectural Heritage (518-834-9328; www.aarch.org; 1745 Main Street, Keeseville) is a park-wide nonprofit organization devoted to historic preservation. Tours of public and private sites in summer and fall, lectures, and workshops are just a few of the programs and services it offers.

ARTS CENTERS AND ARTS COUNCILS The **Westport Heritage House** (westport heritagehouse.com; 6459 Main Street) hosts its annual Spirit of Place art show and organizes monthly artist studio tours during the summer.

The **Essex County Arts Council's events calendar**, at www.essexcountyarts.org, offers a region-wide listing of plays, concerts, craft fairs, and more.

A VINTAGE SCENE OF KEESEVILLE'S MAIN STREET COURTESY OF TED COMSTOCK, SARANAC LAKE

FILM CREDITS

During the silent-film era, the Adirondacks provided a backdrop for popular films, including *The Shooting of Dan McGrew, The Wilderness Woman, Glorious Youth*, and dozens more. The movie industry thrived for more than a decade in unlikely places such as Plattsburgh and Port Henry. Cowboy scenes were staged at Ausable Chasm, "Alaskan" trapper cabins were filmed in Essex County farmyards, and adventures supposedly set in South America, Siberia, and Switzerland took place along the valley. As the cameras rolled, Washington crossed the frozen Delaware—somewhere on the Saranac River. This region again had the spotlight in 2010 when Paul Sorvino, William Sadler, and Nick Wechsler came to the Champlain Valley to film *Mineville*, about a poor family of Irish immigrants who work in the iron-ore mines.

FORT TICONDEROGA Fort Ticonderoga (518-585-2821; www.fortticonderoga.org; 102 Fort Ti Road, off NY 22, Ticonderoga), high above Lake Champlain, is a must-see for Adirondack visitors. In 1755, the French built a fort, Carillon, on the site, and for the next quarter century, the stone fortification was a key location in the struggle to claim North America. The Marquis de Montcalm defended the site against numerous British invaders until 1758, when Lord Jeffery Amherst captured the fort. Ticonderoga was British territory until Ethan Allen and the Green Mountain Boys took the fort "in the name of Jehovah and the great Continental Congress" during the American Revolution. In the early 1800s, the Pell family acquired the ruins and fields where the soldiers once camped. Work was begun in 1908 to rebuild the barracks and parade grounds, making Fort Ticonderoga the nation's first restored historic site (in contrast, Colonial Williamsburg's restoration dates back to the 1930s). In more recent years, the Mars family, and today, a dynamic board of directors, have given the fort a makeover, adding a slick conference center, redesigning exhibits, rebuilding parts of the fortification, rehabbing the Pavilion (an 1830s hotel) at the King's Garden, and focusing on the art of creating historically accurate clothing, shoes, musical instruments, and other aspects of eighteenth- and nineteenth-century military life, which is popular with a burgeoning reenactment crowd.

Inside the barracks are exhibits on the French and Indian War and the American Revolution, from intricately inscribed powder horns to blunderbusses, cannons, and swords. Below the barracks is the subterranean kitchen, which supplied thousands of loaves of bread every day to the standing army. Beneath the walls, on a broad plain facing the lake, is the King's Garden, a gorgeous spot that's been cultivated for hundreds of years and is open for tours. The walled English-style garden dates back to the 1920s and is one of a handful of American places recognized by the Garden Conservancy. When driving the road to the fortification, stop the car and take a moment to read the monuments and absorb the battlefield, hallowed ground where thousands of soldiers fell. The fort is set in a spectacular spot with a magnificent view of the lake, but don't end your visit there. It's worth a side trip up Mount Defiance, near town, to get an even higher perspective. From the top of that hill, a show of British cannons so intimidated the officers at Ticonderoga and Fort Independence, a fort across the lake in Vermont, that colonial troops fled both strongholds (shots were never fired). Bring a pair of binoculars and a picnic lunch.

You can eat a meal at Fort Ti, and there's always action at the fort, including reenactments and tours with costumed interpreters, narrated boat cruises, demonstrations of musketry and cannon firing, and fife-and-drum drills. In late summer and fall, visitors can tackle a corn maze designed in the shape of the fort. The fort opens at 9:30 AM daily, May through October. Admission during peak season: $23 adults, $10 ages 5–12, senior and group discount.

MUSEUMS **Adirondack History Center Museum** (518-873-6466; www.adkhistory center.org; 7590 Court Street/US 9, Elizabethtown), open Memorial Day through Columbus Day, interprets regional history—mining, farming, trapping, logging, recreation—in its exhibits and showcases local artists in the Rosenberg Art Gallery. Its beautiful Colonial Garden of perennials and herbs is modeled after Hampton Court, in England. For Adirondack and genealogical scholars, an excellent library is open by appointment year-round.

In a rehabbed carriage-house next to the historic Moriah Town Hall, the **Iron Center Museum** (518-546-3587; 34 Park Place) explores the local iron-ore mining industry. Open mid-June through mid-October.

The **North Star Underground Railroad Museum** (518-834-5180; www.northcountry undergroundrailroad.com; 1131 Mace Chasm Road, Ausable Chasm) reveals the hidden history of the Champlain Line of the Underground Railroad through the stories of the fugitives who passed through northeastern New York on their way to freedom. Open seven days a week during the summer; closed Monday through Wednesday after Labor Day.

Penfield Homestead Museum (518-597-3804; www.penfieldmuseum.org; 703 Creek Road, Crown Point) has a sign in the front yard that makes an astonishing claim: the site purports to be the birthplace of the Electrical Age. In 1831, Allen Penfield used a crude electromagnet to separate iron ore from its base rock, thus testing electricity in an industrial application for the first time. Ironville today is a lovely, quiet spot so

COURTESY OF FORT TICONDEROGA

WHALLONSBURG GRANGE HALL

About a decade ago, a century-old grange in teensy Whallonsburg finally got the revival it deserved when locals pitched in to embrace it, update it, and use it once again as a hub of the community. Today, the Whallonsburg Grange Hall (518-963-7777; www.thegrangehall.info; 1610 Route 22) has a popular lecture series, is backdrop for classes and workshops, shows movies, hosts plays, music, and square dances, and can be rented for special events.

COURTESY OF NANCIE BATTAGLIA

different from its heyday as the center of a major iron industry from 1830 to 1880, when smoke from the smelters filled the skies and the clatter of rock crushers ceased only after dark. The complex, open June through Columbus Day, is an open-air museum dedicated to the local mines, forges, and old railroads, with an eclectic historical collection in the homestead itself, a white-clapboard Federal building, circa 1826. There's a self-guided walking tour of the 550-acre grounds that takes you for a nice hike in the woods to find remnants of the days of iron. In mid-August, the museum sponsors Heritage Day, a festival of traditional crafts and skills, with wagon rides and a chicken barbecue.

MUSIC **Otis Mountain Get Down** (www.otismountain.com), held in September, is a weekend of camping and wildly eclectic music—from old-time country to punk, and just about everything in between—in Elizabethtown. **Whallonsburg Grange Hall** (518-963-7777; www.thegrangehall.info; 1610 Route 22) hosts musical acts year-round. Westport's Thursday-night **Soundwaves** concert series (soundwaveswestport.tumblr .com) brings music to Ballard Park, overlooking Lake Champlain, every July.

THE SOUNDWAVES CONCERT SERIES BRINGS TUNES TO THE LAKESIDE VIEWS OF WESTPORT'S BALLARD PARK
COURTESY OF BEN STECHSCHULTE

Meadowmount School of Music (518-962-2400; www.meadowmount.com; 1424 Route 10, Westport) was founded by violin great Ivan Galamian. His summer music camp's alumni give a hint of the talent nurtured in the hills of the Boquet Valley: Yo-Yo Ma, Itzhak Perlman, Pinchas Zukerman, Michael Rabin, Lynn Harrell, Jaime Laredo, and Joshua Bell. Distinguished faculty, visiting artists, and promising students—ages eight through 30—give free concerts at the camp's 500-seat Ed Lee and Jean Campe Memorial Concert Hall at 7:30 PM on Wednesday, Friday, and Sunday; the annual scholarship-benefit concert features world-famous string and piano players. Meadowmount is a rare treasure, and if you're visiting the eastern Adirondacks, the programs are worth the drive.

THEATER **Boquet River Theatre Festival** (518-412-2525; www.brtf.com) presents original children's theater in August at the Whallonsburg Grange Hall.

Depot Theatre (518-962-4449; www.depottheatre.org; 6705 Main Street, Westport) has given Westport's Delaware & Hudson depot new vitality as home to a fine professional acting company. The former freight room—with air-conditioning—comes alive with four or five plays each summer.

Essex Theatre Company (518-526-4520; www.essextheatre.org), originally formed to showcase local talent, just celebrated its 25th year. Two productions

THE SUITCASE JUNKET AT OTIS MOUNTAIN GET DOWN, IN ELIZABETHTOWN COURTESY OF MALCOLM WATTS

OUT OF THIS WORLD

If you're keen to explore strange new worlds and boldly go where you haven't gone before, try Trekonderoga (www .startrektour.com), a celebration of the campy 1960s sci-fi hit that beams into Ticonderoga every August. Trekkies can tour carbon-copy layouts of the original series' sets, which have been used to film the *Star Trek New Voyages* fan-fiction serials in nearby Port Henry. There are also special guests—past pop-ins have included Nichelle Nichols (Uhura) and Walter Koenig (Chekov)—panels, screenings, and the most trektastic souvenir opportunity ever, a chance to have your photo snapped in the iconic Captain's Chair.

Just want to check out the sets? Regular tours are offered in spring, summer and fall at 112 Montcalm Street, in Ticonderoga. For times and tickets, visit www .startrektour.com.

are performed at Essex's Masonic Lodge every summer.

The **Adirondack Shakespeare Company** (518-803-HARK; www.adkshakes .org) offers a spring, summer, and fall lineup at venues throughout the area— but their favorite haunt in summer is the Scaroon Manor Amphitheater, a historic open-air performance space in Pottersville, near Schroon Lake.

✳ To Do

Roads with bucolic views for cyclists, a new trail network for hikers, a raging river, challenging rock faces for climbers, a vast lake for every watery or icy pursuit—the Champlain Valley is an all-season playground for outsdoorspeople.

BICYCLING This region offers scenic and historic destinations such as

DEPOT THEATER IS A PROFESSIONAL SUMMER ACTING COMPANY IN WESTPORT'S DELAWARE & HUDSON DEPOT COURTESY OF DEPOT THEATER

THE HIT LIST

Here's a sampling of iconic outdoor adventures for this region:

1. Tackle the Adventure Trail—with cable bridges, a cargo net climb, and edge walks—at Ausable Chasm (518-834-7454; www.ausablechasm.com), "the Grand Canyon of the Adirondacks."

2. Sign up for Champlain Area Trail's (CATS) springtime Grand Hike, a 12-mile hamlet-to-hamlet trek from Wadhams to Essex with a block party waiting at the end. CATS (518-962-2287; www.champlainareatrails.com) has a total of 42 miles of trails to explore.

3. One of the best "bang-for-your-buck" hikes in the region is Rattlesnake Mountain, in Willsboro—it's less than an hour to the summit's spectacular views. Note: this trail is on private land; the owners kindly allow access for hiking, but fires, camping, mountain bikes, ATVs, snowmobiles and hunting are forbidden.

4. A popular place to pedal for stunning views: across the Champlain Bridge, from Crown Point to Addison, Vermont.

5. Experience Fort Ticonderoga's (518-585-2821; www.fortticonderoga.org) Maze by Moonlight in October—a trip through a sprawling corn maze by flashlight, searching for hidden stations to complete the challenge.

HISTORIC AUSABLE CHASM

Willsboro Point, a thumb of land sticking into Lake Champlain, with great views coming and going.

A great resource for rides is *Bicycling the Scenic Byways of the Adirondack North Country* (www.bikethebyways.org), sponsored by the Adirondack North Country Association. Or download **Adirondack Coast Bikeways,** which outlines 14 loops in Essex County, at www.lakechamplainregion.com. For still more trip ideas, ask at regional bike shops; many sponsor guided rides or have their own maps of local favorites.

Always carry plenty of water and a good tool kit. *And wear a helmet!*

BOAT TOURS The season generally runs from early May through October; call ahead for a reservation.

Carillon Cruises (518-585-2821; www.fortticonderoga.org) gives historic tours around Fort Ticonderoga on the *Carillon*.

Lake Champlain Ferries (802-864-9804; www.ferries.com) shuttles cars between Essex, New York, and Charlotte, Vermont; Port Kent, New York, and Burlington, Vermont; and Plattsburgh, New York, and Grand Isle, Vermont. Passengers without cars are welcome.

CANOEING AND KAYAKING Paddling along the Adirondack coast is a grand adventure: **Lake Champlain** is big water, so expect big waves. When you're planning any trip, allow an extra day in case the weather doesn't cooperate. Remember that you're required to carry a life jacket for each person in the boat; lash an extra paddle in your canoe or kayak, too. Bring plenty of food and fuel, a backpacker stove, and rain gear.

The waterways from Old Forge to Lake Champlain make up a stretch of the 740-mile **Northern Forest Canoe Trail** (www.northernforestcanoetrail.org), which begins in Old Forge and ends in northern Maine. And the Boquet River allows for serious kayak action, though some stretches should be reserved for experts only.

CLIMBING Poke-O-Moonshine is an ice- and rock-climbing mecca. And those looking to brush up on skills in the off-season—or to determine if climbing is right for them—can visit the indoor **Crux Champlain Valley Climbing Center** (518-963-4646; www.pokomac.com/the-crux; 56 Rogers Lane), in Willsboro.

LAKE CHAMPLAIN IS A NATURAL WATERPARK COURTESY OF CARL HEILMAN II, WWW.CARLHEILMAN.COM

THE END OF BATS?

Caves inside the Adirondack Park, particularly in the Champlain Valley and in Hague, in Lake George, were once healthy hibernacula for little brown bats, the most common variety in the Northeast. But in the last decade, tens of thousands of these animals have died due to white-nose syndrome. When the bats become infected with this highly contagious fungus, their bodies attack it and slough it off, in the process destroying their wing membranes so they can't fly—or they fly so poorly that they can't feed.

Scientists are frantic to quarantine caves (spelunking in designated Adirondack caves is, at press time, off-limits), to study and understand how to combat the disease. The future for the little brown, among other species, is unclear.

WHITE-NOSE SYNDROME IS PUSHING LITTLE BROWN BATS TO EXTINCTION
COURTESY OF KEVIN MACKENZIE, WWW.MACKENZIEFAMILY.COM

DIVING With all the military action that happened on Champlain in the eighteenth and nineteenth centuries, there's bound to be remnants of ships and battles on the lake bottom. The **Lake Champlain Underwater Historic Preserve**, established in public trust for the people of New York and Vermont, allows divers public access to some of Champlain's shipwrecks. The hub of this preserve is the Lake Champlain Maritime Museum, on the Vermont side of the lake. Check out the museum's website, www.lcmm .org, or call 802-475-2022, for a list of shipwrecks, a map of the preserve, and diving rules and regulations. **Jones' Aqua Sports** (518-963-1150; www.divechamplain.com; 71 Klein Drive, Willsboro) is a dive outfitter, training center, and great resource.

FAMILY FUN In this region of the Adirondacks is a spectacular gorge of carved sandstone cliffs near the park's northeastern corner, and one of the country's oldest tourist destinations, dating back to 1870. At **Ausable Chasm** (518-834-7454; www .ausablechasm.com; 2144 Route 9, Ausable Chasm) you can hike through the formations, check out the rim walk, then ride a raft or inner tube down 2 miles of rapids. Open daily April through mid-November, the chasm costs $17.95 for adults and $9.95 for ages 5–12.

FISHING To get in the proper frame of mind for fishing, nothing beats a trip to a local fish hatchery. The **Essex County Fish Hatchery** (518-597-3844; Creek Road, Crown Point) is open every day. The only fish ladder in the park is on the **Boquet River** (School Street, Willsboro); if you time it just right in the fall, you can watch big salmon ascend the watery staircase.

The **Rotary Fishing Classic** (www.plattsburghrotary.org), sponsored by Plattsburgh Rotary Club, covers all of Lake Champlain, with weigh stations at Port Henry, Essex, and Willsboro, in June. Mega tournaments with big-bucks prizes and corporate

GOLD PRIZE

Each year anglers pull thousands of pounds of yellow perch from the ice of Lake Champlain, a golden prize that pulls hungry crowds into Champlain Valley diners and taverns during the dark days of winter—especially on Fridays during lent. The fillets are deep-fried to deliciousness, and often served with coleslaw and french fries. The following are a couple of joints where you just might catch a perch fry: **DeBro's On the Way Café** (518-597-3545; www.debrosonthewaycafe.com), in Crown Point, and **Hot Biscuit Diner** (518-585-3483; www.hotbiscuitdiner.com), in Ticonderoga.

sponsors, such as **LCI Father's Day Derby** and the **Lake Champlain International Fishing Tournament**, are listed on www.mychamplain.net.

There are many fishing guides and schools in the region, including **Adirondack-Champlain Guide Service** (518-963-7351; www.adirondackchamplainguideservice.com; 4629 Route 22, Willsboro).

GOLF Courses in the Champlain Valley are:

Cobble Hill Golf Course (518-873-9974; 8405 Route 9, Elizabethtown). Nine holes, par-35, 3,000 yards. Completed in 1897, great views of the High Peaks.

Harmony Golf Club, Port Kent Golf Course (518-834-9785; 95 North Street, Port Kent). Nine holes, par-30, 2,000 yards. Close to Vermont ferry.

Moriah Country Club (518-546-9979; 3122 Broad Street, Port Henry). Nine holes, par-32, 2,100 yards. Opened in 1900.

Ticonderoga Country Club (518-585-2801; www.ticonderogagolfcourse.com; 609 Route 9N, Ticonderoga). Eighteen holes, par-71, 6,300 yards.

Westport Country Club (518-962-4470; www.westportcountryclub.com; Liberty Street, Westport). Eighteen holes, par-72, 6,200 yards. Challenging; beautiful views.

Willsboro Golf Club (518-963-8989; 140 Point Road, Willsboro). Nine holes, par-35, 2,600 yards.

KIDS' CAMPS Among the kids' camps in this region is **Camp Dudley** (518-962-4720; www.campdudley.org; 126 Dudley Road), in Westport, the oldest continuously running summer camp in America. It began in New Jersey, it was moved to this site in the Champlain Valley in 1908, and its sister facility, Camp Dudley at Kiniya, is across the lake in Colchester, Vermont. Dudley's grounds total 500 acres and include 2 miles of shoreline, with all shapes and sizes of Adirondack-style buildings. Kids play soccer and tennis, swim and sail the lake, run the 200-meter outdoor track, swing golf clubs on the camp's driving range, and shoot on its rifle range. The late Academy Award nominee Burgess Meredith, who played Sylvester Stallone's boxing coach Mickey in the first three Rocky movies, was a Dudleyite.

Pok-O-MacCready Camps (800-982-3538; www.pokomac.com)—Pok-O-Moonshine for 120 boys; Camp MacCready for about the same number of girls—sit on Long Pond and approximately 350 acres in Willsboro. That's about all the sitting that happens here. Since Pok-O's founding in 1905 and its sister's arrival in 1967, more than 300 of its campers have gone on to become 46ers. The curriculum includes high-adventure canoeing, backpacking, and rock-climbing camps, with emphasis on self-reliance in the wilderness.

HIKING AND BACKPACKING The Adirondack woods are free of many of the natural hazards that you need to worry about in other locales. However, there's some poison ivy in the Champlain Valley region. Eastern timber rattlesnakes are occasionally found here; keep your eyes open when crossing rock outcrops on warm, sunny days. These snakes are quite shy and nonaggressive, but take care not to surprise one. And cases of Lyme disease have been recorded in the Adirondacks; hikers should take precautions against exposing themselves to deer ticks (*Ixodes dammini*) (see page 34).

For folks who wish to hike in the Champlain Valley, the **Champlain Area Trails** (CATS) comprise a new network of well-maintained routes in Essex, Westport, and Willsboro, that are continually being expanded and will eventually connect to other communities in the eastern Adirondacks, as well as in Canada and the Hudson Valley. The CATS have an informative website, www.champlainareatrails.com, with trail descriptions, maps, events, and more.

RUNNING **LaChute Road Runners** (www.lachute.us), based in Ticonderoga, sponsors a variety of area races, such as the **Montcalm Mile Run** down Ticonderoga's main street on the Fourth of July.

SAILING **Lake Champlain** offers good sailing in the midst of beautiful scenery and has marinas for an evening's dockage or equipment repairs. Sailing on island-studded waters can be tricky, since in the lee of an island you stand a good chance of being becalmed. Wind can whip shallow lakes into white-capped mini oceans, too. A portable weather radio should be included in your basic kit; Adirondack forecasts (out of Burlington, Vermont) can be found at 162.40 megahertz.

You can purchase Coast Guard charts for Lake Champlain. Some USGS topographical maps have troughs and shoals marked, but these maps are of limited use to sailors. Your best bet is to ask at boat liveries for lake maps, or to at least find out how to avoid the worst rocks.

For hardware, lines, and other equipment, **Westport Marina** (518-962-4356; www .westportmarina.com; 20 Washington Street, Westport) has a good selection of sailing supplies and rentals.

PLATTSBURGH'S MAYOR'S CUP REGATTA & FESTIVAL IS A TIME-HONORED NORTH COUNTRY TRADITION COURTESY OF ADIRONDACK LIFE

DRAMATIC VIEWS AND ENDLESS ICE DRAW NORDIC SKATERS FROM BOTH SIDES OF LAKE CHAMPLAIN COURTESY OF MARK BOWIE, WWW.MARKBOWIE.COM

WILD FOREST AREAS More than a million acres of public land in the park are designated as wild forest, which is open to snowmobile travel, mountain biking, and other recreation. In the Champlain Valley is the **Hammond Pond Wild Forest** between Paradox and Moriah, with old roads for hiking and ponds for fishing.

ARTISANS **Courtney Fair** (518-391-0371; www.courtneyfair.com; 6588 Main Street), in Westport, makes rustic three-legged stools and simple, elegant farm tables crafted from salvaged lumber.

SPAS AND WELLNESS **Lake Champlain Yoga and Wellness** (518-963-4300; www .lakechamplainyogaandwellness.com; 2310 Main Street), in Essex, offers yoga classes, physical therapy and massage, aromatherapy, meditation—the list goes on.

✳ Lodging

Don't expect many motels and hotels here, but there are a handful of bed & breakfasts and inns. While some visitors lodge across the lake in Vermont or commute from more populated spots in the High Peaks region, the finest way to explore and experience the Champlain Valley is to make the Adirondack coast your headquarters. Here are some highlights.

ELIZABETHTOWN

Get centered at **Namaste Inn Bed & Breakfast** (518-873-2332; www .namasteinnny.com; 12 Footbridge Lane), a restored turn-of-the-century Victorian in a serene setting with two guestrooms—each with a private bath—and a spacious meditation/yoga room. No small children or pets. $$.

Old Mill Bed & Breakfast (518-873-2294; www.adirondackinns.com/oldmill; 8214 River Street) was, in the 1930s and '40s, an art school led by landscape painter Wayman Adams. Now it's a lovely bed & breakfast. Four guest rooms, all with private baths, are in the main house. Breakfast, served on the enclosed patio that has a fountain as its centerpiece, is a highlight. $$.

Stoneleigh Bed & Breakfast (518-873-2669; on Facebook; 18 Stoneleigh

Way) is a beautiful Germanic-looking castle that was built in 1886 for local judge Francis Smith. The house, with babbling Barton Brook in front, has a fine library, as befits a country judge, and several porches and balconies under the tree-shaded, secluded grounds. Downstairs, there's a suite with private bath; upstairs, four spacious rooms share a bath and a half. A separate carriage house with private bath is also available. Ask about the ghost stories. $.

The **Woodruff House Bed & Breakfast** (518-873-6788; 8219 River Street) is an extraordinarily elegant but comfy offering on the Boquet River. The home, built in 1868, is getting rave reviews as a B&B. It has two rooms and two baths that can accommodate up to six people, delicious gourmet country breakfasts, and a quaint backyard that's ideal for an intimate wedding. $$.

ESSEX

The **Cupola House** (518-963-7494; www.thecupolahouse.com; 2278 Main Street), a prim and proper Greek Revival with wonderful two-story porches, has two handsome apartments that are just two blocks from the ferry to Vermont. Both have complete kitchens and full baths and access to the upstairs porch. A lakeside cottage accommodates two to six people. $$$

Essex Inn (518-963-4400; www.essexinnessex.com; 2297 Main Street) is a lovely lodging fronted by stately columns along Main Street, steps from the ferry landing. The inn, which has anchored the most historic hamlet in the park for two centuries—it's rumored to have been a hot hangout for spies during the War of 1812—has 10 beautifully renovated rooms and suites, all with private baths. Its tavern and restaurant (see page 188) are Adirondack rustic, serving meals made with ingredients from local farms. $$$.

LAKE MONSTER

Champ, the legendary monster of Lake Champlain—purported to look something like the Loch Ness Monster—has books, symposiums, T-shirts, and local businesses celebrating its existence. According to one Champ-camp website, the first recorded sighting took place when Samuel de Champlain explored these waters. Check out Bulwagga Bay's Champ sightings plaque, or join in on the fun at Port Henry's Champ Day, held every July.

MORIAH

The **Edgemont B&B** (518-546-4123; www.edgemontbandb.com; 284 Edgemont Road), a turn-of-the-century Victorian mansion overlooking Lake Champlain, has been converted into a charming bed & breakfast with five bedrooms—each with private bath—plus a game room, wraparound porch, and 20 acres of meadows and woods to explore. Billed as "cycling-friendly," the place provides covered parking for bikes, as

THE WOODRUFF HOUSE IS A CHARMING NINETEENTH-CENTURY BED & BREAKFAST IN ELIZABETHTOWN COURTESY OF THE WOODRUFF HOUSE BED & BREAKFAST

well as pumps and other tools, and route maps. $$.

WESTPORT

The **Inn in Westport** (518-335-1966; www .innwestport.com; 1234 Stevenson Road), which dates back to 1855, is just across from Westport's quaint Ballard Park. In this fully renovated historical landmark expect peaceful, refined public areas, a cafe, bookstore, and 10 comfortable rooms—with names such as William Shakespeare, Ayn Rand, Oscar Wilde . . . you get the idea—each with private baths. An outdoor deck allows views of Lake Champlain and, in summer, the bustle of this Adirondack port community. $$.

The **Westport Hotel** (518-962-4001; www.westporthotelny.com; 6691 Main Street), a spacious clapboard building, has been sheltering travelers since 1874, when the railroad came to Westport. Guests can choose from 10 rooms; most have private baths. The on-site Tavern is a welcoming space with good meals. People who are traveling without a car should note that there's daily Amtrak service to Westport, and many of the town's charms, from the Depot Theatre to the lakefront, are nearby. $$.

CAMPGROUNDS Public campgrounds operated by the **Department of Environmental Conservation** (518-402-9428; www.dec.ny.gov), are open from Memorial Day through Labor Day. Reservations can be made for a site in the state campgrounds by contacting **Reserve America** (800-456-CAMP; www .reserveamerica). Its website includes details about every state campground, as do the DEC's campsite listings on its site. If you can't find what you're looking for on Reserve America's site, contact the campground itself.

Ausable Point (518-561-7080; 3346 Lake Shore Road, Peru), on Lake Champlain. Showers, swimming, boat launch, wildlife refuge (a good place to explore by canoe), a great beach for kids.

Crown Point (518-597-3603; 784 Bridge Road, Crown Point), on Lake Champlain. Showers, boat launch, across

WESTPORT'S BALLARD PARK COURTESY OF JO ANN GARDNER

DAYS OF ORE

Approach the Adirondacks from the east—ferrying Lake Champlain from Charlotte, Vermont, to Essex, New York—and you'll see the park's big view of soaring palisades, deep-rooted port towns, and ancient metamorphic foothills that undulate beneath dense forests all the way to the High Peaks. Venture south among the iron-rich hills of Westport, Moriah, and Crown Point to find clues that you're in former big-time mining country—ore outcrops visible along lakeside cliffs were clues for eighteenth-century settlers. In 1776 Benedict Arnold used iron from Moriah to forge hardware for his Revolutionary War fleet on Lake Champlain. After the Champlain Canal opened in 1823, dozens of prospectors shipped ore to ready markets along the Hudson River. Soon local iron was finding its way into everything from transcontinental railroad tracks to cladding for battleships. Eastern Adirondack mines were supplying nearly 9 percent of the nation's iron ore by 1875.

By the early 1900s, most area mines were owned by Port Henry's Witherbee Sherman & Company, which posted agents in New York City to recruit immigrant labor. The company had 1,600 employees by 1917, mined 1.3 million tons that year, and was dispatching 450 railroad cars of ore weekly. Republic Steel took over operations in 1937 but shut down in 1971 when the mines became too deep to compete with open pits in the Midwest. In the end, two centuries of mining tallied 71 million tons of ore—enough to fill a train that could span the continent, and back—leaving an underworld of equivalent volume beneath the foothills of the southeastern Adirondacks. Eleven locomotives and 53 mine cars remain below in the now-flooded system.

Today it's fun to explore communities such as Ironville, Port Henry, Mineville, and Witherbee and watch (from the road) for sealed mineshafts, giant tailings piles, ruins of nineteenth-century blast furnaces, and European-style mansions built by skilled immigrants for wealthy iron investors. Bring a magnet when you visit lakeside parks—you'll be surprised how much iron you can find in a pail of beach sand.

Patrick Farrell's *Through the Light Hole* (North Country Books, 1996) provides a detailed history of eastern Adirondack iron mining. Visit Port Henry's **Iron Center Museum** (www.porthenrymoriah.com) and Ironville's **Penfield Homestead Museum** (www.penfieldmuseum.org) to see exhibits and artifacts.

—*Tom Henry*

from fort, next to good visitor information center.

Lincoln Pond (518-942-5292; 4363 Lincoln Pond Road, Elizabethtown). Swimming, showers, canoe or rowboat rentals; no powerboats allowed.

Putnam Pond (518-585-7280; 763 Putts Pond Road, Ticonderoga). Swimming, showers, canoe or rowboat rentals, boat launch, access to Pharaoh Lake Wilderness Area.

✳ Where to Eat

Warm-weather lakeside dining is a treat here, though there are exceptional eateries tucked inland. Always call ahead, as many of this region's businesses hibernate in winter.

DINING OUT

ELIZABETHTOWN

Deer's Head Inn (518-873-6514; www.thedeershead.com; 7552 Court Street), a rambling inn built in 1808 (the guest registry shows that Grover Cleveland and Benjamin Harrison stayed here), has changed hands through the centuries, but its current owners have transformed the oldest tavern in the Adirondacks into a hip hangout. The emphasis is now on local, regional, and sustainably produced

THE WESTPORT CHAIR

The Westport chair originated around 1903 in the town of the same name on the shore of Lake Champlain. Summer resident Thomas Lee canted the seat and back at several different angles, gathering family members to test each adjustment until he settled on a tilted 100-degree angle, satisfied he had created a relaxing place to sit. He later gifted the design to Harry Bunnell, a local hunting buddy, who got it patented in 1905 and manufactured chairs of hemlock and basswood until 1930. About this time, the Adirondack chair design began its rise, though its origin is a mystery. Westports stamped "Bunnell" can fetch well over $1,000 today.

—*Mary Thill, from "Angle of Repose,"* Adirondack Life

COURTESY OF NANCIE BATTAGLIA

foods, served for breakfast, lunch, and dinner. Cheese, pickled and fresh veggies, meat boards, craft cocktails, poutine, maple lemonade, and imaginative salads add a welcoming flair to regional dining.

ESSEX

The **Old Dock Restaurant** (518-963-4232; on Facebook; 2752 Essex Road), like many of the commercial establishments in Champlain Valley villages, is in a building dating back to the early nineteenth century. It was converted to a restaurant in the 1930s and overlooks the landing of the ferry to Vermont. In good weather, everyone sits outdoors to watch the clouds racing above Vermont's Green Mountains. Lunch and dinner offerings, served when the place is open, mid-May through Labor Day, are varied, although seafood dishes are favorites among diners. Boat slips are available for customers.

The tavern and restaurant at the **Essex Inn** (518-963-4400; www.essexinnessex.com; 2297 Main Street)

DEER'S HEAD INN IS AN ELIZABETHTOWN MAINSTAY COURTESY OF TED COMSTOCK, SARANAC LAKE

offer delicious dishes crafted with the freshest ingredients—the menu lists the local farms that contribute to each plate. The setting is upscale rustic, with fireplaces and handcrafted flourishes, and in summer diners can enjoy their meals on the front porch, overlooking the historic Main Street. The Stables provides a private dining option—with its own wine closet—for groups of up to a dozen.

PORT HENRY

The **Red Brick Cafe** (518-250-0993; villageinnandredbrickcafe.us; 1 Star Way) is a beautiful new destination in town, a historic building that's been artfully renovated with both indoor and outdoor seating. The menu is simple—soups, sandwiches, crepes—but the food is good and the coffee is a cup above.

TICONDEROGA

Charming **Libby's Bakery Cafe** (518-558-1522; www.libbysbakerycafe.com) opened on the ground floor of an attractively renovated old building on Montcalm Street a few years ago, the start of what Ticonderoga boosters hope will be a downtown revitalization. For breakfast,

THE RED BRICK CAFE IS A NEW DESTINATION IN PORT HENRY COURTESY OF RED BRICK CAFE

SMALL FARM RISING

The Adirondack Park is undergoing an agricultural rebirth, with the Champlain Valley as its epicenter. And in the half-decade since Ben Stechschulte's documentary *Small Farm Rising* spotlighted some of the pioneers of the area's local-foods movement, dozens of other small farms have put down stakes here.

Many of these are run by first-generation farmers who are implementing sustainable practices and offering Community Supported Agriculture shares to locals (locals pay an annual CSA fee and receive, in turn, weekly bounty from the farm). Most farms sell at area farmers markets—in the Champlain Valley it's behind the Adirondack History Center Museum, in Elizabethtown, on Fridays, 9 AM to 1 PM, May through October. Some also have farmstands or cafes, even Airbnb rentals.

Restaurants are increasingly incorporating local products, but for truly field-to-fork cuisine, look for pop-up farm dinners held around Essex County. These occasionally happen at The Hub on the Hill (518-418-5564, 545 Middle Road, www.hubonthehill.org), in Essex, an ag-related-business incubator with a store selling everything from **Reber Rock Farm's** sunflower oil to Dak and Dill's pickled garlic scapes to chic tea towels designed by a local artist.

AN AGRICULTURAL RENAISSANCE IS UNDERWAY IN THE CHAMPLAIN VALLEY, WITH THE RISE OF FARMS OPERATED BY FIRST-GENERATION FARMERS, SUCH AS FLEDGING CROW VEGETABLES, IN KEESEVILLE COURTESY OF BEN STECHSCHULTE, WWW.BENSTECHSCHULTE.COM

Essex is also home base to **Essex Farm**, the draft horse–powered CSA operated by Mark and Kristin Kimball. Her 2010 memoir, *The Dirty Life: A Memoir of Farming, Food, and Love*, describes the couple's challenging first years on the farm.

try a flaky croissant or a cinnamon roll with a proper cappuccino. Sandwiches come on house-baked bread, and the soups are made from scratch. Wine and small plates are served Thursday through Saturday evenings. Save room for baklava or another decadent pastry.

WADHAMS

Dogwood Bread Company (518-962-2280; www.dogwoodbread.com; 2576 Route 10) is a place folks go out of their way to visit. Everything is delicious here—bread and other baked goods, soups, sandwiches, and amazing wood-fired pizza (served Friday evenings year-round, and on Wednesdays during the summer).

A pretty stretch of Mace Chasm Road in Keeseville has emerged as another hot spot: **Mace Chasm Farm** has an on-site butcher shop selling cuts of beef, pork, and poultry, plus sausages and charcuterie (518-963-4169; www.macechasmfarm.com). Owners Courtney Grimes-Sutton and Asa Thomas-Train bring their food truck across the road to **Ausable Brewery** on Thursday evenings in summer; grab some tacos and a couple pints of the Badger brothers' latest brews and enjoy the pastoral view. **North Country Creamery**'s Clover Mead Café serves breakfast and lunch; most items feature the farm's cow's-milk yogurts and cheeses, which are also for sale in the adjoining farm store.

Events celebrating the local bounty are a great way to experience the region's reenergized farm scene. Highlights include the Adirondack Harvest Festival, in September, at the Essex County Fairgrounds, in Westport; Bike the Barns, in October (www.adirondack.org/bikethebarns); and the Essex County Cheese Tour, also in October.

A directory of Champlain Valley farms and related events can be found at **Adirondack Harvest**'s website, www.adirondackharvest.com.

MACE CHASM FARM, IN KEESEVILLE, IS PART OF A BURGEONING SMALL-FARM SCENE IN THE CHAMPLAIN VALLEY COURTESY OF BEN STECHSCHULTE

WILLSBORO

Turtle Island Cafe (518-963-7417; www.turtleislandcafe.com; 3790 Main Street) is in a 127-year-old former pharmacy overlooking the Boquet River. It hosts plenty of adventurers, often after they've hiked the Champlain Area Trails. Entrées are crafted from the best local, sustainable ingredients—the burgers are especially popular—and there's a great wine and craft beer selection. Live music on summer Fridays.

CASUAL BITES **Gunnison Lakeshore Orchard** (518-597-9222; 3196 Route 9N), in Crown Point, has delicious homemade cider donuts, as well as pies, fritters, gifts, and, of course, apples.

MICHIGANS

Meat as a condiment is all the rage here. A michigan, whose nomenclature is spiritedly debated, is basically a hot dog with chili—minus the beans or cheese—on top. The following are places where you can try this local favorite: **Gene's Michigan Stand** (518-546-7292), in Port Henry; the **Wind-Chill Factory** (518-585-3044), in Ticonderoga; and **Ethel's Dew Drop Inn** (518-963-8389), in Willsboro.

Beyond the Champlain Valley, Michigans are sold at **Skyline Ice Cream** (518-359-7288), in Tupper Lake; **Teddy's** (518-891-0422), in Bloomingdale; and **Whitebrook Dairy Bar** (518-946-7458), in Wilmington.

COURTESY OF MARK KURTZ, WWW.MARKKURTZ.COM

Pink Pig Cafe (518-962-8833; on Facebook; 2750 Essex Road), in Essex, features yummy baked goods, specialty coffee and smoothies, as well as a simple breakfast and lunch menu that highlights local produce. Pink Pig Cottage Antiques, with cool clothes, jewelry, furniture, and home decor, is attached.

Sitting down at **Foote's Port Henry Diner** (518-546-7600; 5 St. Patrick's Place) is an experience—it's stationed in a historic Ward Dining Car, the horse-drawn predecessor to modern food trucks that made the rounds at local mills in the 1920s. And the joint's from-scratch food is a scrumptious as the setting is unique.

Ticonderoga's **Hot Biscuit Diner** (518-585-3483; hotbiscuitdiner.com; 14 Montcalm Street) is a cheery, checked-tablecloth place. Everything's homemade, from blueberry muffins to the trademark biscuits. No credit cards.

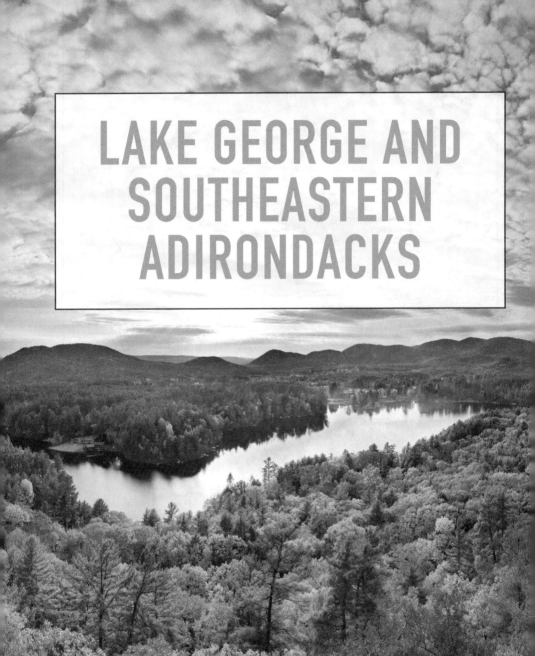

LAKE GEORGE AND SOUTHEASTERN ADIRONDACKS

COURTESY OF JOHNATHAN VESPER
WWW.WILDERNESSPHOTOGRAPHS.COM

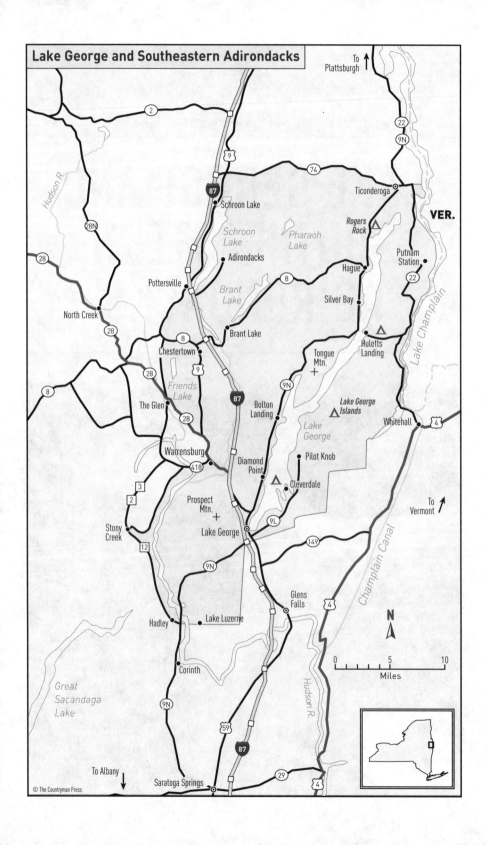

Lake George and Southeastern Adirondacks

To Plattsburgh

VER.

Lake Champlain

To Vermont

To Albany

Schroon Lake

Schroon Lake

Adirondacks

Pottersville

North Creek

Brant Lake

Brant Lake

Chestertown

Friends Lake

The Glen

Warrensburg

Diamond Point

Prospect Mtn.

Stony Creek

Hadley

Lake Luzerne

Corinth

Great Sacandaga Lake

Pharaoh Lake

Rogers Rock

Ticonderoga

Hague

Silver Bay

Huletts Landing

Tongue Mtn.

Bolton Landing

Lake George Islands

Lake George

Pilot Knob

Cleverdale

Lake George

Glens Falls

Putnam Station

Whitehall

Champlain Canal

Hudson R.

Saratoga Springs

© The Countryman Press

N

0   5   10
Miles

LAKE GEORGE AND SOUTHEASTERN ADIRONDACKS

Thomas Jefferson once described Lake George as "without comparison, the most beautiful water I ever saw"—an endorsement tourism officials have gotten mileage out of ever since—and every summer hordes of visitors agree. In winter this region is one big ghost town, but from Memorial Day to Labor Day it is vacation central, vast enough to encompass the touristy chaos of Canada Street plus posh lakeside compounds, friendly family resorts and even pockets of tranquility.

Look past the crowds and the tacky T-shirt shops, and you'll find Lake George village has plenty to offer—concerts and fireworks at the Shepard Park bandshell, a stellar art gallery, and the new Charles R. Wood Park, which hosts a packed calendar of festivals in summer. For kids, the village is a wonderland of mini-golf courses, waterslide parks and candy shops—and, of course, beaches.

Bolton Landing, a few miles north of Lake George village, is a popular resort town with eclectic boutiques, upscale eateries, and a New England seaside vibe.

If it's a quieter scene you're after, head to the eastern or northwestern shores, where communities like Hague, Cleverdale and Huletts Landing more than make up for their lack of tourist amenities with quiet charm and stunning, island-studded views.

A few miles west of Lake George, Lake Luzerne is more low-key but has a handful of worthwhile attractions, including Luzerne Music Center, the Adirondack Folk School, the Hudson River's Rockwell Falls and America's oldest weekly rodeo. To the north, Schroon Lake is a quaint and historical resort town. Architecture buffs should check out Warrensburg, which has a number of stately nineteenth-century homes, from Greek Revival and Gothic cottages to Italianate villas and Queen Anne mansions. The oldest building in Warrensburg, diagonally across from the car dealership on US 9, is a former blacksmith shop, dating back to 1814.

✳ To See

Painter Georgia O'Keeffe experienced Lake George with her photographer husband, Alfred Stieglitz, creating elemental scenes of water, rock, sky, and undulating hills. Although her Adirondack tenure was a short period in a long and productive life, this region launched O'Keeffe's signature style.

Today the Lake George region still has a lively arts scene, with galleries, museums, a folk school, an opera colony, even jazz in the park. The **Lake George Arts Project** (518-668-2616; www.lakegeorgearts.org; Old County Courthouse, 1 Amherst Street, Lake George) has had a lot to do with that, organizing sculpture shows, exhibiting artists with national renown in its Courthouse Gallery, offering free outdoor concerts in Shepard Park—including the **Lake George Jazz Festival**—and throwing fun, well-attended benefits such as the rock-and-roll and chili cook-off called **Bands 'n Beans** (March), as well as the **Black Velvet Art Party** (November), a celebration of terminal tackiness.

BEACHES There are dozens of beaches in the Lake George region—or more, if you consider the private strands that come with lakefront property. The following are a few notable spots for swimming, sunning and sandcastle-building.

In Lake George village, **Million Dollar Beach** is the largest and most popular beach in the region. The state-run facility includes a volleyball court, picnic tables with grills, changing rooms, and a public boat launch.

Bolton Landing has two public beaches. Though a little farther from the center of town, **Veteran's Memorial Park Beach** has a roomier sandy area, plus a playground, a basketball court, picnic tables, and a pavilion.

Schroon Lake's **Town Beach** is set among rolling hills at the base of a grassy park that's perfect for picnics.

CRAFTS AND FINE ARTS INSTRUCTION Adirondack Folk School (518-696-2400; www.adirondackfolkschool.org; 51 Main Street) is a non-accredited, not-for-profit continuing education campus along Lake Luzerne's Main Street, where adults can learn the traditional arts of the Adirondacks. Classes in quilting, building rustic furniture, weaving, blacksmithing, wood carving, playing banjo, caning chairs, braiding rugs, making soap, and basketry are offered year-round.

MUSEUMS The **Sembrich** (518-644-2431; www.operamuseum.org; 4800 Lake Shore Drive, Bolton Landing) celebrates the great Polish soprano Marcella Sembrich, but

THE ADIRONDACK FOLK SCHOOL, IN LAKE LUZERNE, TEACHES ADULTS THE TRADITIONAL ARTS OF THE ADIRONDACKS COURTESY OF THE ADIRONDACK FOLK SCHOOL

also Bolton Landing's early 1900s role as a mecca for opera stars and composers, such as Louise Homer, Samuel Barber, and Gian Carlo Menotti. From 1921 to 1935, Sembrich made her home here. Born Marcella Kochaska, she was a European sensation, and in 1898, she joined New York's Metropolitan Opera. Sembrich founded the vocal departments of the Juilliard School in Manhattan and the Curtis Institute in Philadelphia; during the summers, a select group of students came to her cottage studio. The studio, now a charming little museum, houses a collection of music, furniture, costumes, and opera ephemera related to Sembrich's brilliant career, including tributes from the leading composers of the day. Don't miss a stroll around the lakeside trail for a peaceful moment. Music lectures and a concert series are held in summer. Open mid-June through Labor Day.

In Lake George, in the old courthouse, the **Lake George Historical Association Museum** (518-668-5044; www .lakegeorgehistorical.org; 290 Canada Street) contains three floors of exhibits, including 1845-vintage jail cells in the basement. Also in Lake George is **Fort William Henry Museum** (518-668-5471;

ADIRONDACK SHOOTER

The home base of Carl Heilman II, one of the Adirondacks' most intrepid, talented landscape photographers, is Brant Lake, in the southern Adirondacks. Heilman's a regular contributor to regional publications, such as *Adirondack Life* magazine, and has published numerous coffee-table photography books on this region, plus instructional guides on how to capture these scenes. Order a book—his *Lake George* and *The Adirondacks* are gorgeous—check Heilman's tour schedule, or sign up for one of his popular photo workshops at www.carlheilman.com.

ADIRONDACK PHOTOGRAPHER CARL HEILMAN II OFFERS WORKSHOPS ACROSS THE PARK COURTESY OF CARL HEILMAN II, WWW.CARLHEILMAN.COM

www.fwhmuseum.com; Canada Street), a restored log fortress dedicated to French and Indian War history, with life-size dioramas, assorted armaments, and lots of action: military drills, musket and cannon firing, and fife-and-drum bands. The fort is open daily, spring through fall.

MUSIC On the second weekend in September, the Lake George Arts Project–sponsored (www.lakegeorgearts.org) **Lake George Jazz Festival**, in Shepard Park, is the place to be. The bands—often Latin or Afro-Caribbean stars—are top-notch, the vibe is cool, and the price is free. The arts project also sponsors music in the village park on summer nights, from reggae to blues to Celtic rock.

LAKE GEORGE'S VICARS ISLAND, DEER LEAP, AND SABBATH BAY POINT FROM HARBOR ISLANDS COURTESY OF CARL HEILMAN II, WWW.CARLHEILMAN.COM

Lake George Music Festival (518-791-5089; www.lakegeorgemusicfestival.com) is a nonprofit organization whose mission is to bring classical music to the residents of Lake George Village and surrounding communities. For a week in August, concerts featuring chamber groups and an orchestra are held throughout the southern Adirondacks—in churches, hotels, galleries, schools, and private homes. Performers include professionals from symphonies around the world, plus current music students, who learn from these master musicians.

IN SEPTEMBER, THE LAKE GEORGE ARTS PROJECT SPONSORS THE POPULAR LAKE GEORGE JAZZ FESTIVAL IN SHEPARD PARK COURTESY OF THE LAKE GEORGE ARTS PROJECT; PHOTOGRAPH BY ANDRZEJ PILARCZYK

Luzerne Music Center (518-696-2771; www.luzernemusic.org; 203 Lake Tour Road, Lake Luzerne) is a classical music summer camp and chamber music festival on a 20-acre campus on Lake George. Throughout the summer members of the Philadelphia Orchestra, on faculty at the camp, perform in a chamber music series and give lessons and master classes to campers, ages 11–18. Luzerne's CEO and president is Elizabeth Pitcairn (www.elizabethpitcairn.com), a Luzerne Music Center alumna, an international performer, and owner of the famous Red Mendelssohn, made by Antonio

TIME WARP

Nostalgia buffs can live their vintage-vacation dreams in Lake George village, which has some fabulous examples of midcentury architecture and style. These include the country's last remaining **Howard Johnson's** restaurant (518-668-5418; 2143 US 9); although at press time the fate of the iconic orange-roofed diner was unclear. Though parts of **Surfside on the Lake** (518-668-2442; www.surfsideonthelake.com; 400 Canada Street) were recently demolished and replaced with a sleek, retro-inspired hotel with a rooftop cabana bar, its 1940s-era neon sign was spared. At the other end of Canada Street, the **Tiki Resort** (518-668-5744; www.tikiresort.com; 2 Canada Street) lives on in full faux-Polynesian glory, complete with artificial palm trees, tropical cocktails and a hula-dancing dinner show. But the crème de la kitsch just might be the **Lake George Elvis Festival** (888-406-5885; www .lakegeorgeelvisfest.com), which brings King revelers to Lake George each spring for Elvis look-alike contests, tribute competitions, and vendors peddling black wigs, large sunglasses, and sparkly jumpsuits. Through the years, the event has had various organizers and names, but fans can agree that Lake George and Elvis are a natural fit.

COURTESY OF NANCIE BATTAGLIA

Stradivari in 1720. (Its myth is that the violin, purchased for $1.7 million for Pitcairn by her grandfather at a 1990 Christie's auction, is allegedly painted with the blood of the violin-maker's wife, who died in childbirth. The instrument, which inspired the film *The Red Violin*, received its name for its burgundy varnish.) The Luzerne Music Center's recitals and concerts are superb. Violinists Sarah Chang and Midori; composer John Corigliano, who wrote the score for *The Red Violin*; jazz musician Chris Brubeck; and quintet Canadian Brass are among the acclaimed guest artists who have performed at Luzerne Music Center.

Schroon Lake Arts Council (518-532-9259; schroonlakearts.com; Dock Street, Schroon Lake) presents evening summer concerts, open jams, and dance performances in the historic Boathouse Theater; its festival of folk music, storytelling, and rustic crafts is in August.

Seagle Music Colony (518-532-7875; www.seaglecolony.com; 999 Charley Hill Road, Schroon Lake) was established in 1915 by Oscar Seagle, famed baritone and voice teacher. Vocal music is still the primary program, with coaching and master classes in opera and musical theater for conservatory students and aspiring performers. Some Sunday evenings in the summer, the nondenominational Vespers concerts showcase exceptional choral singing; public concerts featuring scenes from opera and musical theater are held June through August.

NATURE CENTERS **Up Yonda Farm** (518-644-9767; www.upyondafarm.com; 5239 Lake Shore Drive, Bolton Landing) is a lovely lake-view property that functions as an environmental education center. The site, operated by Warren County, is busiest during warm weather, with guided trail walks, after-dark tours, and programs on birds, butterflies, and other beasts.

✳ To Do

Boating galore on a big lake, a historical underwater diving trail, hiking treks up and around one of the most picturesque landscapes in the East, an extreme zip-line, even waterparks and Frankenstein—this region of the park has something for everyone.

BICYCLING There are endless thrilling, gorgeous rides—on skinny tires or fat ones—in these parts. **Pack Forest** in Warrensburg is good for mountain biking. The **Warren County Bikeway** (www.warrencountydpw.com), an old trolley line linking Lake George village with Glens Falls, is a cyclist's dream. It's smooth, peaceful, and well engineered; there are picnic groves, historical markers, and, as you enter the Falls, an ice-cream stand. To the 9-mile bikeway you can add another nine of vehicle-free riding on the **Feeder Canal towpath**. For experienced road riders, climbing **Tongue** on two wheels is a thrill. One popular group trip goes from Bolton, on Route 9N, over the long ridge of Tongue, past Silver Bay to a dock below Ticonderoga. There *The Mohican* picks up weary riders and transports them to the village with a fascinating narrated voyage; there is also the option to do the trip in reverse, with a drop-off in Ticonderoga fol-

lowed by a bike ride back to Lake George. The **Bicycle Discovery Cruise** is 40 miles; the boat ride is five hours. For details and reservations contact Lake George Steamboat Company (518-668-5777; www .lakegeorgesteamboat.com). **The Hub** (518-494-4822; www.thehubadk.com; 27 Market Street), in Brant Lake, is a bike-repair shop, bar and cafe in one, and the starting point of group rides throughout the warmer months; new mountain-bike trails on the small mountain behind the shop should be open by summer 2018.

BOATING This is Lake George, where you've just got to cruise in your Chris-Craft, zip around in your motorboat, or

CLASSIC WATERCRAFT IN LAKE GEORGE COURTESY OF NANCIE BATTAGLIA

LAKE GEORGE STEAMBOAT COMPANY'S PADDLE WHEELER *MINNE-HA-HA*   COURTESY OF NANCIE BATTAGLIA

launch your paddleboat. Many state campgrounds have boat ramps. If you have a reserved campsite, there's no extra charge to launch a boat. Note also that motorboats (over ten horsepower) and sailboats (longer than 18 feet) used on Lake George must have a permit, available from local marinas or the **Lake George Park Commission** (518-668-9347; www.lgpc.state.ny.us).

BOAT TOURS The season generally runs from early May through October, and many cruises require that you call ahead for a reservation. **Lake George Shoreline Cruises** (518-668-4644; www.lakegeorgeshoreline.com; 2 Kurosaka Lane, Lake George) has several boats to choose from, including the adorable *Horicon* and the 400-passenger *Adirondac*. Narrated daytime and dinner cruises, as well as wedding cruises, are available, and the *Horicon* departs at dusk on Thursdays in the summer for fireworks cruises. **Lake George Steamboat Company** (518-668-5777; www.lakegeorgesteamboat .com; 57 Beach Road, Lake George) has three enclosed boats, including the huge *Lac du Saint Sacrement* and the paddle wheeler *Minne-ha-ha*. The *Mohican* makes a four-and-a-half-hour tour of the lake daily in the summer and navigates through the Narrows among the islands each afternoon. In addition to providing shorter narrated trips, boats have cocktail lounges and offer dinner, pizza, and moonlight cruises with live music. Wedding packages are also available.

KIDS' CAMPS **Adirondack Camp** (518-547-8261; www.adirondackcamp.com), at Putnam Station, uses Lake George as its playground. On Pilot Knob, **YMCA Camp Chingachgook** (518-656-9462; www.camp.cdymca.org; 1872 Pilot Knob Road) has been a fixture since 1914. If you're in the Adirondacks during July or August, and would like to visit a particular camp with your prospective happy camper, you should call ahead. See www.acacamps.org for a list of camps accredited by the American Camp Association.

CANOEING AND KAYAKING Where to begin with Lake George? It's vast, it's gorgeous, and the possibilities are endless.

THE WILD SIDE OF LAKE GEORGE

The 70,000-plus-acre **Lake George Wild Forest** is an adventurer's playground. Great hikes surround the lake, especially if you like to climb for rewarding vistas. On the west shore the **Tongue Mountain Range** in the town of Bolton, with First and Fifth Peaks, to name a couple, has numerous vantage points. The summit of the range's **French Point Mountain** shows most of Lake George. To the water's east is **Black Mountain**, the highest rise in the wild forest. Although the fire tower atop it is off-limits, from the rocks to the tower's north is a spectacular 180-degree view of Lake George. Farther south, **Sleeping Beauty**, where peregrine falcons nest on the cliffs, gives a great perspective of the southern basin.

Motorboats rule the southern reach of the lake, but there's quiet water, too. Islands in the **Narrows** are inviting, especially during the off-season, before the Fourth of July and after Labor Day. This stretch is good for kayaking, though beware of waves that can swell to four-foot whitecaps in stormy weather. A tamer paddle, from **Northwest Bay Brook** through the wetlands and into **Northwest Bay**, which opens into Lake George, is a pretty trip. In Hague, **Jabe Pond** is an easy body of water to sample in a canoe, and it's accessible by car.

PILOT KNOB RIDGE PRESERVE IN THE LAKE GEORGE WILD FOREST COURTESY OF CARL HEILMAN II, WWW.CARLHEILMAN.COM

It's dangerous to paddle from the congested village waterfront, where Jet Skis buzz and powerboats throw huge wakes. Head a few miles outside of town to **Lake George Kayak Company** (518-644-9366; www.lakegeorgekayak.com; 5 Boathouse Lake), the go-to spot in Bolton Landing for canoeing, kayaking, and stand-up paddling. The shop provides lessons, guided trips, rentals, and more. The **Adirondack Mountain Club Member Services Center** (518-668-4447; www.adk.org; 814 Goggins Road, Lake George) also offers spring, summer, and fall canoe workshops in different locations for all ages; guided canoe tours are available for women, youth, and Road Scholar (formerly Elderhostel) groups.

When you're planning any trip, allow an extra day in case the weather doesn't cooperate. Remember that you're required to carry a life jacket for each person in the boat; lash an extra paddle in your canoe, too. Bring plenty of food and fuel, a backpacker stove, and rain gear.

ISLAND TIME

There are more than 200 islands in Lake George, ranging from wind-swept rocks sprinkled with blueberry bushes to 30-acre havens with lean-tos. Many are state-owned, available for camping and picnicking for a fee and by reservation. The campsites are in great demand but you can book an island for a day for $10 when you get a permit from the Department of Environmental Conservation office on River Road in Warrensburg or at Long, Narrow, or Glen Island ranger stations. Day permits (good from 9 AM to 9 PM) can be purchased at Norowal Marina, in Bolton Landing.

DIVING No amount of wishful thinking could turn the chilly Adirondack depths into crystal-clear Caribbean seas, but there is plenty to discover beneath the waves in Lake George. In fact, it's the site of New York's first underwater heritage preserve and home to numerous eighteenth- and nineteenth-century shipwrecks. The **Underwater Blueway Trail** promotes and preserves New York's maritime heritage. Shipwrecks and rock formations are marked with buoys, guiding lines, and signage. Volunteers for this project included members of **Bateaux Below**, historians and divers who created dive sites in Lake George beginning in the 1990s. Among the preserve sites at the bottom of Lake George are the 52-foot British artillery ship *Land Tortoise*, which sank in 1758; the Sunken Fleet of 1758, smaller bateaux used to transport troops; and the 45-foot tour boat *Forward*, which sank in the 1930s and is used today as an underwater classroom for beginner divers.

The following dive operators can help with equipment, instruction, and maps to the Underwater Blueway Trail: **Adirondack Scuba** (518-884-4056; www.adirondackscuba.com; 98 Rowland Street, Ballston Spa), **Diamond Divers** (518-505-3483; www.diamonddiverslg.com; Bolton Landing), **Dive Center** (518-562-3483; www.divechamplain.com; 4013 US 9, Plattsburgh), and **Jones' Aqua Sports** (518-963-1150; www.divechamplain.com; 71 Klein Drive, Willsboro). The **New York State Divers Association** (www.scubany.org) also provides scuba diving resources.

FAMILY FUN **Adirondack Extreme Adventure Course** (518-494-7200; www.adirondackextreme.com; 35 Westwood Forest Lane, Bolton Landing) is a high-wire treetop adventure park, with ropes courses and zip-lines for adults and kids. Open Spring through Fall.

Not extreme enough for you? The new **Eagle Flyer** zip-line (518-685-3317; www.adkeagleflyer.com; 5 Mill Road, Lake George) sends intrepid guests soaring 1,000 vertical feet down French Mountain, reaching speeds of 50 miles per hour.

PADDLING AT THE BASE OF DEER LEAP COURTESY OF CARL HEILMAN II, WWW.CARLHEILMAN.COM

Lake George Floating Classroom (518-668-3558; www.lakegeorgeassociation.org), aboard the *Rosalia Anna Ashby,* allows kids and their families to learn about Lake George and how to keep its water clean. Open July and August.

House of Frankenstein Wax Museum (518-668-3377; www.frankensteinwaxmuseum .com; 213 Canada Street, Lake George) is just one of those Lake George places you've got to visit. Open Memorial Day through Halloween.

Magic Forest (518-668-2448; www.magicforestpark.com; US 9, Lake George), for little ones, has rides and games, plus Santa's Hideaway, and is home to the Adirondack Park's only diving horse, Lightning. Open Memorial Day through Labor Day.

Natural Stone Bridge & Caves (518-494-2283; www.stonebridgeandcaves.com; 535 Stone Bridge Road, Pottersville) features caves, with a mineral shop, a playground and picnic area, and mining activities. Open daily mid-May through mid-October, and for self-guided snowshoe tours mid-December through March, weather permitting (closed Christmas Day).

Water Slide World (518-668-4407; www.waterslideworld.net; US 9 and 9L, Lake George) has a wave pool, water slides, and bumper boats. Daily mid-June through Labor Day.

FISHING To get in the proper frame of mind for fishing, nothing beats a trip to a local fish hatchery. In the southeastern Adirondacks, the **Warren County Fish Hatchery** (518-623-5576; 145 Echo Lake Road, Warrensburg) is open daily, with a nice picnic grove.

GOLF In this region the courses include:

Bend of the River Golf Club (518-696-3415; 5 Park Avenue, Hadley). Nine holes, par-35, 2,700 yards. One of the first courses to open in the spring.

Cronin's Golf Resort (518-623-9336; www.croninsgolfresort.com; Golf Course Road, Warrensburg). Eighteen holes, par-70, 6,100 yards. Cottages on-site.

Queensbury Country Club (518-793-3711; www.queensburygolf.com; 907 NY 149, Lake George). Eighteen holes, par-70.

The Sagamore Golf Course (518-743-6380; www.thesagamore.com; Federal Hill Road, Bolton Landing). Eighteen holes, par-70, 6,900 yards. Designed by Donald Ross; challenging and lovely.

Schroon Lake Municipal Golf Course (518-532-9359; 36 Club House Drive, Schroon Lake). Nine holes, par-36, 3,000 yards.

HOUSE OF FRANKENSTEIN WAX MUSEUM, ON CANADA STREET, IS A LAKE GEORGE INSTITUTION COURTESY OF NANCIE BATTAGLIA

Top of the World (518-668-3000; www.topoftheworldgolfresort.com; 441 Lockhart Mountain Road, Lake George). Eighteen holes, par-71, 6,044 yards.

MINIATURE GOLF Historians take note: miniature golf was reputedly launched in downtown Lake George at the intersection of Beach Road and US 9 in the early years of the twentieth century. Lake George remains a hotbed of Adirondack minis, and close to a half-dozen courses are nearby. You can try **Around the World in 18 Holes**

IN BOLTON LANDING, THE SAGAMORE'S 18-HOLE DONALD ROSS–DESIGNED COURSE IS CHALLENGING AND PICTURESQUE COURTESY OF THE SAGAMORE RESORT

(518-668-2531; www.aroundtheworldgolf.com; 72 Beach Road), **Lumberjack Pass Mini Golf** (518-793-7141; www.lumberjackminigolf.com; 1511 US 9), **Goony Golf** (518-668-2589; www.goonygolf.com; US 9), **Pirate's Cove** (518-668-0493; www.piratescove.net; 2115 NY 9N), and **The Fun Spot** (518-792-8989; www.thefunspot.net; 1038 US 9).

HIKING AND BACKPACKING Take note: rattlesnakes live in the Tongue Mountain Range near Lake George; keep your eyes open when crossing rock outcroppings on warm, sunny days. These eastern timber rattlers are quite shy and nonaggressive, but try not to surprise one.

The **Adirondack Mountain Club** (518-668-4447; www.adk.org; 814 Goggins Road, Lake George) offers hikes with naturalists, fall foliage hikes, wilderness overnights, and weekends for women, youth, and senior citizens.

HORSEBACK RIDING AND WAGON TRIPS A legacy of the dude-ranch days in the southeastern Adirondacks, **Painted Pony Rodeo** (518-696-2421; www.paintedponyrodeo .com; 703 Howe Road, Lake Luzerne) presents professional rodeo competitions Wednesday, Friday, and Saturday nights in July and August, rain or shine. This is the home of the country's oldest weekly rodeo, complete with trick riding and roping, clowns and novelty acts. There's more equine action, particularly riding through acres and acres of trails, at the all-inclusive **Stony Creek Ranch Resort** (518-696-2444; www .stonycreekranchresort.com; 465 Warrensburg Road, Stony Creek), formerly 1000 Acre Ranch. **Bennett Riding Stable** (518-696-4444; www.bennettsridingstable.com; 1410 Lake Avenue, Lake Luzerne) gives trail rides. **Circle B Ranch** (518-494-4888; 771 Potter Brook Road, Chestertown) does wagon, sleigh, and hayrides. **Rydin'-Hy** (518-494-2742; www.rydinhy.com; Sherman Lake Road, Warrensburg) gives trail and sleigh rides, although at press time owners were rebuilding the main lodge after a major fire. **Saddle Up Stables** (518-668-4801; www.ridingstables.com; 3513 Lake Shore Drive, Lake George) offers trail rides.

Public horse trails include the **Lake George Trail System** on the east side of Lake George, off Pilot Knob Road, with 41 miles of carriage roads on an old estate, plus lean-tos. Also, **Lake Luzerne**, off NY 9N near Lake Luzerne hamlet, on Fourth Lake, has a campsite with a corral, and 5 miles of trails on state land that connect with many miles of privately owned trails. **Pharaoh Lake Horse Trails**, in the Pharaoh Lake Wilderness Area, east of Schroon Lake, include 12 miles of sandy woods roads, plus lean-tos.

RACES AND SEASONAL SPORTING EVENTS **New Year's Day Polar Plunge Swim** (518-668-5323; www.lakegeorge.com; Shepard Park, Lake George) means hundreds of brave swimmers plunging into icy Lake George.

Prospect Mountain Road Race (www.adirondackrunners.org; Prospect Mountain Memorial Highway, Lake George) sends runners 5.5 miles uphill all the way, in April or early May.

Adirondack Distance Run (www.adirondackrunners.org) is a 10-mile road race along Lake Shore Drive, in June or early July.

Lake George Triathlon (www.adkracemanagement.org) is an Olympic-distance race, in early September.

Adirondack Marathon Distance Festival (www.adirondackmarathon.org), a 26-mile run around Schroon Lake, plus shorter races, happens in September.

SAILING **Lake George** offers great sailing in the midst of beautiful scenery and has marinas for an evening's dockage or equipment repairs. Sailing on island-studded waters can be tricky, since in the lee of an island you stand a good chance of being becalmed. Wind can whip shallow lakes into white-capped mini oceans, too. A portable weather radio should be included in your basic kit; Adirondack forecasts (out of Burlington, Vermont) can be found at 162.40 megahertz.

You can purchase Coast Guard charts for Lakes George and Champlain, but not for most of the small interior lakes. Some USGS topographical maps have troughs and shoals marked, but these maps are of limited use to sailors. Your best bet is to ask at boat liveries for lake maps, or at least find out how to avoid the worst rocks.

For hardware, lines, and other equipment, **Yankee Boating Center** (518-668-2862; www.yankeeboat.com; 3578 Lake Shore Drive, Lake George) is well stocked with everything from the essentials to brand-new boats. It also has a sailing school and rents day sailers and cruisers (the rental center is at 518-668-5696; 3910 Lake Shore Drive, Diamond Point). **Y-Knot Sailing** (518-656-9462; www.yknotsailing.org), at YMCA Camp Chingachgook, in Pilot Knob, offers sailing instruction, races, and workshops to sailors of all levels of experience and physical ability.

SCENIC HIGHWAY Near Lake George village, **Prospect Mountain Veterans Memorial Highway** (518-668-5198; www.visitlakegeorge.com; off US 9) snakes up a small peak to a terrific 100-mile view stretching from the High Peaks to Vermont and the Catskills. It's a state-operated toll road open daily from late May through the fall.

CROSS-COUNTRY SKIING AND SNOWSHOEING **Caroline Fish Memorial Trail** (518-494-2722; Dynamite Hill, NY 8, Chestertown) is lighted for night skiing.

Friends Lake Cross-Country-Ski and Snowshoe Center (518-494-4751; www.friendslake.com; 963 Friends Lake Road, Chestertown) has 32 kilometers of groomed trails; with rentals and instruction.

Rogers Rock State Campground (518-623-1200; NY 9N, Hague) has 10 kilometers of groomed trails; part of the trail is lit for night skiing.

Schroon Lake Ski Trails (518-532-7675) allows backcountry skiing in Pharaoh Lake and Hoffman Notch wilderness areas.

Warren County Trails (518-623-5576; Hudson Avenue, Warrensburg) is a 16-kilometer network along the Hudson River.

WILDERNESS AREAS These portions of the Forest Preserve are 10,000 acres or larger and are open to hiking, cross-country skiing, hunting, fishing, and other similar pursuits, but seaplanes may not land on wilderness ponds, nor are motorized vehicles welcome. In this region, there's **Pharaoh Lake.** Forty-six thousand acres; east of Schroon Lake hamlet. Extensive trail system, 36 lakes and ponds, lean-tos, views from Pharaoh and other nearby mountains.

WILD FOREST AREAS More than a million acres of public land in the park are designated as wild forest, which is open to snowmobile travel, mountain biking, and other recreation:

Lake George. On both the east and west shores of the lake, north of Bolton Landing. Contains the Tongue Mountain Range on the west, and the old Knapp estate, with 40-plus miles of hiking and horse trails, on the east.

Wilcox Lake. West of Stony Creek. Miles of snowmobile trails and old roads; ponds and streams for fishing.

✳ Lodging

Old-school mom-and-pop motels and housekeeping cabins abound on some stretches of this region, and many of them are just fine. But the following are mostly B&Bs—listed here because they're lovely launch pads for whatever your Adirondack adventure may be.

BOLTON LANDING

Boathouse Bed & Breakfast (518-644-2554; www.boathousebb.com; 44 Sagamore Road) was once the summer home of Gold Cup–winning speedboat racer George Reis. This extravagant place offers an absolutely perfect backdrop for a relaxing getaway on Lake George. There are four rooms and a suite, which has an enclosed sun porch, in the main house, all with Jacuzzi tubs, mini fridges, and either queen- or king-size beds. The separate carriage house has two suites, both with lake views, king-size beds, and gas fireplaces. Guests can swim the lake, park their boat in the available slips, soak in the hot tub on the dock, and have free access to the fitness center and indoor pool at the nearby Sagamore. Included in the price are family-style, three-course hot breakfasts. Open February–October. No children. $$$.

The **Sagamore Resort** (518-644-9400; www.thesagamore.com; 110 Sagamore Road) is the latest incarnation of a grand hotel that has overlooked Lake George here for more than a century. Completed in 1883, the grand lodge has survived two fires and weathered the Depression, but gradually declined during the 1970s. Today the Sagamore is the pride of the community. The elegantly appointed

THE SAGAMORE RESORT, FIRST BUILT ON THIS SPOT IN 1883, IS STILL A GRAND HOTEL COURTESY OF THE SAGAMORE RESORT

THE GRAND SAGAMORE RESORT, OVERLOOKING LAKE GEORGE, IS PACKED WITH AMENITIES COURTESY OF THE SAGAMORE RESORT

public areas include a conservatory with lake views, eight restaurants—everything from fine dining to seafood to pub fare (Mister Brown's Pub is a longtime favorite)—a spa, and a gift shop. Guests have 390 deluxe units to choose from, including suites, hotel bedrooms, lakeside lodges, and executive retreats with lofts. The list of Sagamore amenities is impressive: indoor and outdoor pools; a recreation center with miniature golf, a rock-climbing wall, and basketball courts; outdoor tennis courts; playground; a beautiful sandy beach; docks for guests' boats; endless activities and programs for kids; and a Donald Ross–designed championship golf course 2 miles away. Open year-round; in January check out the Glacier Ice Bar and Lounge. $$$–$$$$.

CHESTERTOWN

The **Chester Inn Bed & Breakfast** (518-494-4148; www.thechesterinn.com; 6347 Main Street) is one of Chestertown's beautiful homes listed on the National Register of Historic Places—this

Greek-Revival inn dates back to 1837. Beyond the grand hall, with its mahogany railings and grain-painted woodwork, are four second-floor guest rooms with private baths. Guests are welcome to explore the 13-acre property, which has gardens, a horse barn, a smokehouse, and an early cemetery. $$.

The **Fern Lodge** (518-494-7238; www .thefernlodge.com; 46 Fiddlehead Bay Road) is an over-the-top spot to get away from it all. All five rooms at the lodge on Friends Lake have king-size beds, massive stone fireplaces, lake or mountain views, mini refrigerators for chilling wine or cheese boards, spacious baths with steam showers, Jacuzzi tubs, and elegantly rustic decor. Ramble, cross-country ski, or snowshoe the surrounding 70 acres, stroke the lodge's kayaks out on the lake, hang around the impressive great room, shoot pool, watch movies in the private theater, relax in the sauna, get fit in the exercise room, or browse the fine wine cellar for the perfect vintage. Enjoy an evening boat tour with historic narrative and wine; in the morning linger over an extraordinary

THE FERN LODGE, A FRIENDS LAKE GETAWAY, OFFERS ADIRONDACK-STYLE LUXURY COURTESY OF THE FERN LODGE

multicourse breakfast with homemade breads and pastries. An outdoor hot tub and lakeside lean-to are new. $$$$.

Friends Lake Inn (518-494-4751; www.friendslake.com; 963 Friends Lake Road) has been a hostelry of one kind or another for about 150 years, although its first tenants, the tannery workers, would marvel to see people rather than cowhides soaking in the enormous wooden hot tub outdoors. Today there are 17 comfortable rooms and small suites—either traditional- or Adirondack-style—all with private baths, some with steam showers and whirlpool tubs, fireplaces, private entrances and balconies, and views of Friends Lake. Truly an inn for all seasons, guests can enjoy cross-country skiing or snowshoeing on 32 kilometers of groomed trails in the winter, fishing in the spring, swimming and mountain biking in the summer, and hiking in the fall. $$$$.

Landon Hill Bed & Breakfast (518-494-2599; www.landonhillbnb.com; 10 Landon Hill Road), a lovely Victorian home set among rolling hills on a country lane, is peaceful and comfortable. An oak spiral staircase leads you to the four guest rooms upstairs (all with private baths), and downstairs are a handicapped-accessible guest room and bath. Before the sit-down breakfast, have coffee and homemade muffins by the woodstove. Then, after filling up on quiche and fresh fruit, explore the property's 89 acres, or head for Chestertown's historic district or the nearby Schroon River for fishing and canoeing. Guests can unwind in the outdoor hot tub. Landon Hill is just a mile from I-87, the Northway, so it's a convenient jumping-off spot for further adventures. $$.

DIAMOND POINT

Canoe Island Lodge (518-668-5592; www.canoeislandlodge.com; 3820 Lake Shore Drive) first opened in 1946, after Bill Busch financed the down payment on Canoe Island with a couple hundred bushels of buckwheat. The 21-acre, 25-building complex now offers all kinds of family vacation options, from quaint log cabins to modern suites and private chalets. There are clay tennis courts, a sandy beach on Lake George, hiking trails, and numerous boats to sail. Perhaps the best part of a stay here, though, is the chance to enjoy the lodge's very own three-acre island, about three-quarters of a mile offshore. Shuttle boats take guests to the island where they can swim, snorkel, fish, sunbathe, and explore a beautiful, undeveloped part of the lake. The lodge accommodates about 175 people at peak capacity. Rates include breakfast and dinner plus most activities. Open mid-May–mid-September. $$$.

HAGUE

Ruah Bed & Breakfast (518-543-8816; www.ruahbb.com; 9221 Lake Shore Drive) has amusing legends: this stone mansion was reputedly designed by Stanford White. Part of the estate was won in a poker game. The Lake George monster—the biggest hoax ever seen in northern New York—was created in the studio of the original owner, artist Harry Watrous. Bing Crosby and Jack Dempsey slept here. Stay at Ruah and you'll have your own stories to tell—about visiting a lovely inn overlooking a beautiful lake. The four guest chambers are upstairs and have private baths. The Queen of the Lakes is spacious, with access to the balcony and views from every window. Common areas downstairs include a vast living room with a fieldstone fireplace and an antique grand piano, a cozy library, and an elegant dining room. To give you an idea of the scale of this inn, the veranda stretches across the front of the house and measures about 80 feet long. Open May through January. $$.

Trout House Village Resort (518-543-6088 or 1-800-368-6088; www.trouthouse.com; 9117 Lake Shore Drive), one of the few four-season resorts on the quiet northern portion of Lake George, is a handsomely maintained complex of log cabins and chalets. Many of the cabins have fireplaces, decks, and complete kitchen facilities. There are numerous suites and rooms in the main lodge, all with private baths. There are canoes, rowboats, sailboats, kayaks, bikes, and even a nine-hole putting green for guests. Trout House is a short distance from historic sites such as Fort Ticonderoga and Crown Point, while the Ticonderoga Country Club—a challenging eighteen-hole course—is just up the road. By January, the atmosphere changes from that of an active resort to a quiet country inn, perfect for cold-weather getaways. $$$.

WARRENSBURG

Alynn's Butterfly Inn (518-623-9390; www.alynnsbutterflyinn.com; 69 NY 28) is a classic country-style bed & breakfast, and its huge wraparound porch invites lingering on a summer day to watch real butterflies visiting the garden. All five of the inn's guest chambers are named after native butterflies and have private baths. A full gourmet breakfast is served daily. $$.

The Glen Lodge B & B (800-867-2335; www.theglenlodge.com; 1123 NY 28) is an eco-friendly bed & breakfast (all its power comes from wind) on the Hudson. Its proprietors run Wild Waters rafting company, so ask about the "Rafting and a Room" package. The place can accommodate up to 16 guests in five nice, simple Adirondack-style rooms. $$.

Ridin'-Hy Ranch (518-494-2742; www.ridinhy.com; 64 Ridin'-Hy Ranch Road), an 800-acre complex on Sherman Lake, is a western-style dude ranch that has everything, from a private intermediate-level downhill ski area to rodeos. There are 50 miles of trails for snowmobiling, cross-country skiing, or horseback riding. In warmer weather, guests can swim, row, or water ski on Sherman Lake, and fish in Burnt Pond or the Schroon River. At press time, the owners were rebuilding the main lodge after a major fire. Accommodations include chalets, lodge rooms, and motel units. Rates include all meals and activities. $$$.

Seasons B&B (518-623-3832; www.seasons-bandb.com; 3822 Main Street) has remarkable regional history. James Fenimore Cooper was a guest at this house, which belonged to Peletiah Richards, when he was researching *The Last of the Mohicans*. In those days, the home was among the grandest in town, and later, in the nineteenth century, this place became more elaborate still with the addition of an Italianate tower, a long veranda, and a bay window. Details inside the Seasons include an ornate fireplace in the parlor, a coffered wood ceiling above the staircase, and antiques throughout. There are four guest rooms upstairs, two with private baths and two that share a bath. A section of the house that dates from 1820 has been renovated into a handsome suite with a corner

ROUGHING IT THE EASY WAY

Fancy the idea of balsam-scented slumber without the hassle of setting up camp or the back pain of sleeping on terra too-firma? A handful of glamping—glamorous camping—operations offer luxurious canvas tents outfitted with cushy beds and other creature comforts.

Adirondack Safari (518-240-8010; www.adirondacksafari.com; 346 Schroon River Road, Warrensburg) is an upscale campground, with 40 furnished tents, including suites that sleep four to six guests; an outdoor lounge with live entertainment on weekends; and well-maintained bathroom and shower facilities. Campsites come with a charcoal grill and fire pit; food is not included. $$.

With six canvas cabins tucked in the woods, **Camp Orenda** (518-251-5001; www.camporenda.com; 90 Armstrong Road, Johnsburg) offers a quieter experience. Nightly rates include three meals a day from the backcountry kitchen, including a to-go lunch. Guests can use the camp's canoes and kayaks on Garnet Lake; go on a rock-climbing, white-water rafting or hiking adventure; or arrange for an in-tent massage. $$$.

Posh Primitive (518-744-6808; www.poshprimitive.com; 435 Stock Farm Road, Chestertown) prides itself on its garden-to-table cuisine and Great Camp–inspired accents in its four rustic platform tents. The friendly hosts provide everything you need for a pampered vacation in the great outdoors. $$$.

fireplace in the living room, queen-size bed, and spacious bathroom with double whirlpool and separate shower. Guests are treated to a fine, full breakfast. $$.

CAMPGROUNDS The **Department of Environmental Conservation** (518-402-9428; www.dec.ny.gov) operates public campgrounds in the park, all of which are open from Memorial Day through Labor Day. Many campgrounds open earlier, and some operate late into the fall.

Facilities at state campgrounds include a picnic table and grill at each site, water spigots for every ten sites or so, and lavatories. Camping is allowed year-round on state land, but you need a permit to stay more than three days in one backcountry spot or if you are camping with a group of more than six people. You may camp in the backcountry provided you pitch your tent at least 150 feet from any trail, stream, lake, or other water body.

Reservations can be made for a site in the state campgrounds by contacting **Reserve America** (800-456-CAMP; www.reserveamerica), though DEC

campgrounds will cheerfully take you on a first-come, first-served basis if space is available. Before July 4 and after September 1, it's usually easy to find a nice site without a reservation.

Eagle Point (518-494-2220; US 9, Pottersville). On Schroon Lake. Boat launch, showers, swimming.

Hearthstone Point (518-668-5193; 3298 Lake Shore Drive, Lake George). On Lake George. Showers, swimming.

Lake George Battleground (518-668-3348; 2224 US 9, Lake George). Historic site. Showers. An easy walk to downtown and docks where tour boats leave from.

Lake George Islands (numerous sites on Narrow Island, 518-499-1288; Glen Island, 518-644-9696; and Long Island, 518-656-9426; 18 Boathouse Lane, Bolton Landing). Access by boat, tents only, swimming. No dogs allowed.

Luzerne (518-696-2031; 892 Lake Avenue, Lake Luzerne). On Fourth Lake. A Hudson River impoundment. Showers, swimming, canoe and rowboat launch. No powerboats allowed.

Rogers Rock (518-585-6746; 9894 Lake Shore Drive, Hague). Historic site on Lake George. Boat launch, access to rock-climbing cliff.

Scaroon Manor (518-494-2631; 8727 NY 9, Pottersville). On Schroon Lake. A historic resort that appeared in the 1957 movie *Marjorie Morningstar*, it was turned into a campground in 2011. All campsites and facilities are designed to be accessible to those with wheelchairs or walking aids.

✳ Where to Eat

Beware of tourist traps that dish out pricey, lousy dinners. The following are among the consistently good restaurants where you can expect a delicious meal, cool ambience, and character.

DINING OUT

BOLTON LANDING

The **Algonquin**—referred to as "The A" by locals—on Lake George's Huddle Bay, is a bustling lakeside institution that continues to attract waterfront diners all summer long (518-644-9442; www .the algonquin.com; 4770 Lake Shore Drive). Many guests prefer to arrive by boat. The menu's "beginnings" range from chicken wings to baked brie. Dinner entrées include chicken parmigiana, horseradish-encrusted salmon, and strip steak. Burgers, sandwiches, and flatbread pizzas round out the menu. The newly remodeled Topside Grille features the Hacker-Craft Bar, with decor inspired by the iconic mahogany boats; make a reservation online. Open mid-April through Columbus Day.

Cate's Italian Garden Restaurant and Bar (518-644-2041; www .catesitaliangarden.com; 4952 Lake Shore Drive) has a spacious covered terrace between the building and the street that hums with the activity of a popular tourist town. Inside, the small dining room is crowded with art posters and Italian bric-a-brac. The pizza here is the best around, or you can get full-course dinners. Specials are consistently delicious—be sure to ask about the lasagna.

Chateau on the Lake (518-644-7094; www.blchateau.com; 15 Allens Alley), a boutique inn and fine dining restaurant, has gotten rave reviews since opening in 2014. This intimate spot is tucked away from the hubbub of Lake Shore Drive and serves traditional European-style dishes with innovative twists. For starters, the New Zealand lamb lollipops are a popular item. Entrées on the seasonal menu may include chicken forêt with a cremini mushroom risotto or pistachio-encrusted salmon; foie gras can be added to any entrée. Try "Casual Wednesdays" in summer for lakeside music, small bites and drink specials.

CHESTERTOWN

Main Street Ice Cream Parlor & Restaurant (518-494-7940; www .mainstreeticecreamparlor.com; 6339 Main Street) is a family affair: Bruce and Helena Robbins took charge of the popular eatery from Bruce's parents a few years back. The cheerful yellow building was originally a schoolhouse, and the place is chockablock with local antiques and vintage signs. The focal point of the big, bright dining room is an old-school soda fountain dishing out sundaes, floats, and malts, and the kitchen makes fantastic deli sandwiches, homemade soups, and burgers. The signature Pack Basket is roast turkey with trimmings and cranberry mayo on a kaiser roll, and

THE SEXIEST CHEESE IN AMERICA

Turns out *Esquire* magazine's pick for "the sexiest cheese in America" is made in this region, in Thurman, by Nettle Meadow Farm (518-623-3372; www .nettlemeadow.com). Bring the famous Kunik or the farm's other artisan cheeses home as a delicious Adirondack souvenir.

DISTILLERIES

There's a bit of a boozy renaissance in the Adirondacks, as a fine crop of distilleries has taken root across the park. In the Lake George area, there's Springbrook Hollow Farm Distillery (518-338-3130; www.springbrookhollow.com; 133 Clements Road, Queensbury), with a line of vodka, liqueurs, gin, moonshine, and bourbon—crafted with local ingredients—served up in a beautifully restored nineteenth-century barn, and Lake George Distilling Company (518-639-1025; www.lakegeorgedistillingcompany.com; distillery is at 11262 Route 149, Fort Ann; store is at 329 Canada Street, Lake George) producing a variety of whiskey, bourbon, and rye. See adkcraftbev.com for more regional distilleries, as well as breweries and wineries.

other sandwiches are on Rock Hill Bakehouse bread, the best in the region.

LAKE GEORGE

Adirondack Brewery & Pub (518-668-0002; www.adkbrewery.com; 33 Canada Street) has a North Woods atmosphere, with log pillars and twig screens, creating just enough privacy and sense of separation from the bar. You may wish to remain at the bar, however, given the tasty assortment of beers brewed on the premises. The kitchen does well with a variety of thick sandwiches and handmade burgers. Takeout—even the beer, in growlers—is available.

Bistro LeRoux (518-798-2982; www.bistroleroux.com; 668 Route 149) is a little off the beaten path. The bistro's earthy space is chef-owned and -operated, serving tasty fare that's a world away from the heavy Italian offerings of other area restaurants: the seasonal menu might include cabernet-braised short ribs, summer vegetable risotto, or seared wild salmon with chili verde. Truffled *pommes frites* are a perennial favorite.

The **Boathouse** (800-853-1632; www.lakegeorgeboathouse.com; 3210 Lake Shore Drive), during high season (it's closed in winter), often has watercraft lined up waiting to put in at the restaurant's dock. The food—mostly seafood, chicken, and steak, all well prepared—is worth the wait, whether you arrive by Chris-Craft or car. The main dining room is a massive post-and-beam boathouse built in the late 1800s, once owned by *New York Times* publisher Adolph Ochs; umbrella-shaded seating is available dockside.

The Inn at Erlowest (518-668-5928; www.theinnaterlowest.com; 3178 Lake Shore Drive) is one of the fanciest places around. This mansion, more than a century old, was a private residence until 1999. The Erlowest is now a four-star bed & breakfast, with several elegant private dining rooms—stunning backdrops for romantic dinners, small receptions, and other affairs. The lake itself isn't visible from the restaurant, but guests can sip pre-meal cocktails on the mansion's Grand Patio, where there's a gorgeous Lake George view. The inn's wine list is extensive; meals are truly an experience. The menu changes each season, but starters may include pork tenderloin with a charred nectarine, blood orange, and fig conserve, or seared wild striped bass with beet puree, summer peas, and radish. Lighter fare—charred tomato risotto, vegetable spring rolls—is served in the cozy Library Bar.

Pizza Jerks (518-668-4411; www.pizzajerks.com; 59 Iroquois Street) serves fresh, delicious pies; management swears its pies are better than anyone else's, or your money back. You can get grub to go, have it delivered, or eat in. Try the specialty pizzas, such as the Tree Hugger (fresh spinach, tomato, pesto, garlic, and onions), the Carcass (every meat in the shop), or the Rasta (Jamaican jerk-seasoned chicken, onion, green peppers, and pineapple). They'll even make any pizza vegan, using non-dairy cheese.

RACHAEL RAY'S ADIRONDACK ROOTS

Celebrity chef and talk show host Rachael Ray grew up in Lake George—she even worked at the local HoJo's—and keeps a woodsy and unassuming cabin in Lake Luzerne. Ray's grandfather Emmanuel was a stonemason who emigrated from Sicily to the Adirondacks. "[He and his brothers] worked their way up the Hudson and came upon Lake George and they loved it," she says. "In Ti, there was a community of Italian immigrants." There, he raised his ten kids, helped rebuild Fort Ticonderoga, and worked on the area's most elaborate homes until moving in with Ray's family in Lake George.

"His friends would come over and I'd sit up with all these old men as they smoked their pipes and played cards all night. My grandfather knew everything about everything: cooking, landscaping, gardening. He taught my mother everything he knew. Anyway, I was really bored when I went to school because I had been hanging out with 80-year-old Italian men, and I thought they were my contemporaries."

That experience has much to do with Ray's cooking, influenced by flavors she's familiar with—"lots of olive oil and garlic." She says, "My style of cooking definitely reflects where I live. It's very earthy. I lean toward the woodsy spices: rosemary and thyme and sage. And I chop everything big. Most of the year I live off one-pot menus like soups and stews and things that go hand in hand with living on a mountain."

Adirondack cuisine, says Ray, is more about atmosphere than ingredients. Of Jacobs and Toney Meat Store of the North, in Warrensburg, Ray says, "A sandwich there is twice the size of your skull!" Also in Warrensburg, Oscar's Smoke House—"their smoked turkey breast, their Canadian bacon; everything they make is fantabulous. That horseradish cheddar, give me a break with that!" And she says everyone should put a calendar from Martha's Dandee Cream ice cream, in Queensbury, on the fridge and plan "what flavors are what days so you don't miss the peanut butter days or the black raspberry days."

LAKE LUZERNE

UpRiver Cafe (518-696-3667; 29 Main Street) has good lunches and delicious dinners that might include almond-encrusted salmon in a Thai peanut sauce, or duck in a maple glaze. The deck out back overlooks a pretty stretch of the Hudson River with Rockwell Falls, and diners agree this is a sweet spot for fine fare. Luzerne Music Center concert-goers can bring their Monday night series tickets and get a discounted meal.

POTTERSVILLE

Café Adirondack (518-494-5800; www .cafeadirondack.com, 5 Olmstedville Road) specializes in "Coastal Southern cuisine." Recommended in summer are the cafe's Seafood Diablo and its seared tuna, not to mention reservations—though it recently moved to roomier digs across town. Open year-round, with a chef's tasting menu on Thursdays in the off-season.

SCHROON LAKE

Pitkin's (518-532-7918; 1085 Main Street) is the place where the homemade soups are thick with real stuff (not cornstarch), pies are heavenly, and coleslaw and potato salad and barbecue are the best around. This place might look like your average North Country diner with giant lake trout and panoramic photos on the walls, but you get authentic Texas-style barbecue, beef brisket, pork ribs, and chicken. On Thursday nights in the summer, the line of ribs fans snakes down Main Street in anticipation of the Thursday rib special, and the wait for a table can be long.

Sticks & Stones Wood Fired Bistro & Bar (518-532-9663; www

.adirondacksticksandstones.com; 739 US 9) is the place to go with a crowd who can't agree; there's something for everyone. Traditionalists will find their steak done just right; creative salads, such as spinach and quinoa with apples in a lemon balsamic dressing, satisfy light eaters; and any of the delicious wood-fired pizzas can be made gluten-free. The roomy dining space has a warm, Adirondack lodge feel, with peeled log beams, a stone fireplace, and antler chandeliers.

STONY CREEK

Stony Creek Inn & Restaurant (518-696-2394; www.stonycreekinn.net; 6 Roaring Branch Road), a 150-year-old southern Adirondack institution, is one of the neatest spots between Saratoga and Montreal. On Sunday night, when there's great Mexican food and local bands, the joint really jumps. Long a mecca for square dancers and the home stage for the regionally renowned Stony Creek Band, the inn presents everything from straight country to rhythm and blues, old-time fiddle to salsa. All this music—a rarity in the area—attracts crowds from far and wide. Along with hot tunes, the Stony Creek Inn has some unbeatable specials: check out Wednesday's "Five & Dime" menu, which offers $5 burgers (in all sorts of styles) and $10 dinners (roast tip sirloin, chicken, etc.). Open May to December. Closed Mondays and Tuesdays.

CASUAL BITES In Bolton Landing, **Frederick's** is open year-round and is a casual lakeside spot for cocktails (518-644-3484; www.fredericksrestaurant.com; 4870 Lake Shore Drive). The **Hague Firehouse Restaurant** (518-543-6266; www.haguefirehouse.com; 9813 Graphite Mountain Road) is a modern and airy summer dinner spot in a renovated firehouse; try to snag a table on the brookside patio and order the local perch or other casual fare. **The Hub**, in Brant Lake, is a combination bike shop, café, and bar, serving breakfast, hearty panini, and flatbread pizzas, plus local craft brews on tap (518-494-4822; www.thehubadk.com; 27 Market Street). In Warrensburg, **Lizzie Keays** (518-504-4043; www.lizziekeays.com; 89 River Street) serves tasty meals in the refurbished Empire Shirt Factory. Also in Warrensburg, the historic **Grist Mill** (518-623-8005; www.gristmillny.com; 100 River Street) is now an upscale restaurant; it still has grindstones, conveyors, chutes, and grain-grinding apparatus, plus a great river setting. And family-run **Oscar's Adirondack Smoke House** (1-800-627-3431; www.oscarsadksmokehouse.com; 22 Raymond Lane) is a regional institution. When Rachael Ray's in town, she stops here for smoked bacon and aged Cheddar cheese.

Look for **Paradox Brewery**'s craft brews at local restaurants, or stop by their taproom, on the road between Schroon Lake and Pottersville, to taste unique seasonal beers like Dark Bay Stout, brewed with cacao nibs and orange zest (518-351-5036; 154 Route 9; www.paradoxbrewery.com).

✳ Selective Shopping

Canada Street, Lake George village's main drag, is a Day-Glo kaleidoscope of T-shirt sellers, ice-cream stands, and souvenir joints. If you can't decide what to get the folks back home there's a psychic advisor who might be able to help. More traditional Adirondackana can be found outside the village. Antiques, also. And for shopaholics who need their outlet-shopping fix, there's that, too.

ADIRONDACKANA AND ANTIQUES In Lake George, **Ralph Kylloe Antiques and Rustics Gallery** (518-696-4100; www.ralphkylloe.com; 1796 NY 9N) is Adirondackanapalooza, with its exceptional rustic furniture and decor for the home.

Antiques-shoppers should check out the excellent **Black Bass Antiques** (518-644-2389; www.blackbassantiques.com; 4940 Lake Shore Drive), in Bolton Landing, for books, antique fishing tackle, Lake George souvenirs and photographs, and other general Adirondack items.

In Schroon, **Pine Cone Mercantile** (518-532-0220; 1079 Main Street) has a tasteful selection of modern-rustic home goods and stylish gifts.

Warrensburg is home to **Discoveries** (518-623-4567; www.discoveriesusa.com; 4498 NY 9), with its miscellany from kitchen to bath, glassware, sporting goods, and furniture. **Riverside Gallery** (518-623-2026; www.riversidegallery.com; 2 Elm Street) sells old prints, paintings, reproduction furniture, picture framing, and Adirondack gifts.

BOAT BUILDERS In Brant Lake, Gar Woods are constructed and restored by the talented Turcotte brothers' **Gar Wood Custom Boats** (518-494-2966; www.garwoodcustomboats.com; 20 Duell Hill Road).

The **Hacker Boat Company** (518-543-6732; www.hackerboat.com; 8 Delaware Avenue) houses new and used Hacker-Crafts, plus memorabilia and art, at its Silver Bay showroom and headquarters.

Reuben Smith's Tumblehome Boatshop (518-623-5050; www.tumblehomeboats.com; 684 NY 28), in Warrensburg, does high-end restoration and builds historic and classic wooden boats.

CLOTHING The masses seem to go to **"Million Dollar Half Mile,"** and it's just a quick toss of the gold card from Lake George Village. Separate plazas on both sides of US 9 (near its intersection with NY 149) add up to outlet heaven for the dedicated shopper. See a full list of the current stores—among them, J. Crew, Banana Republic, Carter's, Coach, L.L. Bean, Harry & David, Lane Bryant, Yankee Candle—at several complexes of outlet malls at www.factoryoutletsoflakegeorge.com.

FAIRS AND FLEA MARKETS Garage-salers take note: **World's Largest Garage Sale** (518-623-2161; www.warrensburgchamber.com; throughout Warrensburg) is the mother of all town-wide sales. The traffic backs up to Northway Exit 23 for this blowout, the first weekend in October. More than one thousand vendors, plus many local families, offer a bewildering array of items for sale. Plan to walk once you get to town; there are shuttle buses from the parking lots. **Christmas in Warrensburg** (www.warrensburgchamber.com) includes crafts sales, and area shops open extended hours the first weekend in December.

FURNITURE MAKERS Among the furniture makers in this region—which you should contact before visiting, as many studios are in private homes—are **Thomas W. Brady** (518-644-9801; www.tombradyfurniture.com; 4635 Lake Shore Drive), of Bolton, who makes elegant contemporary furniture; and Barry Gregson's **Adirondack Rustics Gallery** (518-532-9384; www.adirondackrustics.com; 727 Charley Hill Road), in Schroon, where you can find rustic tables, chairs, settees, beds, corner cupboards, and sideboards—all made of burls, cedar, white-birch bark, and assorted woods.

GENERAL STORES **Adirondack General Store** (518-494-4408; www.adkgeneralstore.com; 899 East Shore Drive, Schroon Lake), a company store for a tannery dating back to the 1850s, is now an authentic country store that mixes the antique and the modern in a charming blend. You can hang out by the woodstove when it's cold, read the paper on the porch when it's warm, buy a nice gift, or get milk, eggs, bread, and such for camping in Pharaoh Lake Wilderness Area. The deli's very good.

Deau's Mt. Severance Country Store (518-351-5066; 1375 NY 9)—formerly just Mt. Severance Country Store—reopened under new management in late 2016.

Along with gas and groceries, the shop has a deli and bakery serving up breakfast sandwiches, hot lunch specials, and soups.

The Hague Market (518-543-6555; www.haguemarket.com; 844 Graphite Mountain Road) bills itself as the Adirondacks' oldest running general store, with organic and conventional groceries, home-baked goodies, and a deli, plus gifts and clothing in the boutique upstairs.

POTTERY Pottery dinnerware can be found in Chestertown at David and Sharon Coleman's **Fawn Ridge Pottery** (518-494-4373; www.fawn-ridge-pottery.com; 34 Fawn Ridge Road).

In Brant Lake, Janelle Beaulieu's **Stuck in the Mud Pottery** (518-831-0438; www.stuckinthemudpottery.com; 6578 NY 8) has been featured in *Fine Cooking* magazine and on the website www.Food52.com. Her chic, modern designs are sold nationwide.

✳ Special Events

Lake George Winter Carnival (518-240-0809; www.lakegeorgewintercarnival.com) every Saturday in February, has kid-oriented activities, fireworks, music, races, and a polar bear plunge.

Bands 'n Beans (518-668-2616; www.lakegeorgearts.org) is a Lake George Arts Project benefit that includes numerous local bands and a massive chili cook-off at Roaring Brook Ranch, in Lake George, in March.

Americade (518-798-7888; www.americade.com) is reportedly the world's largest multibrand motorcycle-touring rally. Held in and around Lake George in early June, there are guided rides on Adirondack backroads, seminars, swap meets, contests, music, parades, and banquets. Bikes range from tasteful special-edition Harleys worth tens of thousands of dollars to rusty "rat bikes" that look like found-object sculptures.

AMERICADE, IN LAKE GEORGE EACH JUNE, IS REPORTEDLY THE WORLD'S LARGEST MULTIBRAND MOTORCYCLE-TOURING RALLY COURTESY OF AMERICADE

The **Adirondack Wine & Food Festival** (518-668-9463 x 15; www .adirondackwineandfoodfestival.com) showcases the region's wineries, craft breweries, distilleries, food vendors and food trucks. Held at the end of June at the Charles R. Wood Park Festival Commons, the weekend event features tastings, cooking demonstrations, and a family tent to keep the kids entertained.

Stony Creek Mountain Days (518-696-3575; www.stonycreekny.org) highlights Adirondack skills and pastimes with lumberjack contests, craft demonstrations, square dancing, and storytelling, followed by fireworks, held in Stony Creek the first weekend in August.

Adirondack Folk Music Festival (518-532-9259; www.schroonlakearts com) is an all-day affair in Schroon Lake that also includes rustic furniture and crafts, in mid-August.

INDEX

Italics indicate illustrations.

NOV 3 0 2018